American Childhood

American Childhood

ESSAYS ON
CHILDREN'S LITERATURE
OF THE NINETEENTH AND
TWENTIETH CENTURIES

Anne Scott MacLeod

The University of Georgia Press
ATHENS & LONDON

© 1994 by the University of Georgia Press
Athens, Georgia 30602
All rights reserved
Designed by Kathi L. Dailey
Set in Primer by Tseng Information Systems, Inc.
Printed and bound by Thomson-Shore, Inc.
The paper in this book meets the guidelines for
permanence and durability of the Committee on
Production Guidelines for Book Longevity of the
Council on Library Resources.

Printed in the United States of America

98 97 96 95 94 C 5 4 3 2 1
00 99 98 97 96 P 5 4 3 2 1

Library of Congress Cataloging in Publication Data

MacLeod, Anne Scott.
American childood : essays on children's literature of the
nineteenth and twentieth centuries / Anne Scott MacLeod.
p. cm.
Includes bibliographical references and index.
ISBN 0-8203-1551-6 (alk. paper)
ISBN 0-8203-1803-5 (pbk.: alk. paper)
1. Children's literature, American—History and criticism.
2. American literature—19th century—History and criticism.
3. American literature—20th century—History and criticism.
4. Children—United States—Books and reading.
I. Title.
PS490.M29 1994
810.9'9282—dc20   92-38269

British Library Cataloging in Publication Data available

Contents

Preface / vii

AMERICAN GIRLS

American Girlhood in the Nineteenth Century:
Caddie Woodlawn's Sisters / 3

Nancy Drew and Her Rivals: No Contest / 30

Girls' Novels in Post–World War II America / 49

AMERICAN BOYS

Bad Boys: Tom Bailey and Tom Sawyer / 69

Good Democrats: Ragged Dick and Little Lord Fauntleroy / 77

CHILDREN IN FICTION AND FACT

Children's Literature for a New Nation, 1820–1860 / 87

Child and Conscience / 99

Children, Adults, and Reading at the Turn of the Century / 114

Images: American Children in the Early
Nineteenth Century / 127

A WORLD APART

The Children of Children's Literature in the
Nineteenth Century / 143

Family Stories, 1920–1940 / 157

Censorship and Children's Literature / 173

THE END OF INNOCENCE

Ice Axes: Robert Cormier and the Adolescent Novel / 189

The Transformation of Childhood in Twentieth-Century
Children's Literature / 198

Epilogue / 210

Notes / 217

Index / 235

Preface

The essays brought together in this book were written over a period of about fifteen years. All of them reflect my interest in the connections between American children's books and the culture that produced them. While the focus moves between the nineteenth and the twentieth centuries, and from individual books and authors to groups of books defined by kind, by audience, or by period, these essays are related by a point of view. When I read books written for children, I look for authors' views, certainly, but I also try to discover what the culture is saying about itself, about the present and the future, and about the nature and purposes of childhood.

It is popular these days to say that children's books "reflect" their culture, but the description oversimplifies a complex relationship. Children's literature does, certainly, represent the society that produces it, but it does so partially and with many ambiguities and evasions. No metaphor as direct as "reflection" can convey the subtleties of the connections between children's books and culture. Writing for children, adults bring to bear their own experience of childhood, their ideas of what childhood is or ought to be, their commitment to the conventions of their own time, and their concerns for their own society's problems and progress. In other words, authors of children's books consciously take into account myriad extrinsic considerations that they might or might not bring to writing for adults. Indeed, most writers for children practice some degree of self-censorship. They often tell children the truth, but it is seldom the whole truth.

Yet the very act of writing is revelatory. Whatever the authors' intentions, attitudes escape the restraining net of convention. Reading widely in the children's literature of a period, one catches the characteristic tone: optimistic or pessimistic; confident or anxious; celebratory or critical or fearful. If most children's literature stays well within socially conventional bounds at the intentional level, as I believe it does (I cannot agree with those who claim that this literature is purposefully subversive), the less conscious levels often carry more unpredictable messages. What is endlessly interesting is the complex relationship among the conscious attitudes expressed in children's books, the often unconscious subtexts, and the realities of the surrounding culture. Children's books do not mirror their culture, but they do always, no matter how indirectly, convey some of its central truths.

The source for most of these pieces is the domestic novel for children—the "family story" that is set in a period more or less contemporary with the time of publication and meant for readers of middle to teen years. These books tell me most about the complex, ever-changing interplay between conventional attitudes toward children and the literature published for them. This fiction most clearly represents the prevailing mainstream concept of childhood in any period.

Concepts of childhood change as societies change. Children themselves are often recognizable across time and culture—the reluctant schoolboy who drags his feet through medieval literature still looks familiar today; so does little Hartley Coleridge, whirling and shouting in the wind as his romantic father looks on. Yet it is culture that determines how children experience childhood. Even biology does not set the agenda: childhood is not necessarily identical to the period from birth to puberty. It may be shorter or longer or indeterminate; it may end, culturally speaking, at seven or thirteen or twenty-one (or even later, as in American society, which often refers to thirty-five- or forty-year-olds as "kids"). Childhood may be sheltered or unprotected, privileged, spartan, or genuinely poor. Adults may regard children as sinners or saints, genetically programmed or tabula rasa. American children have lived many different kinds of childhood.

Most of these essays locate and describe shifts in the American concept of childhood over nearly two centuries as those shifts have been recorded in children's literature; they are arranged in this collection according to their conceptual connections. Others, though they also begin with children's literature, have a somewhat broader focus. Examining the image of children and childhood as it appears in children's books, I became curious about how the realities of childhood compared with the images in the books. I have no illusions about the difficulties of satisfying my curiosity. Children's lives are mysterious to most adults even when the children are here and now; the lives of children in the past are notoriously problematic to research. I have used autobiography, in spite of its reputation for unreliability, since it offers one of the few avenues into the experience of childhoods long past and because it seems to me that autobiography, like fiction, tells a good deal of truth if it is read widely and with attention to what is between the lines as well as to what is in them. Several essays bring the abstractions of children's fiction together with the homely details of autobiography (and, in one case, with the asperity of foreign visitors' comments) to offer a glimpse of American children of the early nineteenth century as they lived in their families and communities.

Throughout, a cultural-historical interest defines my research approach to children's literature. I recognize the particularity of my kind of truth and its partial nature as well; none of these essays exhausts its subject. When I look at the children's books of any era, I begin not with a hypothesis about what, exactly, the literature will tell me but only with the belief that it will illuminate some aspects of the society of its time. I try to hear what the books say, and then I reflect on its meaning as I understand it. Someone else, listening differently, might hear other voices and find other meanings. The one certainty is that children's books are peculiarly revealing about some of the deepest currents of a society's life. Children are our past and our future; in them we invest our hopes and fears, for ourselves and for the world. The literature we write for children is inevitably permeated by our most fundamental emotional attitudes toward ourselves, toward our society, and, of course, toward childhood.

American Girls

American Girlhood in the Nineteenth Century: Caddie Woodlawn's Sisters

>E)(

Caddie Woodlawn, a historical novel for children written by Carol Brink in 1935, held for many years the status of a minor classic of children's literature. Its portrayal of a girl growing up on a pioneer farm in Wisconsin in the mid-1860s was presumed to be faithful both factually and in spirit to the realities of children's lives in the United States of the period. Briefly, the narrative centers on a young girl who has been allowed to grow up side-by-side with her brothers, running free as they run free (and as her two sisters do not) because her father hoped that such an outdoor life would improve her fragile health. At the time of the story, Caddie is twelve and approaching puberty; her mother is becoming less and less tolerant of her untrammeled ways. The climax of the novel comes about when Caddie and her brothers conspire in some minor meanness to a visiting girl cousin, but only Caddie is punished for it by their mother. As Caddie smarts under this injustice, her father comes and talks to her, letting her know that the time has come when her life must begin to change, describing the special, separate, and, in his description, exalted role that women play in the adult world. It is women, he tells her, "who keep the world sweet and beautiful. Women's task is to teach men and boys gentleness and courtesy and love and kindness. It's a big task, too, Caddie—harder than cutting trees or building mills or damming rivers. . . . A woman's work is something fine and noble to grow up to, and it is just as important as a man's. . . . No man could ever do it so well."[1]

But women's work, Mr. Woodlawn makes clear without saying so, requires skills and a discipline impossible to acquire in the free life his daughter had led so far. The real burden of her father's talk is to tell Caddie that her childhood, and with it her freedom, is about to end: "How about it, Caddie," he asks, "Have we run with the colts long enough?" (p. 240).

Mr. Woodlawn's lecture on womanly responsibilities is quite in line with the mid-nineteenth-century conception of what was called "woman's sphere."[2] The idea of woman's place as separate and different from the rest of the universe was central to nineteenth-century society, and there is no lack of evidence on the point. Magazines, journals, newspapers, novels, advice books of every kind expounded endlessly on the subject, and most of these expositions, barring those by rebellious women, described the duties and dimensions of women's work very much as Mr. Woodlawn did. His was indeed the bargain offered nineteenth-century women: influence in exchange for freedom; a role as "inspiration" in place of real power; gratitude and affection from family rather than worldly reward or renown. General consensus in America held that woman's sphere was moral rather than intellectual, domestic rather than worldly; her power was indirect; her contribution to the world was through husband and children, her reward their love and respect. What Caddie heard was the lesson every nineteenth-century American girl learned at some time before she embarked on her adult life. So far the novel is on sound historical ground.

But the premise of the novel as a whole is that Caddie's childhood freedom was highly unusual in the United States of 1865. Her two sisters, whose lives are shown as housebound and mother-modeled, are clearly meant to represent a more standard nineteenth-century upbringing for girls. The notion that family discipline divided along sex lines is central to the story: "We expect more of girls than of boys," Caddie's father tells her (pp. 239–40). When she accepts her girlhood (as opposed to an asexual childhood), the author of the novel makes it clear, Caddie is accepting both greater restrictions on her freedom and higher standards for her behavior.

I suspect that most Americans share these assumptions about nineteenth-century childhood, and particularly about the difference between girls' and boys' experience in that era. Reading backward from the restrictions imposed on adult women, it is perhaps natural to assume that strict limits were also put on girls from the beginning. We tend to believe that the lives of young girls were like the lives of adult women, bounded by the household and its duties.

But was it true? Are we right to assume that because nineteenth-century womanhood was confined within narrow limits, a nineteenth-century girlhood was no more than an apprenticeship to the same limitations? Is it a fact that girls were more restricted than boys, that they were less physically active and less enterprising, that they were confined to the household and its "womanly" duties while their brothers roamed more freely, learned more eclectically, tested themselves and their skills more thoroughly?

Having asked this much, we come to the next question: how do we find out? If historical evidence for the conventional view of woman's place is voluminous, the same cannot be said for the realities of children's lives in a past time. Few children leave documented accounts of their lives; even journals and diaries were more likely to be kept by adolescents than by children younger than, say, thirteen or fourteen. Whatever the evidence that allows us to describe how children lived in the past, it is almost at some remove from the children themselves.

Fortunately, one source, while removed, is still reasonably direct. Autobiography written by women who grew up in the United States during the nineteenth century before about 1875 is rich with information about how girls lived before their adolescent years. Many American women wrote such memoirs in their later years, to preserve for their children and grandchildren, if not for a wider audience, some account of lives lived in a rapidly changing country. The authors were a diverse lot, from the daughters of pioneers, whose schooling was at best sketchy, to women who had enjoyed the most comfortable homes and the best education the country had to offer girls at the time, as well as many more whose circumstances fell somewhere in between extremes. All but a handful can be called "middle class" as that term applies to the fluid and flexible social structure of nineteenth-century America. In these autobiographies where women recorded their childhood memories, often in considerable detail, we may catch a glimpse of the ordinary lives of middle-class American girls, remembered, it is true, by adults, but remembered by the adults who had themselves experienced the childhood they described.

Many autobiographies of childhood before 1875 suggest that Carol Brink's assumptions about an American girlhood, however logical they may seem in the light of adult social-sexual arrangements in the nineteenth century, must not be accepted uncritically. Far from being unique, what I think of as the Caddie Woodlawn Syndrome seems to have been common in America during that period. In a surprising number of memoirs is an account of just such an experience of childhood freedom followed by just the same closing of the doors as the girl neared puberty. If autobiography can be accepted as any kind of sample of common practice, then it would seem that in a good many households the sharp differentiation between appropriate behavior and activity for prepubescent boys and girls was not as firmly applied as we often suppose. Many American women could and did look back to their childhood years as a period of physical and psychic freedom unmatched by anything in their later life.

They recorded that freedom with a joy that rings down through the years and out of the pages of their autobiographies. Instead of being confined to house and hearth, many girls, like Caddie, "lived as much as possible in the open" and thrived on it. Carolyn Briggs, growing up in Northampton, Massachusetts, had her freedom as a gift from the family doctor, who thought her threatened by consumption, and decreed that she live "out of doors as much as possible, without regard to weather, always being well wrapped up with flannel underclothing . . . and . . . long sleeves. . . . How I blessed the dear man for giving me my freedom," she added fervently.[3]

For many others, doctors' orders were not necessary; many American families allowed their little girls to live nearly as unfettered and vigorous an outdoor life as their brothers. Country children in particular roamed their world without much restriction. "Our family discipline was not more rigid than it was in other families, and I was not under special supervision," wrote Caroline Creevey of her Connecticut childhood. And Elizabeth Allan echoed in her memoirs of a Virginia childhood: "I suppose someone must have had an eye on me, but I was conscious of no surveillance, and I roamed at large until the boys got out of 'school,' when I attached myself resolutely to them, doubtless becoming a great nuisance." Once a week, Caroline Briggs lost her accustomed freedom to Sunday strictures. Her description of that privation emphasizes her usual liberty: "At sunset Saturday night, the straightjacket was put on . . . [and] all the joy of life was laid aside." Fortunately, Caroline's mother was not overly doctrinaire. Once Sunday dinner was over, "wisely and well, my mother let me run like a young calf in the meadow back of the house. So the nice clothes were all taken off, and I was given my freedom. I thank God for that every year of my life."[4]

What these girls did with their freedom was what children have always done; there would be nothing remarkable in their remembered activities had they been girls of a later period or boys of any time. It is only because they were nineteenth-century girls that we are surprised to read that they dammed streams, fished and trapped, swam in ponds and rivers in summer, sledded and skated in winter. "For fair weather," wrote Creevey, "there were the orchard, the garden, the groves of chestnut and other trees, . . . the field and woods. . . . In winter our own hill afforded fine coasting, and big sleds with bright, smooth runners were cherished by girls as well as boys."[5]

Any image of prim and proper little girls who imbibed with their mother's milk a deep concern for the state of their clothing dissolves before the autobiographical accounts. These American girls climbed trees, fell into rain barrels, fished in the horse troughs. "We played I Spy, mumblety-peg, stalked about on forked-stick stilts, skinned up the trees, bent limbs for a teeter, climbed on and jumped off the stable roof," recalled Sarah Bonebright. With the clarity of hindsight, they recorded years later how they had abused their clothes: "I often climbed trees and tore my clothes," wrote one, and Anna Clary told of climbing a tree with her skirt filled with grapes. After a while she slid down the tree trunk, to the considerable detriment of both grapes and dress.[6]

City children—a minority in nineteenth-century accounts, as they were in the population—obviously had less of the natural world available to them, but they were not necessarily housebound or sedentary for that reason. Una Hunt grew up in Cincinnati in the 1870s and 1880s, climbing "every tree and shed in the neighborhood." There is no reason to assume that the trees and sheds were low, easy ones, either, since she also recorded that "I was often badly hurt, but after each fall, when vinegar and brown papers had been applied, [my mother's] only comment was 'You must learn to climb better,' and I did."[7] She topped her career by climbing to the tip of the church belfry, where she panicked and had to be helped down. Her mother drew the line then, but only at belfries; and Una went back to slightly less exalted heights.

This girl, like some others, also invented some vigorous indoor sports, not always with family approval. She and the other children in her family liked best what they called "indoor coasting." They used tea trays to slide down the stairs, but only, she confessed, when the family was all out. Elizabeth Allan stayed home from church one Sunday during a visit with some city cousins. Long afterward, she remembered the "wild hilarity" of the afternoon in the 1850s. "I initiated my city cousins in the fun of playing 'Wild Indian.' . . . I amazed them by leaping from tops of high bureaus and tables, and boasting how many more spots in the carpet I could jump over than their prim little legs could encompass." Later her "Presbyterian conscience pricked [her] sharply," not for the wildness of the games, however, but because they had been played on a Sunday.[8]

Nineteenth-century American families did differentiate in their treatment of girls and boys; most twentieth-century families do also. But the distinctions insisted upon in nineteenth-century America may have been fewer and less strict than we commonly suppose while children were preadolescent. Even the strictures against boys and girls playing together, familiar from novels and memoirs, seem to have been unevenly applied. Some girls were indeed forbidden to play with boys, unless perhaps with their brothers, but others chose boys as companions and met no objection from their parents.

Most nineteenth-century children knew work at least as well as play. In a woman's memoirs of childhood, we expect to read that domestic chores dominated her share of the work, and it is true that nearly every autobiography written by a woman records some housekeeping skills acquired young. Girls learned how to knit, sew, and cook, to wash clothes, clean house, and preserve food. They gathered eggs and picked berries, washed dishes, and carried wood for the kitchen stove. They were expected to help care for younger children in the family, sometimes to the point where a woman referred to a younger brother or sister as "my child." Under normal circumstances, the tasks, though constant, were not overly arduous. When the mother of the family was ill or dead, however, the weight of domestic responsibility on a young girl might be considerably heavier. Several accounts tell of virtually full responsibility for housekeeping passed to girls at an early age.

The point about housework, however, was not whether girls were expected to do some of it, or even a good deal of it, as children; of course they were. Children's help was indispensable in most American homes where servants were few and chores were endless. The question is whether work was divided along strict sex lines, with some activities reserved strictly for one sex or another. And here the answer is less absolute. In some rural families, at least, autobiographies indicated that boys helped with domestic work before they were old enough to work beside their fathers in the fields. And while most girls learned housekeeping in the expectation that they would eventually have houses to keep, their autobiographies show that they also learned other, less domestic skills during their childhood years. Virginia-born Ellen Mordecai was brought up by her aunts after her mother's death. They were capable women, who could "do anything," according to Mordecai, and they taught her to fish and trap. Ellen was deft with wild things. She caught a woodpecker in her hand once, just to admire his feathers. Once, she climbed a tree to investigate a hole. She put her hand in, felt something soft, and ran back home for a large silver spoon. Up in the tree again, she put the spoon gently into the hole, to scoop up several baby flying squirrels. These, too, she admired without harming and put back into the tree. And Ellen, taught by her aunts, fished enthusiastically, as they did.[9]

The parents of Frances Willard (who ultimately became president of the Women's Christian Temperance Union) enforced no connection at all between sex and kinds of work. "Mother did not talk to us as girls, but simply as human beings, and it never occurred to me that I ought to 'know house-work' and do it. Mary took to it kindly by nature; I did not, and each one had her way. Mother never said 'you must cook, you must sweep, you must sew' but she studied what we liked to do and kept us at it with no trying at all. I knew all the carpenter's tools and handled them: made carts and sleds, cross-guns and whip handles. . . . But a needle and a dishcloth I could not abide— chiefly, perhaps, because I was bound to live out-of-doors."[10] Sunday dinner preparation in the Willard household rotated among mother, father, and Oliver, the latter two being, in Frances's words, "famous cooks." The Willards represented a thoroughly open-minded attitude toward child nurture which cannot be considered typical of American households in general. Yet their approach, and that of others more conventional, suggests that American parents were often flexible and common-sensical, rather than rigidly doctrinaire in teaching skills or allocating tasks to children. Many parents seem to have been willing to consider convenience and children's tastes rather than some arbitrary view of what was "suitable" work for girls or boys.

This kind of pragmatic latitude is a key note in many American women's childhood memories. The early years of childhood offered a certain psychic as well as a physical freedom to most American children. "We were a neighborhood of large families," wrote Lucy Larcom in *A New England Girlhood*, "and most of us enjoyed the privilege of 'a little wholesome neglect.' Our tether was a long one, and when, grown a little older, we occasionally asked to have it lengthened, a maternal 'I don't care' amounted to almost unlimited liberty." Larcom, who read mostly English books as a child, contrasted the picture of an English childhood she found there with her own American experience: "We did not think those English children had so good a time as we did; they had to be so prim and methodical. It seemed to us that the little folks across the water never allowed to romp and run wild. . . . [We had] a vague idea that this freedom of ours was the natural inheritance of republican children only."[11]

Though the children of pioneering families faced greater hazards than did those of long-settled places, their parents were no more inclined to hover over them, according to Sarah Bonebright, who grew up on a pioneer farm in Iowa. "We had received instructions and the warning admonition from our parents and were expected to circumvent the [wild] creatures or avoid the danger." Girls as well as boys were expected to cope. Bonebright told of being sent on an errand three-quarters of a mile away, across the river and deep in the woods. She lost her way, making three false starts before finding it again, and was home late. "I do not recall that I was questioned about the delay, or that anxiety was expressed at my unusually long absence. I had accomplished the mission. To be able to 'make a shift' for any contingency was expected of both young and old."[12]

In fact, in view of the common belief that a Victorian upbringing was strict and narrow, especially for girls, the record of parental attitudes that can be found in many memoirs is enlightening. The autobiographies rarely report physical punishment, and then only for serious or extremely exasperating behavior. Alice Kingsbury's laconic remark, "Our parents never cared much about punishing us," was echoed by other authors. Kingsbury, recalling that she was spanked only once, wrote: "Usually when I had a tantrum, my mother took me in her arms and sat in a rocking chair, rocking and singing to me." Ellen Mordecai called her home "happy and indulgent," and Una Hunt wrote that the children of her family were "never ordered to do anything or told arbitrarily that we must obey."[13]

This is not to say that children were undisciplined. Hunt's parents, like most others of these accounts, expected a good deal of their children in many ways, including a sensitive awareness of right and wrong. In fact, most autobiographies suggest that nineteenth-century children developed tender consciences early in life. But many parents seem to have tempered their expectations with a sympathetic tolerance and a feeling for child nature that we (rather arrogantly) think of as wholly modern. Rachel Butz, for example, was withdrawn from her first school because her teacher was overly stern.

Her parents, she wrote, "had the good sense to let me remain [home] until I could have a teacher who . . . could understand the wants and needs of childhood." Later when she went away to boarding school, she suffered acutely from homesickness. "I had lived such a free, joyous life that . . . restrictions were hard to bear." She returned home before the end of the first term, with her parents' consent. With the sensitive conscience trained into so many children of the time, she deplored her own "failure," but she was grateful for her parents' leniency. "They did what was right for my highest good. . . . I am thankful for their sympathy." This is by no means an isolated story; many women recalled such sympathetic understanding. Laura Richards, daughter of Samuel Gridley and Julia Ward Howe, remembered herself at four or five, afraid of the dark. More than once, she went "into the lighted drawing room, among all the silks and satins, arrayed in . . . a 'leg-nightgown,' demanding her mother. . . . and I remember that she always got her mother, too."[14]

But this "free, joyous life" described again and again in American women's autobiographies came to an end for them, as it did for Caddie Woodlawn, when they crossed the fateful line that marked the end of childhood and the beginning of young womanhood. Timing varied, but not the outcome. For some, the doors closed at thirteen; for others not until fifteen or even later, but close it inevitably did once the claims and constraints of nineteenth-century womanhood were laid upon the growing girl.

Most authors say only a very little about the loss of their freedom, which is perhaps not surprising, since every girl was well aware of the dimensions of "woman's sphere" long before she reached puberty. Generally, the regrets must be read between the lines of these women's memoirs, in the passionately fond recollections of girlhood freedom. But those who recorded the moment of change and their feelings about it often gave a glimpse of the conflict they faced. Rachel Butz called her adolescence "that most trying and uncomfortable age, when physically I was almost a woman, but at heart, was still a child." Lucy Larcom was more specific: "The transition from childhood to girlhood, when a girl had an almost unlimited freedom of out-of-door life, is practically the toning down of a mild sort of barbarianism. . . . I clung to the child's inalienable privilege of running half wild; and when I found that I was really growing up, I felt quite rebellious." Even late in life, Ellen Mordecai spoke with fierce regret of the close of childhood. Her thirteenth year ended her "happy-go-lucky, carefree childhood." She wrote, "In memory's book, that leaf wears forever a margin of black." [15]

Of them all, it was Frances Willard who lodged the most heartfelt protest. She mourned not just the loss of childhood freedom, but what that loss meant to her as an adult human being: "No girl went through a harder experience than I, when my free, out-of-door life had to cease, and the long skirts and clubbed-up hair spiked with hairpins had to be endured. The half of that down-heartedness has never been told and never can be. I always believed that if I had been left alone and allowed as a woman what I had as a girl, a free life in the country, where a human being might grow, body and soul, as a tree grows, I would have been ten times more of a person in every way." [16] Not every woman's memoirs spoke so forcefully of their author's reaction to the profound alterations that adolescence brought. Many recorded without comment their authors' entirely conventional adult lives as wives and mothers, offering no hint of whether they resented or regretted a social system that gave and then abruptly retracted the gift of freedom. To understand the meaning of their loss—and it must have had meaning for every woman who experienced it—we must turn to less direct testimony.

One resource, oblique yet revealing, exists in the form of children's books. The latter half of the nineteenth century saw the beginnings of a great age of children's fiction, an outpouring of literature written by middle-class adults for middle-class children, much of it in the tradition of domestic realism, which was intended to be true to the common reality of daily life. As an index to reality in any period, children's fiction is admittedly problematical—indirect, allusive, edited, and perhaps idealized by its authors, often burdened with didactic intent. But it is also rich in emotional truth. In any period, authors writing realistic fiction for children tend to recreate the shape and feeling of their own childhood. Constructing literary childhood, adults often replay the patterns of their own early lives, sometimes romanticizing, sometimes justifying them, sometimes bringing them to a more satisfactory conclusion than they achieved in reality. Realistic children's fiction, then, is another avenue to an understanding of nineteenth-century women's feelings about their own childhood experiences. Women who wrote children's stories of everyday life in the latter half of the nineteenth century usually described childhood of a generation earlier, drawing upon the memories of their own young lives. Their stories of childhood and adolescence resonate with feeling; in them are clues to their authors' attitudes toward their early years, unconscious as well as conscious, which can hardly be reached by a straighter path.

It is surely significant that so many women who wrote "girls' stories" chose as their subject the transition from childhood to adolescence, or, more accurately, to young adulthood. The typical nineteenth-century girls' story was seldom about very young children, nor did it deal with a heroine who was wholly within young adulthood. Until about the turn of the century, when the earlier years of childhood gained favor with writers, the characteristic girls' novel centered on heroines of about twelve to sixteen years old, girls who stood just at the end of childhood and on the verge of young womanhood.

The stories were, typically, intensely domestic and interior. Where the boys' books increasingly revolved around a young man's encounter with the outside world—in the army, in the West, in the city—and around active, extroverted adventure, girls' novels focused on character and relationships, as, of course, girls' lives did as they approached womanhood. And within the context of character and relationships, nineteenth-century writers repeatedly identified the decisive moment in a girl's life as that time when she left behind the relatively undifferentiated personality of childhood to take on the required characteristics of an adult woman. They saw this transition as a dramatic event in a girl's life; certainly they saw it as the supremely fitting moment for a didactic message defining the obligations and the limitations of a woman's future.

Louisa May Alcott was one of the earliest, and is doubtless the best known today, of the nineteenth-century women who wrote such novels for children. Alcott's books were sufficiently entertaining so as to make readers, even today, tend to overlook how much preaching is in them. In fact, they were quite didactic; Alcott consistently pushed her convictions on upbringing, family life, womanly virtue, and other values in her writing for children. While in some respects her views were advanced, even feminist—she always endorsed the idea of independence for women and was always as interested in work for women as for men—in her children's books, at least, Alcott generally upheld the conventional tenets of nineteenth-century womanhood. The portraits of admirable women and children are immensely (and consciously) instructive as models of conventional ideals. Yet between the lines of these stories, it is often possible to catch signs of Alcott's less openly acknowledged responses to the limitations women faced in her era.

Her first and most enduringly popular story for girls is, of course, *Little Women*. As a quasi-autobiographical novel, it is both more revealing and more carefully hedged against revelation than her less autobiographical books. In *Little Women*, Alcott retraced and also reshaped the patterns of her own life; truth and wish were bound together.

Characterization is at the heart of the book's remarkable perennial appeal. As every reader recognizes, Jo March is the author, the author is Jo March, and so is every girl that reads the book. It is Jo—her roughness, her ambition, her earnest yearning to be good; and above all, her humanness, good, bad, and mistaken—to whom every reader responds. Meg is admirable, Amy exasperating, and Beth too perfect to be believed, but Jo is drawn from Alcott's own character and feelings; her character has a vivid reality still.

Without recapitulating the familiar story, one can note that *Little Women* is again the story of girls who stand just on the brink of young adulthood. Alcott conveys in some detail the texture of the March girls' childhood existence, and then carries her story forward to their young womanhood and their destinies as women. Through Jo's eyes we see the transition of that passage for Louisa May Alcott.

The dominant emotion is a passionate regret for the childhood about to be left behind, for the family unity about to be splintered as the girls move toward their separate futures. Meg's marriage signals the inevitable destruction of childhood, and Jo is frankly jealous, not of Meg as she assumes an adult role, but of John, who is taking Meg away.[17] Jo's reaction to her own growing up recalls several autobiographical accounts. Like Lucy Larcom, Frances Willard, Ellen

Mordecai, and others, Jo resists and resents the approach of adult-hood. Partly, of course, the resistance can be read as a shrinking from the greater responsibilities, both social and sexual, of adult life, but much of it is to the loss of freedom. Unlike the twentieth-century child, who usually sees adult status as liberation, nineteenth-century women more often identified freedom with childhood and clung to it as long as they could. Generations of girls sympathized with Jo's plea to "let me be a little girl as long as I can," and with her wish that "wearing flatirons on our heads would keep us from growing up," because they knew, as she did, that adolescence was the beginning of limitations and restraints that would last the rest of their lives. Adolescence was the fork in the road where boys' and girls' paths di-verged, as Jo ruefully acknowledged when Laurie proposed that they run away together. "If I was a boy, we'd run away together, and have a capital time; but as I'm a miserable girl, I must be proper, and stay at home. . . . 'Prunes and prisms' are my doom." [18]

Jo's rebellion against the restrictions of "woman's sphere" came directly from Alcott's own heart; Jo's emotions are usually an accu-rate record of her own adolescent feelings. Since she was writing fiction, however, she could extend to Jo the compromise between am-bition and acceptance that she never found for herself, as she did in Jo's marriage to Professor Bhaer. For over a hundred years, roman-tic readers have groaned over Jo's rejection of handsome, devoted, wealthy Laurie, but Alcott knew her own mind. Marriage with Laurie would have made Jo a feminine success in conventional terms, cer-tainly; she would have been beloved, no doubt, and comfortably well-off, but she would also have been idle. As Mrs. Laurence, she would have had no function in the world beyond the domestic doorstep. Marriage to the unromantic Professor, on the other hand, gave her domestic happiness in the form of affection and children, but with it, work. Jo acquires husband and vocation together, while Alcott, who found no such bargain in real life, remained unmarried.

Jack and Jill, a more purely fictional story by Alcott, offered little compromise and less hope to freedom-loving girls. This novel, one of Alcott's lesser-known books, concentrates on the process of trans-forming an untamed girl into a promising adolescent. In a sense, it is the second half of the Caddie Woodlawn story. Where Brink devoted most of her story to Caddie's experiences as a free and enterprising child, Alcott begins her tale only moments before the crisis that precipitates change, and spends the bulk of the book showing how and to what end Jill's character is reformed.

The story revolves mainly around Jill, secondarily around her two girl friends, Merry and Molly. Jack and a couple of other boys play a part as well, but their roles are subordinate to the girls'. The central and certainly the most keenly felt theme is exactly the transition girls must make between childhood and young adulthood, precisely the changes adolescence must bring to the ways of a lively, spirited girl. In Jill's case, and to a lesser extent in Molly's as well, that transition reiterates the patterns so often laid out in autobiography. Both Jill and Molly are weaned from their childhood "wildness" in the course of the story, tamed and constrained into the beginnings of acceptable womanhood.

Alcott gives only the briefest glimpse of Jill before the sledding accident that brings about her transformation, but that glimpse is revealing. As Jack and Jill, inseparable friends, are sledding, Jill is challenged by a boy who says she "wouldn't dare" to attempt a difficult run. Jill responds vigorously: "I won't be told I don't dare by any boy in the world," she declares. She is "as brave and strong" as anyone, and she demands that Jack take her down that risky run [19] Jack demurs, because the hill is dangerous, but willful Jill prevails, and down the hill they go, twice safely, but the third time to disaster. The sled hits a fence, goes over a steep bank, and shatters. Jack suffers a broken leg, which will immobilize him for a time, but Jill injures her back and finds herself facing the certainty of months in bed and the possibility of permanent crippling.

Brief as it is—the whole action takes but a chapter to tell—the sledding scene establishes all the strong (and unsuitable) elements in Jill's character that will be corrected in the story to come. Jill is "headstrong," proud, willful, dominant, and competitive: one could hardly draw a better roster of unacceptable characteristics for a nineteenth-century woman.

The rest of the book recounts Jill's months of recuperation and her education in patience, obedience, resignation, and concern for others. The transformation is dramatic. To her mother, preaccident

Jill is "as wild a little savage as I'd like to see," while 200 pages later, Jill can see herself as "a sort of missionary" whose "constant well-doing" has made her "a joy and comfort to all who know and love her."[20] Moralistic it surely is, yet Alcott tells the story with a certain realism. She never minimizes the hardness of the lessons for a spirited girl. Jill suffers pain, fear, boredom, lapses of virtue, and bitter self-reproach; there is no sentimental suggestion that the damping down of a vigorous and willful personality is either swift or simple.

In the best nineteenth-century tradition, most of this education in womanliness takes place through the example of an ideal woman. Jack's mother, Mrs. Minot, leads Jill through her painful experience with precepts and kind encouragement. She also supplies a model for Jill to emulate by telling her of a woman she knew who had been crippled at fifteen, and yet was happy. "'Why, how could she be? What did she do?' cried Jill. 'She was so patient, other people were ashamed to complain of their small worries; so cheerful, that her own great one grew lighter; so industrious, that she made both money and friends by pretty things she worked and sold to her many visitors. And, best of all, so wise and sweet that she seemed to get good out of everything, and make her poor room a sort of chapel where people went for comfort, counsel, and an example of a pious life.'"[21]

Here is the formula by which women "make the world sweet and beautiful," as Mr. Woodlawn had said. Here are the traits of patience, cheerfulness, industry, and the ability to "get good out of everything," which are the hallmark of womanhood and which are also, of course, diametrically opposed to Jill's childhood character.

Molly's and Merry's stories supply the other piece of Mr. Wood-lawn's list of womanly duties, the gentling of men and boys, and the bringing of an order to their lives that they, according to one of the most cherished tenets of the nineteenth-century code, cannot manage on their own. Both girls turn themselves into "notable house-wives," making home pleasant for their male relatives and reaping their reward in love. With Molly, Mrs. Minot succeeds in making "a tidy little girl out of . . . the greatest tomboy in town," while Merry learns to put limits on her aspirations, giving over dreams of being "a queen or a great lady" in favor of more modest goals: "Now I don't care for that sort of splendor. I like to make things pretty at home, and know they all depend on me, and love me very much. Queens are not happy; but I am."[22]

Again, it is the patterns that interest us, the parallels between Alcott's story and the autobiographies. Alcott assumes the openness of childhood as a familiar, acceptable phenomenon. For all her moralism, nowhere does she deplore childhood freedom, even if Molly and Jill are "wild" or "tomboyish" as a result of it. Indeed, she has one old woman observe to another that "them wild little tykes often turn out smart women."[23] It is all a matter of timing. At the time of the story, all three girls are fifteen—and fifteen is, in every Alcott book, the moment of transition from childhood to young adult status. What was acceptable in children is not tolerable in young women; it is time, this story says, just as *Caddie Woodlawn* did, for new directions.

Jack and Jill illustrates well the characteristic ambivalence of an author who remembered her own rebelliousness against the prevailing social code, but who had to accommodate it in some fashion. In Merry, Alcott shows the conventional training of a girl played out to its logical end of marriage and contentment within the bounds of conventional society. In Molly, who remained a "merry spinster all her days," she suggests an alternative way of life, not rejecting social convention, but evading the specific restrictions and demands of womanly subordination in marriage. Moreover, Alcott heartily asserts the possibility of the choice as a happy, fulfilling one, for Molly and for the community as well. In Jill, she equivocates. Jill is tamed, quenched, and pressed into the mold of a nineteenth-century woman who has learned to play her subordinate role and put the happiness of others above her own. For her efforts, the rehabilitated "savage" is rewarded with the natural companion of her life, Jack. But just when the picture seems complete, and Jill's enforced education in passivity an unqualified success, Alcott retrieves a small piece of the resistant independence that identified her with her creator in the first place. As she matured, Alcott tells us, Jill "was very ambitious in spite of the newly acquired meekness, which was all the more becoming because her natural liveliness often broke out like sunshine through a veil of light clouds." Still, the ambition apparently breaks no barriers: Alcott tells us only that Jill married Jack and became "a very happy and useful woman."[24]

But it is at the level of metaphor that Louisa May Alcott's less conscious or, at least, less consciously expressed, attitudes appear. The central metaphor of *Jack and Jill* is certainly striking: a crippled woman is held up as a model of womanhood, and Jill's education in feminine virtue is a direct result of her own crippling. Though she eventually recovers physically, the transformation of Jill's character is permanent and laudable, in the conventional terms in which Alcott is dealing. The message is unmistakable: the characteristics of a permanent invalid making the best of her lot are a useful example for all women.

A second image, used by Mrs. Minot, is equally arresting. "I'm not sure," says Mrs. Minot to Jill, toward the end of the novel, "that I won't put you in a pretty cage and send you to the cattle show, as a sample of what we can do in the way of taming a wild bird till it is nearly as meek as a dove." Whatever level of Alcott's being produced this thought, it is memorable, as is Alcott's telling remark that Jill "had learned to love her cage now."[25]

Oddly enough, Alcott's *Jack and Jill* parallels closely an earlier and very popular girls' story by Susan Coolidge (Sarah C. Woolsey). *What Katy Did*, which was published in 1872, eight years before Alcott's book, tells a remarkably similar story of a vigorous, tomboyish girl who learns her womanly role when she is invalided with an injured spine. Woolsey spends more time with her heroine before her accident than Alcott did, giving her readers an opportunity to know this lively personality before it is pressed into the standard mold. And a very engaging personality it is, too. Katy is a character straight out of many nineteenth-century autobiographies: she "tore her dress every day, hated sewing, and didn't care a button about being called 'good.'" Her mother is dead, and her father encourages his children's vigor: "He wished to have the children hardy and bold, and encouraged climbing and rough plays, in spite of the bumps and ragged clothes which resulted." Katy is the leader of the pack, and full of heady ambition. "There were always so many delightful schemes rioting in her brain, that all she wished for were ten pairs of hands to carry them out. . . . she was fond of building castles in the air, and dreaming of the time when something she had done would make her famous." She means to "do something grand" with her life, perhaps "nursing in a hospital, like Miss Nightingale" or possibly she will "paint pictures, or sing, or scalp—sculp." She isn't sure what it will be, only that "it will be *something*."[26]

The story finds Katy at twelve, with obviously much to learn about womanly virtue. Her education begins, as Jill's did, as the result of an accident. Like Jill, Katy brings about her injury by her headstrong insistence on her own way. Like Jill, again, she takes as her model a permanent cripple—"Cousin Helen"—who teaches, in person in this case, the lessons of patience, cheerfulness, and care for the needs of others for whom she is the center of the household in spite of being bedridden. Under such tutelage, Katy's ambition is replaced by attention to others, a far better occupation for a woman, according to Cousin Helen, than "scurrying and bustling over [her] own affairs." Katy learns, as every nineteenth-century woman had to learn, that her "own affairs" were never of real consequence, that she must always be ready to put them aside to tend to other people, taking her reward in love. In a remarkable passage, Cousin Helen suggests that her own invalidism was more pleasing to her father than blooming health ever was: "He had been proud of his active, healthy girl, but I think she was never such a comfort to him as his sick one, lying there in her bed."[27]

Katy absorbs these lessons thoroughly, though it takes four years of invalidism to do it. By the time she is able to walk again, she has taken over the running of the Carr household, and becomes a substitute mother to her sisters and brothers: "To all the . . . children, Katy was . . . the centre and the sun. They all revolved about her, and trusted her for everything." Her description now, "the gentle expression of her eyes, the womanly look, the pleasant voice, the politeness, the tact in advising others, without seeming to advise," tells us that "The School of Pain," as Cousin Helen called it, has educated her well in the nineteenth-century ideal of womanhood.[28]

Louisa May Alcott and Sarah Woolsey were illuminating, if unwitting, witnesses to women's reactions to the patterns their society imposed on them. How guilelessly and yet how plainly these authors drew the analogy between physical crippling and the limitations a girl faced as she approached womanhood! And how revealing was their chosen literary metaphor of their own ambivalence toward the code that governed women's lives. Writers of children's books rarely preach rebellion, nor did these two. They intended their stories to put forth the most conventional concept of women's special place and particular virtues; they meant to use fiction to guide the young into acceptable paths. Yet to the modern reader, if not to their contemporaries, their strong personalities transcended their intentions. No one today can read these two novels, so much alike, without hearing the piercing, if unconscious, cry of outrage beneath the smooth and proper surface.

A generation later, two books appeared within a few years of one another as curiously alike and as representative of their era as *Jack and Jill* and *What Katy Did*. Both were enormously popular girls' books that announced some changes on the theme of spirited young girls verging toward womanhood and that accurately reflected some subtle but fundamental shifts in conventional attitudes toward children. Whether, in the end, either of them held out more hope to their heroines for an adult life with more options for their particular qualities is doubtful, I think, though both aspired to do so.

Rebecca of Sunnybrook Farm (1903) by Kate Douglas Wiggin and *Anne of Green Gables* (1908) by L. M. Montgomery are assembled of virtually identical elements. Both tell stories of little girls who leave rather straitened circumstances (Anne is an orphan, Rebecca comes from a family over-supplied with children and under-supplied with the means to raise and educate them) for new homes that are by no means rich, but that can offer a chance for education. The locale in each case is a village, and the woman into whose care the child is delivered is, in both books, a crusty, exacting spinster whose heart has withered for lack of a woman's normal accoutrements; that is, husband, children, and the giving and receiving of human affection. The span of time covered is also similar in the two novels; each takes the heroine from about her eleventh to her seventeenth year, showing again the passage from childhood to young womanhood.

Both books are primarily character studies. Of the two, *Rebecca* is better written, more realistic, and less sentimental than *Anne,* but in all other respects the characterizations are practically interchangeable and belong firmly within the romantic tradition. Anne and Rebecca embody the idea of childhood that celebrated the child as child, and saw a child as perfect in itself, in harmony with itself and with nature: innocent, spontaneous, imaginative, loving. Each eleven years old, highly verbal, poetic, and imaginative, the little girls make a vivid contrast to the cramped and colorless adults around them. Their stories show them touching and in some cases transforming the lives of others, bringing happiness to adults who have lost the innate joyousness of childhood, and, in fact, nearly lost the knack of being truly alive. Rebecca and Anne grow, learn, and of course suffer mishaps and correction of their childish mistakes, but they are never really wrong or bad. They have no true "faults", they only make mistakes on the way to learning the complicated rules of adult society, which is, often as not, more truly at fault than they are, since it is less simple and natural than childhood. They are William Blake's vision of children: "Innocence! Honest, open, seeking the vigorous joys of morning light."[29]

As romantic children, Rebecca and Anne are of a quite different order of being from the children of Alcott's books. Louisa May Alcott, born in 1833, was a full generation older than Kate Douglas Wiggin. The view of childhood in her writing for children belongs to the rationalistic, preromantic view that dominated children's books until the latter part of the nineteenth century. It is an attitude accepting of childhood and children, but it is not romantic. Alcott's opinion of her young heroines has none of the doting fondness of Wiggin's feeling for Rebecca or Montgomery's for Anne. Likeable as Jo March is, she cannot be mistaken for the author's idea of perfection.

The very title, *Little Women*, is indicative: to Alcott, as to most Americans of her time, children were adults-in-process, apprentices to the rigors and demands of adult life. It was not a matter of viewing children as "little adults"; that was not a nineteenth-century attitude. It is simply that Alcott, like many of her contemporaries, saw childhood primarily as a period of preparation; children were properly engaged in learning, becoming, forming a worthy character for the future; certainly they were not considered finished and wholly admirable as they were.

Alcott's attitude toward her characters' faults illustrates the point. Without suggesting that perfection was a likely human attainment, she nevertheless saw Meg's envy, Jo's temper, and Amy's selfishness and vanity as serious matters that it was absolutely necessary to correct. Even Beth's timidity had to be conquered in some degree. It was the responsibility of adults to help children overcome their character flaws, to guide them along the right paths to creditable adulthood, as Mrs. March and Mrs. Minot do; there was no suggestion that the children were naturally better than adults. In the nature of things, a child was pupil to an adult.

Once romantic attitudes had penetrated the literature, however, the picture children's books presented of adult responsibility toward children altered subtly but profoundly. The right sort of adult could still act as guide and mentor to a child, but the effort had changed from molding childish character into acceptable moral and social form to easing it toward adulthood without destroying the special virtues inherent in children. In the romantic view, the best (though the least likely) adult character was one that preserved most completely the qualities of childhood. Adam Ladd, obviously Rebecca's future husband, and Miss Maxwell, her devoted teacher, had many conversations about Rebecca as she neared young womanhood, all of which centered on how she should be educated without obliterating or dampening her special personality. Or, to be more exact, they regretfully conceded the reality of Rebecca's growing up, and tried to decide how they might help her negotiate her inevitable maturity while protecting the perfection of her childhood being.

Though Montgomery's sequels to *Anne of Green Gables* carry her protagonist into adult life, it is clear that she and Wiggin alike were most entranced with their heroines as children. It was childhood that gave full scope to Rebecca's and Anne's personalities. During those years, their dramatic and poetic imaginations were not unduly constrained by consciousness of conventional expectations. They prattled on, using extraordinary vocabularies gleaned from omnivorous reading, unconsciously amusing and charming those adults perceptive enough to appreciate them. They were strong-minded and full of enterprise and too innocent yet to know that leadership was not for females. They summarized in themselves all that their authors thought attractive and promising in a child.

The question, therefore, is: what became of all this as these girls neared womanhood? In the answer to that question lies a volume of commentary, whether or not the authors intended it so, on how little had changed since Louisa May Alcott looked for a satisfactory, if fictional, niche for Jo's forceful character, and since she and Sarah Woolsey could draw a close parallel between womanly virtue and physical crippling.

By the time Wiggin and Montgomery wrote, enterprising or needy girls had a few more acceptable opportunities to consider than had their mothers and grandmothers. Anne and Rebecca both acquired the education that was accessible to girls by the end of the century, though it was clear in both books that scholarships or private benevolence were necessary if girls as poor as these were to go to school past the local grammar school. And both girls looked forward to paid work as teachers; they did not have to choose from the limited and distasteful array of occupations the March girls faced: governess, seamstress, companion, or (possibly with luck, talent, and determination) a writer.

Yet the narrowness of the future choices available to Rebecca and Anne is quite apparent when one considers what expectations a boy with their talents would have had without question. In childhood, the two girls demonstrate intelligence, energy, and a capacity for leadership that their companions concede without jealousy. Such qualities in a boy would all but assure an interesting, probably a public career. Not so for these girls, as their creators tacitly concede in their descriptions of their heroines' adolescence. As the girls grow older, their personalities become less emphatic. Their colorful (and undeniably intrusive) qualities of mind and imagination dim to "dreaminess" in their mid-teens, while their ambition turns toward conventionally acceptable careers as teachers. They never rebel and never yearn for what they cannot have; indeed, they never even recognize that there is work in the world for which they are suited by nature but from which they are prevented by social convention.

Nor does their ambition in any way interfere with their acceptance of the traditional womanly responsibility to care for others if the need arises. Anne and Rebecca were openly ambitious throughout their school years; they were even, though less openly, competitive. And each won by her efforts the offer of a choice teaching position as she left high school. But before she can collect the reward of her talent and hard work by moving into a paid employment, each girl is faced with a crisis in the form of a seriously ailing relative who needs care. In both cases, the girls respond without hesitation, cheerfully shelving previous plans and undertaking a sacrificial role as a matter of course. It is as though the authors wanted to demonstrate that neither ambition nor achievement had destroyed the selfless sense of duty that was the core of the nineteenth-century womanly model. It was, too, as though these authors saw a period of self-abnegation as a necessary stage in a girl's way to womanhood, just as Alcott and Woolsey had a generation before. Less overtly than their predecessors, but still clearly enough to be understood, Wiggin and Montgomery conveyed the message that the paths a woman trod were likely to be steep and stony for a girl just leaving the freer territory of childhood.

Perhaps for this reason, Kate Douglas Wiggin declined to deal at all with Rebecca's life as an adult. In the original *Rebecca* book, she rounded off her story with Rebecca's graduation from high school at seventeen. Adam Ladd's interest in Rebecca as a woman is plainly enough indicated, but Wiggin was not ready to go further. Though Adam finds Rebecca "all-beautiful and all-womanly," the time is not yet: "He had looked into her eyes and they were still those of a child; there was no knowledge of the world in their shining depths, no experience of men or women, no passion, nor comprehension of it." And so the book ends, with Rebecca still a child.[30]

New Chronicles of Rebecca does not, as readers might have expected, pick up where the first book left off. Instead, Wiggin dips back into Rebecca's young years for more anecdotes, as charming and amusing as those of the first book, of Rebecca's childhood. Once more, Wiggin brings Rebecca up to the age of seventeen, and this time also to the betrothal of her "bosom friend" of childhood. The story ends on a note of nostalgic sadness. Rebecca, watching Emma Jane and her fiancé walk away arm in arm, feels her childhood is slipping away "like a thing real and visible . . . slipping down the grassy riverbanks, . . . the summer night."[31]

The mood is wistful, rather than passionately regretful. It is much less clear here than in *Little Women* what is being lost as childhood "slips away." Jo March knew very well what she mourned: the intact family of her childhood and the freedom to behave according to her nature rather than to a prescribed code for her sex. And Jo, within the strictures of nineteenth-century behavior (and of nineteenth-century children's books) was rebellious and resentful at her loss. Anne and Rebecca are not rebellious; their passage into adult life is made to seem gradual and free of conflict. Though their strong personalities would seem to presage a struggle over the need to trim their sails to the prevailing nineteenth-century wind, Wiggin and Montgomery will not have it so. Anne and Rebecca are romantic children, whose in-born natures are beyond reproach; not they, then, but their creators, must accommodate convention. These girls must ease into adolescence and then into maturity without strife or storm; they must become the most desirable models of young womanhood without seeming to give up any of their childhood perfection, and so they do. For all their vibrancy as children, Anne and Rebecca sail into their womanly backwaters without a murmur.

If the pattern I have described was common in the lives of nineteenth-century American girls—as I think it was—it may seem strange that only a few adult women openly revolted against it. At first glance and from the distance of our own time, a system that allowed for so much freedom at one stage of life and so little at the next would seem destined to produce resentment and rebellion.

But human reaction is rarely so simple or so linear in its logic. Like most people who live in a reasonably coherent and consistent culture, nineteenth-century American girls accepted the view of life their culture presented to them, and with it, the view of woman's proper role. Not only accepted: they absorbed and internalized it and eventually passed it on to a new generation. The books they wrote for children suggest how the processes of adaptation and accommodation actually worked.

Little Women, for example, shows the process underway as the girls, including Jo, try to emulate the example of their model of womanly behavior, their mother. Jo's "boyishness" has been well tolerated, apparently, in her family; no shame or disapproval of it is ever expressed by her parents. But Meg, who at the time of the story is close to the ideal of adult womanhood herself, tries to cure Jo of her whistling and her "wildness," pointing out that she must relinquish such ways now that she is growing up. Though she resists,

Jo does understand that the moment is approaching when it will no longer be excusable for her to be rough, abrupt, ill-kempt, bluntly tactless. Her bitter disappointment when Aunt Carroll chooses Amy for the European tour Jo had hoped to make, because of Jo's own outspoken and all-too-independent opinions, points up the high cost of nonconformity for a girl.

And if the price of nonconformity was high, so too was the cost of conscious resentment. Raised in a society largely united on the acceptable role for women, wooed by a social code that made a virtue of dependency and exalted the submissive and unselfish qualities of ideal womanhood, faced with the discomfort of putting themselves outside convention if they rebelled against their fate, many women must have chosen not to look too closely at the discrepancies between the expectations of their humanity, on the one hand, and their sex, on the other. The briefest pair of sentences in the diary of a young southern girl gives a telling glimpse of the decision many women made, consciously or unconsciously, to accept their social destiny for the sake of their own peace. In 1862, Lucy Breckinridge wrote, "I read some in Michelet's book on 'Woman.' I do not like that kind of reading. It scares me of myself, and makes me rebel against my lot." Lucy Breckinridge was not at all optimistic about the happiness of women's lives, as her diary makes abundantly clear. ("Poor women! Why did God curse them so much harder than men?") But she had few, very few, alternatives to choose from, and she knew it. No wonder a book that outlined women's disadvantages so complacently "scared her of herself."[32]

Yet not to opt for an open rebellion against injustice was not quite to neutralize resentment. Pushed out of sight it might have been; obliterated, it probably was not. Women's resentment of their lot must have surfaced in dozens of ways we can only guess at. It surely emerged, as we have seen, in children's books, and often, paradoxically enough, in the very stories that were written with conscious intent to perpetuate the conventional ideal. Responses ranging from outrage to something like mourning run just under the surface of books utterly conventional in their openly asserted attitudes. At the very least, women's sense of loss fed the nostalgia for childhood that children's books often expressed. The child who read late nineteenth-century books could hardly avoid the conclusion that the end of childhood was also the end of the best part of life. Certainly, a girl was unlikely to miss the message that puberty would be for her the beginning of her imprisonment in a "woman's sphere." She would surely understand that for her the central task of adolescence as defined by her culture was to trim her qualities of mind and character, whatever they might be, to fit the model society had prepared for her.

It was 1777 when Hannah More delivered herself of some profoundly dampening comments on the upbringing of girls: "That bold, enterprising spirit, which is so much admired in boys, should not, when it happens to discover itself in the other sex, be encouraged, but suppressed. Girls should be taught to give up their opinions betimes. . . . It is of the greatest importance to their future happiness, that they should acquire a submissive temper, and a forbearing spirit; for it is a lesson the world will not fail to make them frequently practise, when they come abroad into it, and they will not practise it the worse for having learnt it the sooner."[33] More than a century later, Rebecca Randall acknowledged that More's prescription had by no means passed out of date. "All of us can have the ornament of a meek and lovely spirit," she observed, and added, with her customary accuracy, "especially girls, who have more use for it than boys."[34]

The evidence suggests that American girls often enjoyed a season of freedom before they had to face up altogether to what More and Rebecca agreed was the lot of their sex. But sooner or later, the most blithesome girl had to recognize the reality that awaited her. And whether she chose to rebel against or to accede to the demands of her culture, a nineteenth-century girl could not but realize, with all her sex, that after childhood, gender (to paraphrase Freud) was inexorably destiny.

Nancy Drew and Her Rivals: No Contest

$\searrow\!\!\!\!\nearrow$

If imitation is the sincerest form of flattery, then Harriet S. Adams may have been, next to Hemingway, the most sincerely flattered author of the 1930s. Though her father, Edward Stratemeyer, founder of the Stratemeyer Syndicate, originated the Nancy Drew mystery series with three books published shortly before his death in 1930, thereafter, according to Adams, Nancy Drew was her own personal project.[1]

It was a project that lit a beacon in the publishing world. Even before 1934, when Nancy Drew outsold every other juvenile title on the Christmas book list, new girl sleuth series had begun to multiply, most of them bearing a remarkably close resemblance to the Nancy Drew pattern. None of the imitations, however, not even the Stratemeyer Syndicate's own, proved as immediately popular as Nancy Drew, and none has ever rivaled her legendary grip on her audience. Nancy Drew not only outsold her competitors by far but she pushed most of them out of the marketplace within a few years of their appearance. The rare survivors never offered serious challenge to Nancy's position as reigning queen of the juvenile formula fiction world.

The basics of the Nancy Drew design are familiar. Nancy is an attractive sixteen-year-old girl who lives with her widowed, "famous lawyer" father, Carson Drew, and their "elderly housekeeper," Hannah Gruen. It is a privileged existence of financial ease and extraordinary independence, which Nancy uses to pursue her calling as an amateur sleuth. Each story is a showcase for Nancy's straight thinking, remarkable competence, and unshakable dignity, and every adventure ends with Nancy admired and applauded by all. Though she has friends, in particular her special "chums," Bess and George, and an unemphatic boy friend, Ned, Nancy operates essentially alone, doing most of the acting and all of the thinking in her detecting adventures. The series, too, is focused. A Nancy Drew mystery is only that, never a school story or a romance or a career novel with a bit of mystery thrown in.

The outline of the successful pattern is clear enough: the one-parent, two-chum, one-boyfriend, comfortable, middle-class girl sleuth soon became a standard figure in series fiction. Some series stressed their heroines' independence, as the Drew books did, and most supplied the admiration that surrounds Nancy Drew like a cloud of sweet scent. Yet all of the imitators weakened important parts of the formula. The autonomy that was Nancy's without question, for example, and the single focus of the narratives were blurred in other series, though in retrospect, at least, both look like key elements in the Nancy Drew success story.

In fact, the most moderate literary Darwinist would have to conclude that Nancy Drew's capacity for survival came from sources never identified by would-be imitators. Even experienced hack writers missed the magic, largely because they did not read the deeper messages in the books. They recognized the pieces but not the puzzle; they saw the surface without suspecting the undercurrent.

To examine the failed specimens, then, is to come closer to understanding the essential ingredients in a recipe that could not, apparently, be altered very much without losing some of its peculiar charm. It is also a way of looking again at the underlying message in the Nancy Drew books—surely the most interesting mystery about them—since that message says something about how and why they spoke to their readers so successfully.

Of the many Nancy Drew imitations, *Kay Tracey* came closest to reproducing exactly the obvious features of the original. This Stratemeyer series, written under the pseudonym Frances K. Judd, began in 1934 and ended eight years later. The protagonist, Kay, is sixteen, as Nancy was until the 1950s, with "beautiful brown eyes and light, waving hair . . . golden in the sun," and "possessed of great energy and resourcefulness." She has two devoted girl chums and a vague boyfriend named Ronald Earle. A slight variation on the model has Kay's father dead and Kay living with her mother and Cousin Bill, a "rising young lawyer."[2]

The rigorously genteel diction is vintage Stratemeyer: "We have been objects of curiosity, if not of derision," says Betty, one of the high school friends, who often "murmurs" her remarks.[3] An acquaintance, inviting Kay to the opera, tells her that "*Faust* is being rendered," and Kay herself inquires of a police officer whether a fire was "of incendiary origin."[4]

Some of the admirable simplicity of the Nancy Drew narratives has been lost, however, as well as Adams's consistent emphasis on her sleuth's rational detection methods. Kay Tracey plots make heavy demands on reader credulity, with coincidence and "hunches" accounting for most of Kay's solutions—which often seem laboriously long in coming. In theory, at least, Nancy Drew proceeds along a different tack. It would be hard to argue that Nancy Drew narratives are, in fact, tightly woven or highly credible or that Nancy is really less dependent than Kay is on happy chance. Nevertheless, a Nancy Drew mystery *tells* readers that Nancy works by logical reasoning from clues she has trained herself to see, even as others pass them by: "Nancy never guessed at anything."[5] Except for her ability to discern criminality at a glance, Nancy's prowess as a sleuth is, the books insist, a matter of close observation and clear thinking. Not luck, but reason, is Nancy's handmaiden.

When she isn't lurching from coincidence to happenstance, Kay Tracey stands, like her model, in a constant shower of praise. The author tells us that Kay is "courageous," "calm," and "extremely popular"; that her voice has the "ring of authority"; and that she drives a car "skillfully through traffic." So far, so good—but Nancy's real advantages have slipped through the net.

The stories fail to support the kind of authority and autonomy Nancy enjoys without question. The car is not Kay's—it is Cousin Bill's; the praise from other characters, especially male characters, is often thinned by condescension: "For a cousin, and a girl cousin at that," says the rising young lawyer, "you are unusually shrewd."[6] Kay's authority is also undercut by her clear identification as a school-girl. Though Nancy and Kay are the same age, Nancy is never connected with school; she carries no books, takes no exams. School is hardly a major consideration in Kay's life, but it does crop up now and then, reminding the reader, however fleetingly, of the prosaic realities of high school existence, which rarely includes high adventure or an authoritative voice in the affairs of adults.

Changing the widowed parent from father to mother was also unwise. There is cachet as well as convenience in having a "prominent attorney" father, who admires even as he keeps out of the way, who offers strength and reassurance but at sufficient distance to insure that the limelight is always Nancy's. Kay's mother has no cachet at all, though she carries nonintervention to the point of idiocy. Hearing of Kay's "exciting experience" of being hit over the head, drugged, and/ or hypnotized at a Chinese estate, her reaction is outstandingly—and typically—flaccid: "I am afraid that I sometimes grant you too much freedom, Kay," she "declares" plaintively. "If anything should happen to you I'd never forgive myself." Yet even so spineless a mother as Mrs. Tracey occasionally draws the line: "Kay simply cannot miss another day of school," she finally "interposes," and, briefly but distinctly, the reader hears again the thud of reality.[7]

Realism, even if of a dilute quality, may also have demolished the Penny Nichols series—there were only four titles published between 1936 and 1939—though it is what makes these stories rather engaging to an adult reader. Penny, the creation of Mildred A. Wirt ("Joan Clark"), has blue eyes, golden curls, no mother, a car, and a father who is a professional detective—all pretty familiar so far. But Penny's "rattletrap roadster," which she "paid for herself by teaching swimming at the YWCA," breaks down often, keeping her chronically short of cash, a more likely condition for a 1930s teenager than Nancy's enviable solvency. In fact, a sense of reality tempers most of this series's borrowing from the Nancy Drew model. Though Penny has "rare freedom" and "the complete confidence of her father," neither Penny's freedom nor her father's confidence is quite as complete as Nancy Drew's. Mr. Nichols often behaves like a real—albeit indulgent—father and sometimes like a real detective. He turns down Penny's bid to be present while he interviews a member of a car theft ring, since the man "would never talk as freely" if she were there. When she proposes to hide in the closet to listen, he dismisses the idea "as a trifle too theatrical for my taste." Nor does he talk to Penny about his cases, as Carson Drew does with Nancy; on the contrary, he sometimes withholds information: "Not that I don't trust you, but sometimes an unguarded word will destroy the work of weeks." As a matter of fact, "Penny knew that her father regarded her interest in the . . . case with amusement. He was humoring her in her desire to play at being a detective. . . . he did not really believe that her contributions were of great value."[8]

More dampening still, Mr. Nichols challenges the notion that crooks "look like" crooks ("Appearances are often deceitful, Penny") or that Penny can be sure that someone "isn't the criminal type." "And just what is the criminal type? Give me a definition," he asks exasperatingly, adding, in a most parental way, "I'm merely trying to teach you to think and not to arrive at conclusions through impulse or emotion."[9] Alas, Nancy Drew's success rate would have been cut in half had she not known "instinctively" who was and was not a crook.

Though Penny has some adventures, some of them quite like Nancy's, others slightly more plausible, and though she reaps the familiar praise for her luck and information, reality impinges on her constantly. She isn't always right and she is firmly under adult authority. Unlike Hannah Gruen, the Nicholses' "elderly housekeeper" feels free not only to scold Penny but also to prevent her from "investigating" a prowler outside the house. "You'll do nothing of the kind. We'll lock all the doors and not stir from the house until your father returns," says she.[10] And they do.

Adults do not turn to Penny for advice or help; her investigating efforts are viewed with tolerance at best and her achievements received with surprise. Her sleuthing is not invariably exciting. During a tedious wait for action, she sighs, "I don't believe I'm cut out to be a lady detective." To which her father replies with unglamorous accuracy, "A detective must learn to spend half of his time just waiting."[11] In short, everything about Penny Nichols—her possessions, talents, accomplishments, and experiences—is nearer human scale than is the case with Nancy Drew, and it is especially near teenage human scale. Penny's relationship to the adult world is perilously close to believable—no advantage in a genre whose central attraction is wish fulfillment.

Stratemeyer series books are dependably long on wish fulfillment; it was not an overdose of realism that weakened the Dana Girls as rivals to Nancy Drew. These mysteries, another Stratemeyer product designed to capitalize on the Nancy Drew phenomenon, were also supervised by Harriet Adams under the Carolyn Keene pseudonym. The publishing history suggests reasonable profitability; the series began in 1934 and was still appearing in 1979, though at only half the rate of the Nancy Drews.

In spite of Adams's guiding hand, the Dana girls are but pallid followers in the dazzling train of Nancy Drew. Though the stories share, predictably enough, a number of features with their model, the focus has been diffused. These books were apparently meant to combine the attractions of girl detective fiction with the boardingschool story—a genre fading in popularity by the 1930s—but the result was more a compromise than a fresh triumph. The device of using two protagonists rather than one has some attractions. The usual chums are unnecessary, and it's probably fun to think of having adventures with a congenial sister. On the other hand, sisters need to make more or less equal contributions to solving mysteries, where chums could be used to highlight the lone heroine's superior qualities, as Bess and George set off Nancy's. The Dana sisters cannot avoid sharing center stage; if Nancy does, it is through her own generosity—just another jewel in her crown.

As for the boarding school, no matter that it is "imposing," amazingly undemanding, and infinitely accommodating about letting the sister sleuths out of class to pursue their mysteries, it is still a school. It gives exams, and for the sisters to be loosed for a day of vigorous detective work requires adult intervention. Their genial guardian, Uncle Ned (surely a major part of the wish fulfillment in these books), is always happy to plead their case, and they actually miss very little of whatever excitement there is. Nevertheless, the school's presence weakens the mysteries, as the mysteries detract from the school story; the adult involvement takes some of the play away from the young protagonists, and the multiplicity of themes and characters blurs patterns that are sharply defined in the Nancy Drew books.

Lillian Garis's *Melody Lane* mysteries, published by Grosset and Dunlap from 1933 to 1940, also feature sisters, Cecy and Carol, who have a car, a widowed father, and a housekeeper with minimal authority over them. Though these stories were not Syndicate produced, the odd-flavored class consciousness so common to Stratemeyer books is rampant here as well. A 1935 title describes a caretaker "pleasant of face and manner yet sufficiently respectful to show . . . that he was a caretaker. He had the estate-retainer appearance and his little wife, who patted along back of him, seemed anxious to please." The xenophobia is also familiar, with *swarthiness* and *foreign* used as pejorative terms. Cecy refers to "queer dark women," remarking that she "never did like these foreign beauties." [12]

About there, however, close parallels between Garis's series and Nancy Drew end. Compared with any Stratemeyer book, Garis's are wordy and slow-paced; action waits upon aimless conversations and inconsequential business. The defect is surprising since Lillian Garis had written for Stratemeyer and ought to have understood the primacy of fast action in the Syndicate successes. Melody Lane plots are—by series standards—complex, with many secondary characters whose motivation is often unclear. Diction is quite unlike that in most Stratemeyer stories and is especially unlike that in the Nancy Drews. While adults speak with reasonable formality, young characters, including Cecy, use slang freely: "swell," "bucks," "kid," and "dead ringer." Among themselves, the girls chatter constantly about clothes and "cute boys."

But the most fundamental difference between Garis's girls and Nancy Drew is their distinctly secondary role vis-à-vis males, whether men or boys. Girls meet disparagement on every hand, from their own sex as often as from males. "Mere females should keep out of the way of vast machines," "Girls always have so many little things on their minds they just might neglect the real big ones," and "silly girl stunts" are all typical remarks—and two of the three come from the mouths of females. Girls scream and dither in tense situations, while boys act "calmly, as boys always do in an emergency," and men solve problems that baffle women and girls. Small wonder that somebody in a Garis book is forever exclaiming that "it was such a relief to have a man there."[13]

The plot action, such as it is, reinforces the idea that girls are inept, reactors rather than initiators. Cecy and Carol are sometimes brave, sometimes not, but nearly always they respond to situations rather than undertaking action—a very non–Nancy Drew approach. Nowhere in Garis's series is there the continuous tribute to her heroines' competence, courage, style, and renown that can be found in every chapter of every Nancy Drew mystery. And indeed, frivolous, small-minded, and dependent as they are, these girls have little claim to such paeans as Nancy earns on all sides at all times.

On the other hand, the author of the Dorothy Dixon mysteries surely went too far in the opposite direction. This series—written by "Dorothy Wayne" (pseudonym for Noel E. Sainsbury, Jr.) and published by the Goldsmith Publishing Company—lived and died, like a mayfly, in a single season; all four titles came out in 1933.[14] The books are a startling departure from other would-be Nancy Drew duplicates. If the Melody Lane sisters are less carefully genteel than Nancy Drew, Dorothy Dixon is in another league altogether. Dorothy—a sixteen-year-old "fly-girl" who owns a plane, knows jujitsu, throws a knife with deadly accuracy, and frequently carries a gun—operates at the far edge of seemliness for a girl of her era. Brusque, sarcastic, and aggressive, she bosses her "feminine" friend, Betty (whom she calls a "fluffball") unmercifully. Like Nancy, Dorothy is famous for solving mysteries ("nice ladylike reputation, what?"), but her temper is uneven and her language relentlessly tough and slangy.[15]

Improbable as it may seem, Dorothy has a boyfriend who collaborates on some adventures, though without calling forth much maidenly gratitude from Dorothy. Once, on a desperate climb up a rocky cliff in the dark, friend Bill points out that most of Dorothy's skirt has been torn away. "What of it?" replies Dorothy with her

usual grace. "There's a perfectly good pair of bloomers underneath."
Edward Stratemeyer would have fainted dead away.[16]

In the staid company of 1930s series books, the Dorothy Dixons
stand out as bizarre indeed. One cannot imagine Nancy proposi-
tioned by a young gangster, as Dorothy is, and the mind lulled
by Stratemeyer propriety boggles at Dorothy's laughing reply that
she is "expensive." Capping even this remarkable exchange is the
wrestling match between the gangster and Dorothy—which she, of
course, wins.[17]

Over all, these books are so far from the hackneyed, imitative safety
of most series stereotypes of girls that I have speculated whether
Mr. Sainsbury felt a sociologist's curiosity about the audience for girl
sleuth tales. Certainly, he never made his heroine play second fiddle
to male dominance. As Bill so truly says, "It's your show." "Attaboy!"
says Dorothy.[18]

But the Dorothy Dixon mysteries—which are quite awful, however
liberated—overreached the mark or overstrained reader credulity,
probably both. Perhaps Nancy Drew fans could believe in a roadster
but not a plane; more likely, they recognized that a Dorothy Dixon's
brash self-assertion went well beyond anything their own society was
prepared to tolerate in girls, so they could neither believe nor em-
brace this thorny model, even wishfully. Even as fantasy, Dorothy
Dixon was well outside the pale.

Evidence that the world was not yet ready for Dorothy Dixon might
be found in the Judy Bolton series by Margaret Sutton, which began
in 1932 and lasted until 1967. Fly-girl Dorothy, who had a "long
arm . . . unbending as tempered steel," had a will and an ego to
match.[19] Judy, on the other hand, though billed as the solver of the
mysteries published in her name, is prey to every standard feminine
weakness; no one could mistake her for a feminist outpost.

In fairness, these books should not be judged primarily as imitations of the Nancy Drew pattern, although Judy's sleuthing was an
important part of every story. Sutton filled out the usually spare series
formulas with more, and with more complex characters, as well as
moving her main character along life's road from high school girl
to young married woman. The earliest books were as much school
stories as detective yarns, and soon, as Judy's acquaintance with Peter

Dobbs developed, they became romances—of a very tame sort—as much as mysteries.

Except for the first few books, then, Judy is older than most of the girl sleuths who emulated Nancy Drew, and her age, if not her temperament, confers the requisite independence. Judy, however, squanders her independence on Peter, even taking typing and short-hand that she may help him in his office, "acting as his secretary, she proudly told friends."[20]

From the mildest feminist point of view, the Judy Bolton stories are discouraging, though certainly typical of their period. Judy is jeal-ous, unreasonable, and dependent. It is impossible to imagine Nancy Drew confessing that she is "afraid of thunder" and "snuggling a little closer to [anybody] as he drove the car" or sobbing on Ned's shoulder as Judy sobs on Peter's when he comes to the "haunted" house of strange noises.[21] One must assume that the appeal of these books was largely that of a conventional "girl's story," with family, school, and romance formulas heightened a little by mystery. It is not sur-prising that Sutton's book-a-year contract with Grosset and Dunlap was canceled in 1967.

Nancy Drew's success eluded every one of her rivals. Even those that survived past the 1930s never approached the Nancy Drew sales and certainly never wrote themselves on youthful hearts as Nancy did. Something in the Nancy Drew stories set them apart from others of the genre, making them deeply satisfying, not just to the genera-tion of girls who read them first, but to millions of girls who came after and who read them with the same passionate absorption in a very dif-ferent cultural climate. The non–Nancy Drew girl detective stories go a long way toward clarifying what that special something was.

What seem to me to be the telling differences between Nancy and her cohorts fall, very roughly, into two categories. The first is au-tonomy; the second is a steady and profound but largely covert and, I think, largely inadvertent feminism.

The imitators didn't miss the point about autonomy—which was, after all, plain as a pikestaff in every Nancy Drew story—but neither did they get it right. They were quite willing to lop off a parent; only Judy Bolton has a full set, and she soon outgrows their authority, but they never freed their heroines entirely from adult authority. Some saddled them with single parents who worried or set limits. Some showed them against school backgrounds or allowed them to be ruled occasionally by housekeepers, employers, or officials. In the Penny Nichols books, Mildred Wirt asserted her heroine's freedom, but her story constantly contradicts her, as Penny meets at every turn some adult afflicted with a normal sense of responsibility toward her youth and inexperience.

Dorothy Dixon is an exception to some of this, as she is to most generalizations; adults hardly figure in her stories, and school is never mentioned. She has the requisite single parent, a bank president father, very rich and very rarely an active part of her life. He is readily squashed. When he objects to the idea of her confronting the smugglers who tried to machine-gun her plane, she says, "Daddy, *don't* be ridic," in a tone "tolerantly amused," and he immediately subsides. If she wants some little thing—her own plane, for example—she wheedles, and he grants her wish, remarking fatuously that she has him wound around her little finger.[22]

This kind of exchange, of course, misses the mark as badly as Mrs. Tracey's ineffectual handwringing over Kay's pea-brained quests and not only because wheedling seems wildly out of keeping with Dorothy's character. The point about Nancy Drew's freedom is not just, or even mainly, its completeness but its dignity. Nancy's independence is not a gift coaxed from dim or fond adults. Autonomy is her *right*, won by her responsible and intelligent management of practically everything, and it is never seriously questioned. The enviable ease with which she exercises her total independence of adult authority is as impressive as the independence itself. In a typical passage, Nancy, fresh from some adventure involving a rainstorm, has begun a conversation with her father when Hannah intervenes with maternal solicitude: "You run up and take off those damp clothes at once, and take a hot bath before you catch cold!" But Nancy meets this modest demand with an aplomb born of certainty: " 'I'm not wet, but thank you for the advice!' Nancy laughed, 'I'm just as cozy here as can be.' "[23] And that's all there is to it: no argument, no defiance, no resentment, just a flat, good-natured, absolute refusal.

Even the obligatory discussions with Carson Drew about Nancy's sleuthing plans are more occasions for Carson Drew to express a loving concern for her welfare than his cue to lay down the law about risks she must not take. Again, the emotional level of these exchanges is low: "Oh Dad, I'll be all right," is usually sufficient to reassure Carson Drew. If not, he gives her a gun for her protection, otherwise trusting her "good judgment" to keep her safe.

At sixteen, Nancy suffers none of the irritating, arbitrary limitations that normally surround the young. She behaves like an adult in all matters of consequence; even more important for her readers, I suspect, she is treated like an adult. The occasional exceptions to this rule, mostly in early books and mostly by uncomprehending policemen, offer an opportunity for comeuppance scenes in which the doubters are reduced to confusion when they discover who it is they have scorned while Nancy retains "the composure of a queen." Crooks, of course, fall into the error of thinking that they are dealing with a "mere girl," but Nancy's flashing eye and crushing dignity soon alert them to their mistake: "Nancy's eyes narrowed. [The villain] hesitated. Something warned him that he was not dealing with a girl who could be bluffed."[24]

In short, Nancy transcends youth, moving through life with assurance and without struggle. Though she courts adventure and faces threats, she never has to contend with the humiliations, self-doubt, and uncertainties common to her age; she never has to plead, bluster, or fight for her independence. She is always right—the hallmark of adulthood to a child—always effective. Only villains, dumb policemen, and the nouveau riche ever oppose or dislike her. All socially acceptable people, rich or poor, powerful or suitably grateful, admire her and accept her autonomy.

The feminist aspects of Nancy Drew's allure are more complicated than those of her autonomy. In fact, *feminism,* as we usually use the term, often seems hardly to apply, yet the strongest messages in Nancy Drew *are* feminist—and absolutely central to the phenomenal appeal of the stories. I am not in a position to say how conscious or, at least, how crusading a feminist Harriet Adams was. But if she had set out to convey a strong feminist message through the books she edited, presumably the Dana girls would have expressed it, too—and they do not. Though their heroines are successful sleuths, they are also subject to the routine condescension girls encountered in the 1930s books, even those written expressly for girls. Nancy Drew never is. It is as though the character Edward Stratemeyer created carried with her a certain internal logic to which Adams responded; responded indeed, to the point of heightening the effects and curbing lapses in the original. All the early stories intensify, in small but significant ways, the characterization Stratemeyer began.

Stratemeyer, for example, called Nancy "unusually pretty." Adams favors "attractive," generally, and often leaves it at that; when she enlarges on the subject, however, she suggests the real source of beauty: "though [Nancy] could not be termed beautiful, her face was more interesting than that of either of her companions." Stratemeyer also established Nancy as "unusually capable" at sixteen, saluting her "habit of thinking things through to their logical conclusion."[25] Nevertheless, he often referred to her ideas as "intuitions" and tended to attribute to Carson Drew both her abilities ("probably inherited from her father") and the respect she commanded. After his death the Nancy Drew series emphasized skills and thinking more than "intuition," and usually took pains to describe Nancy's competence as a result of self-training: "she had developed an amazing ability to fight her own battles in the world"; "[she had] trained her powers of observation"; "good fortune attended her largely because of her own efforts." The series consistently stresses intention over happenstance. When George exclaims, "Oh, Nancy, I believe you've stumbled upon a real clue," Bess corrects her promptly: "She didn't exactly stumble. . . . She reasoned it all out."[26] A cold-eyed reader might see the long arm of chance in every chapter, but Adams rarely admits that it is there.

Stratemeyer's grasp of the legend he was—all unwittingly—fashioning was not always as sure as Adams's. It is startling to find even a brief excursion into pathos in a Nancy Drew mystery, but the first book has one: locked in a closet by a crook, "at first, Nancy was too frightened to think logically. She beat frantically upon the door with her fists. . . . At last, exhausted . . . , she fell down upon the floor, a dejected, crushed little figure."[27] It is a moment Adams never reproduced. Nancy has fears, even flashes of panic in various tight spots, but never again is she pitiful. Imprisoned in a cistern, she wastes no time in hysteria. "I'll depend on nobody—I must work myself out of this place."[28] And she does, with will power, physical strength, and resourcefulness. The persona that developed over the first ten years of the series had to do with triumph, not sympathy.

Nancy's universal competence is the most evident of the themes in the series that might be called feminist. The appeal for girl readers is beyond question; it would have spoken to them at any time, but the message was doubtless especially welcome in an era when such a characterization of a girl had so little company. The feminist current runs stronger than that, however.

Crusader or not, Harriet Adams took Stratemeyer's promising beginning and built on it until Nancy Drew was a model of strength and achievement that must have stirred every one of her readers at some level. With emphasis but not stridency, the books countered every stereotype of "feminine" weakness, including such standard fictional attributes as frivolity, vanity, squeamishness, and irrationality, quite as much as dependence and incompetence. More quietly yet, and more remarkably, still without disturbing the conventional surface of the stories or blundering beyond acceptability, the narratives included scene after scene of sex role reversal.

From the beginning the series established Nancy's seriousness, a quality granted freely to boys and men in fiction but rarely to young girls "The news reel . . . held Nancy's attention for a time, but as soon as a comedy was flashed on the screen, she lost interest." A film on New York society bores her. George and Bess, always representatives of the norm, enjoy such fare and often fritter their time away in light pursuits. Characteristically, when the three girls are en route to Arizona by train, George and Bess play bridge with other travelers while Nancy retires to the observation car to read up on the West. A full-fledged participant in the working—which is to say adult—world, Nancy is restless when not engaged in sleuthing; by the end of a vacation, she finds the "steady routine of fun . . . slightly monotonous." George and Bess, of course, bemoan the end of their holidays.[29]

Nancy's qualities are constantly highlighted by those of less serious-minded friends. As befits her vocation as a professional and in contrast to others of her age and sex, Nancy is disciplined, self-controlled, and prudent. Fond as she is of Helen Corning, her close friend in several early books, Nancy tells her little about the mystery she is investigating because Helen is a "natural born gossip. . . . it would be impossible for her to keep the matter to herself." Even when verbally assaulted by a low-class woman, Nancy can remember her purpose and control her response: "Nancy, how could you keep your temper?" exclaims Bess. To which Nancy replies, "What good would getting angry have done? . . . I found a clue by keeping the reins tight on my temper."[30]

Serious, competent, disciplined, and determined, Nancy already stands well apart from the usual characterizations of girls in formula fiction. But to observe her in action as she goes about her self-appointed business of sleuthing is to recognize how completely she has traded in the standard feminine role for an equally standard masculine part, not just in her initiative and courage, but in other ways as well, particularly vis-à-vis her closest "chums"—and Ned.

Even when not detecting, Nancy takes on roles normally awarded only to males. At Shadow Ranch, though all the girls except Bess join in the roundup, only Nancy is allowed to "cut-out," and she does it with her usual style: "Nancy rode fearlessly into the herd. . . . If she was uneasy, she did not show it, working deliberately and with cool calculation." Later, when four girls go into the mountains, Nancy takes along a revolver, with which she competently shoots a lynx. Later still, when the girls are badly lost, Nancy recognizes the part she must play. "Sensing that the morale of the group was about to break, Nancy knew she must assume definite leadership. Though her own courage was at low ebb, she must not disclose by word or action that she feared the worst." Finally, in one of the many confrontation scenes, Nancy actually socks the villain: "her fist landed squarely under Zang's chin. . . . he . . . sagged to the floor."[31] This last was perhaps a little extreme for Mrs. Adams; I don't find many instances of direct physical assault on villains, even by the redoubtable Nancy Drew.

But the role reversal is more interesting in the one-to-one exchanges between Nancy and her friends. It is easy to miss because the parts played really have nothing to do with sex and everything to do with character. Given Nancy Drew's confident, assertive personality, her behavior follows quite naturally and in no way seems "masculine."

In *Larkspur Lane,* Nancy is accompanied on her increasingly dangerous investigations by Helen Corning, who is cast in the highly recognizable female supporting role: admiring, anxious, respectful, and inconsequential. "She did not venture to question her chum, whose face was set in determined lines. 'Nancy, you are so brave and capable,' Helen sighed. Nancy made no reply." And again: "Helen wisely left Nancy to her own thoughts, waiting meekly in the car." And yet again: "Nancy was so engrossed in her plans that she did not answer [Helen's questions], so Helen resigned herself to silence."[32]

The duet continues as Nancy proposes to leave Helen over her protests: "'I'm afraid, and I don't want you to go alone . . . ,' [Helen] sobbed." Nancy reassures, but Helen goes on worrying and objecting until Nancy loses patience: "Oh, do brace up," she says sharply. "Helen could not refrain from weeping a little." Once Nancy has the intended rescue in hand, she tells Helen to go while she stays to see things through. Again Helen protests, anxiously, but Nancy is adamant. "'I—I—' began Helen, but Nancy leaned in and choked her off with a kiss. 'Please hurry,' she urged."[33]

None of this would be at all remarkable were a male protagonist in Nancy's place. The counterpoint of courage against fear, protest against impatient reassurance, is all very familiar, as is the meek silence in the presence of a deeply preoccupied hero—when the hero is masculine. Women, on the other hand, are usually expected to be attentive and responsive to others at all times; no one hesitates to interrupt a woman, since her occupations are judged neither important nor demanding enough to require real concentration. Nancy Drew, filling the role of hero, is also transcending her sex.

As for Ned, I think that no one was very interested in him, any more than many male authors are interested in the women they supply as appendages to their male heroes. Ned is necessary only because Nancy Drew must not lack any advantage a girl of her age might want; he is really just an attribute, like her golden hair and general popularity with her peers.

He gets short shrift, poor lad, from Adams, who never cares enough to make him anything but bland, obliging, and boring, as he does from Nancy who keeps him well down on her list of priorities. In *Larkspur Lane* Nancy remarks to Helen that she had called Ned and told him "something" of her plan. "He didn't agree with [it] at all, yet what can he do about changing it?" she says offhandedly. He offers to go with her as she explores, but she puts him off: "You may be of greater help in the reserve line of attack, as they say in the army."[34]

Role reversal hits a high point in *The Haunted Bridge*, with Nancy vigorously sleuthing and organizing while Ned plays the dull ancillary roles normally filled by girls. When an old man must be nursed in a cabin well away from the action, Nancy assigns Ned to do it. " 'I don't seem to be of much use for anything else,' Ned muttered. . . . [Nancy] gave the boy a warm smile and bade him take good care of the patient." After several days, she relents enough to offer him a night out. They are going to a dance at the resort hotel, but Nancy's mind, as usual, is on more serious things than dances or Ned. When he presents himself and asks how she likes his new suit, her reaction is absentminded: " 'You look handsome in it,' Nancy praised, without noting in detail what he wore."

And of course she does precious little dancing. She and Ned spend most of the time in the garden, "concealed" in some bush, waiting for a suspect to appear. She is not altogether heartless. Seeing Ned "glance wistfully toward the lighted ballroom," Nancy says, kindly, "Won't you go inside and dance?" But Ned says he would rather stay· with her; he knows his place, after all: "You tell me what to do and I'll obey orders with no questions asked."[35]

Ned's irrelevance varies from book to book. He is sometimes given a part to play in a last-minute rescue; Nancy is sometimes more complimentary toward him. But the balance of power is never altered in any real sense; it is always Nancy who thinks, directs, and acts. Her attitude toward Ned is amiable but preoccupied: as late as 1948, she forgets a long-standing date with him.[36] Ned is, basically, ornamental.

Naked and in full view, sex role reversal would have been radical stuff for 1930s series books—for any children's book, for that matter. But of course, in Nancy Drew, it was never bare and open; it was thoroughly veiled by layers of conventional propriety. Except for her taste for sleuthing, Nancy sends few outward signals that she is not bound by every standard, even stuffy, social expectation. Her language is ever formal and correct; she eschews slang, even of the mildest sort, approves of people of "good family" and good taste, and disapproves of those whose clothes or voices are loud or whose furniture is gaudy. For all her accomplishments, she is modest, as becomes a young maiden, always "flushing" at the praise so frequently heaped on her, always giving credit to others for the help she hardly needed. Not the faintest hint of masculinity emanates from Nancy. She never looks "slim and boyish in jodhpurs" as Dorothy Dixon does; she wears "frocks," "sports dresses," and an "exquisitely furred coat." She shops—quite a lot, actually—and thinks about what clothes she will take to the Emerson dance. Chum George may "scoff at anything feminine," but Nancy does not. Her behavior is exemplary, her opinions unexceptional, and her acceptance in society complete. A reader of Nancy Drew was unlikely to feel herself in the presence of radicalism.

What was achieved in Nancy Drew was, apparently, as accidental as it was monumental. Mrs. Adams always disclaimed any conscious intent to make Nancy "liberated," and the disclaimer is entirely believable. Under her editorship, the Syndicate's portraits of other women and of society in general seem ample evidence that Adams was neither a feminist nor any other kind of social radical. Yet Nancy Drew is the very embodiment of every girl's deepest yearning. As an image that combines the fundamental impulse of feminism with utter conventionality, she represents a wish that may be as unrecognized by the reader as it was by the author but a wish that is nevertheless felt at some level by every woman faced with the disadvantages of her sex.

It has always puzzled me that Freud found it so difficult to know "what women want." A woman of his own time could have told him: "The woman who wants to be a man—what is it that she really wants? . . . She wants to be what she may be and ought to be, a fully developed human being . . . , not to be a male. It is man who keeps insisting on the distinction of sex—woman would willingly forget it."[37] Harriet Adams might have told him, too, though not in such clear abstractions. But the answer was there to read in every Nancy Drew book—and in the sales figures they generated.

Women, and girls who are beginning to look toward being women, want what Nancy has. They want to be women *and* people; they do not want to have to choose as though the two were incompatible. They want to be taken seriously, given credit for what they accomplish; they want to be who they are with no more arbitrary restraints and preconceived expectations than men must contend with. They want to take part in the world directly, not to be pushed to the periphery, always and ever assigned a supporting role.

And they want all this without having to put themselves outside the normal rules of acceptance in society. They want to be accepted as women without struggle or disapproval or isolation at the same time they function as people. Nancy Drew's allure derives directly from these wants; she is the idealized expression of these yearnings as they translate to formula fiction.

In formula fiction, realism is irrelevant, and complexity is a mistake; the difficulties of change—the process, conflict, and nuances of social reality—are not acknowledged. Nancy Drew is hardly fully developed as either fiction or reality, but she is unmistakably the image, however abstract, of a young woman who is able to forget the "distinction of sex"—at least so far as that "distinction" has been rewritten as limitation. As a girl who suffers none of the social drawbacks of her sex, who functions as only men are normally permitted to function in her society without losing the least part of her acceptability as a woman, Nancy Drew is herself the dominant message of the series.

The genius of the series, even if it was unconscious, was to offer a dazzling creation wrapped in a cloak of such thick conventionality that neither author nor readers were ever obliged to look directly at its light. But the glow that escaped the muffling sufficed, and it gave the Nancy Drew mysteries a radiance her imitators never had.

Girls' Novels in
Post–World War II America

><€ ><

Oh adolescence, adolescence! I wince before thy
    incandescence!
Thou standst with loafer-flattened feet
Where bras and funny papers meet

                                        Ogden Nash

The teenage girls' novel took its present form in the post–World
War II era.[1] It had antecedents; American fiction for and about adolescent girls dates back at least as far as Louisa May Alcott's novels for
the young. But postwar novels were new in their tighter focus—on
a single protagonist, on a brief time period (a few weeks or months,
rather than years), and above all on adolescence as adolescence. And
these characteristics remain typical, though in all other respects the
postwar literature seems to belong to another world.

For today's reader, post–World War II girls' novels written from
about 1945 to 1965 are powerful measures of how social change has
reordered adolescence in a quarter of a century. The manners, the
mores, the configuration of the family, parents' and children's expectations of one another, and the very tone of discourse in adolescent

fiction have changed utterly since the mid-1960s, so that postwar stories read now like letters from another country where the climate is milder and the road to maturity less stony than it is here.

Postwar literature also demonstrates with particular clarity the ambiguity of children's literature as cultural documentation. Written mostly (though not exclusively) for girls and by women, the books in many ways echoed themes pervasive in the popular culture of the period. Domesticity dominated the fiction, which took a hopeful view of the world, avoiding conflict and providing reassuring, happy endings. Serious or controversial issues were not the stuff of these novels; family and private happiness were. So much would seem to identify the literature with its time; the fervent, optimistic domesticity of the postwar era is after all a byword in American cultural history. An uncritical enthusiasm for a conservative (and highly idealized) view of family life, and a preoccupation with personal satisfactions, are as typical of the period as of the books.

Yet in nearly every other way, postwar fiction seems detached from its surroundings. With only a few exceptions, the stories said nothing about the political and social realities that remade a world or, for that matter, about those reshaping the society at home. Material prosperity, the cold war, the nuclear threat, world power, McCarthyism, civil rights, suburbanism, TV—all are hard to find in the literature as a whole. Even in a politically quiescent atmosphere, and even for a literature traditionally more concerned with individual experience than with social issues, postwar writing for teens was remarkable for its silences and was exceptionally unrevealing about the anxieties of its time, anxieties that often had to do quite directly with the young: war, both potential and actual; juvenile delinquency and rebellion; changing social mores.

The teen novel was one artifact of an adolescent culture that burst into being after the Second World War. Postwar prosperity altered decisively how children and, more particularly, how adolescents lived in American society. To begin with, more of them went to school and for longer. In 1940, about three-quarters of all American children went to high school; by 1960, 87 percent did. Social class as well as numbers transformed the high school scene. At the beginning of the

1930s, only about 50 percent of working-class children attended high school; three decades later, the proportion was closer to 90 percent. By 1960, high school had become a nearly universal experience for American adolescents.

The number of teenagers in the working economy rose dramatically after 1942. The first four decades of the twentieth century had seen the young increasingly removed from the labor market by child labor laws, compulsory high school laws, and a steady decline in the demand for agricultural labor. The war years reversed that trend, offering new opportunities for teenagers to work, especially part-time. By the mid-1960s, about half of all American high-school-aged youngsters held jobs sometime during the year.

In the same period, the age of marriage fell to a record low, in part because teenage marriages increased sharply after the war. The mid-1950s saw 14 million girls engaged by age seventeen; most of them would be married by the time they were eighteen. Throughout the 1950s, Americans married earlier than did their counterparts in other Western nations.[2]

Taken together, these statistics outline a social phenomenon: the development of a distinctive teenage culture, a culture that was something of a paradox. On the one hand, American children were staying in school longer, living in their parental homes longer, and postponing full-time employment and full-fledged responsibility as adults. At the same time, they married young, often establishing families within a few years of leaving high school. Even while they were still in school and living at home, many postwar teens enjoyed an economic power at odds with their dependent status. Growing up in an expanding economy, they were not asked to contribute their earnings to the general family welfare, as earlier generations of young workers had, but could spend their money on their own enjoyment.

And so they did. Teenagers became a whole new commercial market for manufacturers of everything from radios and records to bobby socks and penny loafers. They bought cars—not new cars but that great American bargain, the clunker, which gave them endless mechanical trouble but also an unprecedented mobility and, with it, an unprecedented freedom from direct adult supervision. No wonder that many adults, with some uneasiness, began to see teenagers as a separate cultural group, whose language, clothes, music, and outlook differed from those of the rest of the society.

These developments did not escape publishers. As prosperity stimulated the production of children's books, authors and publishers made a bid for the new teenage market by dividing the ever-popular family story into two forms, one aimed at children below twelve, which kept a focus on the family as a whole, and one directed to teens, which made an adolescent the central character. Girls' novels were a subset, by far the largest, of the literature aimed at teenagers.

The typical postwar teen novel has as its protagonist a girl of fifteen or sixteen who lives quite happily with her parents and a brother or sister or two and goes quite happily to high school, where she has a few friends but not, usually, either enormous popularity or a settled boyfriend.[3] She feels these lacks keenly, having reached a period of uncertainty about herself and about the values that have served her well up to this time. Uncertainty is the emblem of adolescence for the authors, most of whom define it, implicitly but exclusively, as social uncertainty. The plot covers a few weeks or months and centers upon the resolution of a very mild personal crisis. The crisis, like the uncertainty, is neither intellectual nor spiritual but social; the protagonist must define who she is and where she fits in the teenage milieu and, by extension, in the broader society.

Around this simple standard plot authors wrote exemplary tales showing the difference between sound and unsound values and promoting the wisdom of self-acceptance. The heroines are of the girl-next-door variety, neither glamorous nor sophisticated nor original, though at some point in the story they yearn to be one or all of these. Jane Purdy, in Beverly Cleary's *Fifteen*, compares herself unhappily to Marcy, a "cashmere sweater type" who dates all the "most popular boys in school" and has her name in the school paper every week. "Jane had her name in the school paper when she served on the clean-up committee after the freshman tea. Marcy belonged. Jane did not."[4] The distinction is basic to high school life. Mary Fred Malone, of *Meet the Malones,* knows as well as Jane Purdy where she does and does not fit; she's a "mop-squeezer." "That was Harkness High jargon. The studes were the spectacled grinds with high grades. The mop-squeezers were the girls who served on committees, who worked on the paper, who did the grubby behind-the-scene jobs."[5] The third category, the "queens," needs no explanation.

The emphasis on social place in the high school is characteristic. Social structures in school are vivid; other aspects of school life are dimmer. Considering that it was the amount of time spent in school that bonded adolescents together, it is surprising how rarely the classroom appears in this fiction. Except that some heroines like their English classes, nothing much is said about teachers, classrooms, or what is (or is not) learned. Conversations at the lockers and an occasional sighting of extracurricular activities such as newspapers or dances are all there is of school in most books. And in fact, by the 1950s, the shared experience of high school *was* more likely to be social than intellectual. High school was no longer for the special few who expected to go on to college; it was for everyone, college-bound or not. Even those who expected to go on to college were neither as small nor as elite a group as they would have been before postwar prosperity and the GI Bill broadened both aspirations and opportunity. Intellectual ambition was not the glue that held high school culture together. As writers of teen novels knew, it was social relations—relations, that is, with their peers—that made American teenagers a group.

Apart from the sharply drawn categories of high school society, home is more vivid than school in these novels, and it is here that continuity with the literature of the prewar period is strongest. Until about the mid-1960s, girls' novels, like other family stories, throw a golden light on families. Almost without exception, home is happy, supportive, tolerant, and secure. There are some small concessions to the tradition of adolescent as moody or impatient with parental authority, but the examples are usually so very gentle that a veteran of more recent literature might miss them altogether. "Jane stared defiantly at her mother and father. 'You just don't want me to have any fun!' Jane knew when she said this that it was not true. Her mother and father were both anxious for her to have a good time, but somehow this was the sort of thing she had found herself saying to them lately."[6]

Such faint negatives are more than offset by lots of explicit gratitude toward parents. L'Engle's Austin children contemplate their own good fortune often: "We have Mother and Father and we have each other. . . . think how lucky that makes us." "[Mom and Dad] are really sweet, as parents go," says a DuJardin heroine.[7]

Protagonists in this fiction have good reason to be pleased with their parents, who ride out the changes of adolescence with an aplomb that is unshakable, if somewhat patronizing. In Betty Cavanna's *Accent on April*, sixteen-year-old Kathy bemoans her seventeen-year-old brother's changed behavior. He was an ideal brother, but now he has become very critical of her. "He'll outgrow it, pet," her mother assures her, "It's just a phase. This is Jon's year for discovering the life of the mind. He thinks we're just frivolous women. People mature on different levels."[8]

As this passage suggests, the voice in the adolescent novel is primarily the voice of an adult. Unlike contemporary adolescent literature, in which the first-person narrative is well-nigh standard, the postwar novel more often uses third person, with unabashed overtones of the author's point of view. Model adult attitudes are set out by the fictional parents, whose virtues, like their personalities, are soothing rather than colorful. Parents look on adolescence as a phase—odd, perhaps, even a little troubling, but still only a stage that their children must pass through on the way to adulthood. They are patient and understanding, helpful when they can be, tolerant when their help is not wanted. Authors, in the guise of fictional parents, evidently trusted girls to weather adolescence without serious difficulty and to grow into responsible adults whose lives would closely resemble those of their parents.

Realistic children's literature nearly always bends toward socializing the young, imparting values, and distinguishing desirable behavior from the deplorable. The literary mechanisms for accomplishing these tasks vary from era to era, but one perennially popular way is for the narrative to lead its major character from a mistaken understanding of happiness to a true one. Postwar girls' novels do this in predictable, repeated patterns.

To find her place in her small world—which guarantees that she will know her place in the larger world—the heroine of a teen novel must first understand what kind of person she is. In most cases, she already has a pretty clear idea about this as the story begins, since the merciless hierarchies of high school are inescapable and she does not dispute them. She defines herself as average, though the author is usually careful to let the reader know that she is pretty, if not beautiful, and bright enough to get along well in high school, though she may struggle with math. Sometimes she enjoys a small talent for something, like dog portraits or English composition or painting stage scenery, but she is never burdened by a major gift or a burning ambition.

The real task facing the heroine is not so much discovering as accepting what and who she is and cleaving to the values she has learned at home. Her passage to that acceptance is the story. What happens in most teen novels is what happened when Meg March went to Vanity Fair. The heroine turns away, temporarily, from the right values toward the wrong. She tries to be something she isn't or falls in love with the wrong sort of boy, mistaking looks or popularity for true worth. Thus, Jean, in *Jean and Johnny*, believes that she has found Love and the Right Boy in handsome, popular Johnny, only to discover that Johnny cares exclusively for Johnny and that her illusions have made her temporarily blind to real character in the form of a shorter, plainer, but more honest boy.[9] Mary Fred Malone's lapse is yet more reminiscent of Meg's. Not only is she enthralled with the Wrong Boy, but (like Meg), she turns herself into a "queen" with fine clothes and unaccustomed makeup, when by nature she is really a "mop-squeezer." She—and, not incidentally, her family—suffers before she stops being "a traitor to herself [and those] who . . . turned to her." The decision to revert to type always brings happiness, as Mary Fred discovers: "Why, it's more fun to be home and doing things. . . . It's more fun being with Ander than it is with Dike."[10]

A generation with raised consciousness has ruefully (and rightly) observed that the validation of self that is the essential ingredient of every teen novel in this period requires the girl to win the approval of a respectable boy. The attitude, of course, belongs to the era, which "saw a resurgence [after the war years] of a traditional emphasis on woman's role."[11] "Traditional" is something of an understatement. Like film, TV, and popular journalism, postwar adolescent fiction glorified the domesticated woman. Gender roles were absolutely defined: for husband and wife, for brother and sister, and in any dating situation. Books were full of generalizations, half-jocular (but only half), which began with "men always" and "women never." No one ever objected, just as no one ever stepped out of his or her traditional place. Few fictional mothers worked, unless at a sideline and at home. Those few who did work outside the home had jobs, usually part-time, not careers; they posed no challenge to the traditional male breadwinner. Fictional families were usually two-parent, and if one parent was missing, it was through death, not divorce. The only mention of divorce was in connection with minor characters, giving the protagonist an opportunity to reflect on her own good fortune in having an intact family.

The reality of early marriage was an integral part of the literature, a little displaced from center but very much present. Parental relationships were nearly always tolerant, affectionate, and secure, subtly underscoring the long-term rewards of matrimony. The marriage of an older sister or brother, fairly common as a subplot in the fiction, offered romance, excitement, and a glimpse of the bliss and attention the protagonist could look forward to—perhaps quite soon. In Cleary's *Sister of the Bride,* the older sister is eighteen, a first-year student at Berkeley. The radiance of the wedding far outshines the slight gloom cast by the adults who sigh over the tender age of the bride. Adolescent novels rarely admitted real conflict between college and marriage, even young marriage. They hardly ever advised against early marriage, and they took the high school romances that are central to the stories quite seriously. The passing nature of teen romance was not emphasized; a naive reader of the novels could well have believed that first love was the only love possible. Without any demographic figures at hand, it would be entirely possible to deduce the declining age of marriage from postwar girls' stories.

But not the cold war, the civil rights movement, the Korean "conflict," or even the enormous postwar prosperity: adolescent fiction was not a simple "reflection" of the postwar era. While some sociological facts of American society emerged clearly, others surfaced only occasionally and still others were altogether absent. The explosion of suburban development after World War II hardly registered even as late as 1960. There were no scraped tracts of look-alike houses in the literature. Most authors looked backward for their settings to leafy, pleasant neighborhoods, "neither very rich nor very poor," in small towns or cities, and to houses that were not new, and certainly not split-level, but old and roomy and comfortable, if a little shabby. Postwar materialism, with its new appliances, new cars, and upward economic mobility, is undetectable. Weber's Malones and Cleary's various heroines baby-sit or otherwise earn their own money for clothes or excursions outside the family budget. A Cavanna protagonist wears an old (but becoming) cotton dress to her first high school dance.[12] Fathers' occupations, which range from postman to professor to newspaperman to doctor, provide an adequate style of living but not a lavish one. Until at least the end of the 1950s, most of these novels treated money matters, if not anxiously, at least consciously; the feeling was often closer to pre- than to postwar.

Serious issues were elusive, to say the least. One does not look for in-depth discussions of doomsday in an adolescent novel, but it would not be unreasonable to expect to find some traces of cold war anxiety in the literature. Young people in their teens were, after all, next in line; there was still a draft, and high school boys who were fifteen were only three years from eligibility. Though teenagers surely worried about war, the atomic bomb, and the draft, most of the literature written for them skirted such uncomfortable subjects. The civil rights movement was nearly as invisible. Adele DeLeeuw's novel *The Barred Road* (1954) was exceptional in the 1950s for approaching the subject of racism, yet the book is more notable for its novelty than for its boldness. DeLeeuw's handling of her subject was far too cautious to pose any threat to middle-class prejudices, conscious or unconscious. Juvenile delinquency, which attracted congressional and media attention off and on throughout the 1950s, surfaced only occasionally in girls' novels, to be quickly dismissed as irrelevant to the story's protagonists and, by extension, to its readers. Cleary's Jane Purdy easily persuades her parents that delinquency has nothing to do with their daughter, while L'Engle's Austin family learns that "hoods" can be handled with dispatch by an authoritative adult, at least if the adult is Dr. Austin, who is "used to being obeyed . . . [and] has a black belt in Judo."[13]

Judging from the quantities of published material on the subject, postwar American society had a consuming interest in adolescence, part fond, part fearful. Popular and learned opinion makers alike discussed teenagers endlessly, and if they did not agree about whether adolescents were mostly harmless or really dangerous, they did generally agree on the distinctive characteristics that marked the stage of life: emerging sexuality, a need to establish identity, and a tendency to rebel against authority. Erik Erikson's influential *Childhood and Society,* published in 1950, described psychological development as a series of stages defined by tasks. The adolescent's main task, according to Erikson, is to achieve identity, to clarify himself in relation to self, society, and peers. The adolescent must reconcile the morality he learned as a child with the ethical system he will adopt as an adult. So, Erikson said, the adolescent is concerned with ideas and choices: "It is an ideological mind," he observed. Erikson also characterized adolescent rebellion as part of a normal developmental pattern; as one historian has observed, he made "rebellion acceptable." Max Lerner concurred, observing that "every adolescent must pass through two critical periods: one when he identifies with a model—a father, an older brother, a teacher—the second when he disassociates himself from his model, rebels against him, reasserts his own selfhood."[14]

The masculine pronoun is no accident here; the influential theorists of human development constructed their ideas of adolescence primarily on the male model. Adolescence in the abstract operated in the active voice, asserting selfhood, constructing personal ethics, rebelling against constricting patterns of family and childhood. But the forceful images of adolescence that gave it its reputation for tumult came through in the language describing male adolescence.

Neither the language nor the images survived with the same force in girls' books; there adolescent characteristics were softened or deflected to accommodate accepted cultural ideas of girl- and womanhood. The clearest case is that of sexuality. Open acknowledgment of sexual changes or sexual feelings was out of the question; the subject was never raised as such. Authors handled the consequences of puberty symbolically, showing their heroines awakening to a concern with their physical appearance, to an interest in dating and, most of all, to a yearning to be admired by an attractive boy.

The sexual power of adolescent girls acknowledged one way or another in literature through the ages is missing in the teen novel. Louisa May Alcott gave her girls "influence" with which to improve boys, "influence" being the nineteenth-century euphemism for power when it was ascribed to a woman. Postwar fiction concedes not even this much to the "good" girls. Novels by Weber and DeLeeuw, in fact, give the influence for good to boys who use it to squelch girls who step out of character. Only the "queens," the girls who know how to dress and toss their hair, consciously use their power to attract male attention: "queens had a preening awareness of the other sex." [15] Girls' stories did not approve that brand of awareness. Whenever a "good" girl imitates the flirts, she is always brought back in line by uncomfortable consequences and is pretty often reprimanded by a high-minded boy. Sexuality was a dangerous commodity.

Real rebellion was as taboo as sexuality. The literature gave faint assent to the Erikson model but no more. Girls' rebellions are usually no more than brief flashes of mild exasperation followed by contrite reflections on how lucky they really are in their families. Serious conflict, especially conflict between generations, did not happen. Good parents (and the main character's parents were always good) managed their families through tolerance and understanding. The rule was to reconcile differences and avoid confrontation, an ideal entirely attainable, given the acquiescent nature of fictional adolescents.

But it is in the matter of identity as the major task of adolescence that the stringent limits in girls' fiction become most clearly apparent. To form an identity implies making choices, which in turn implies the existence of alternative possibilities and the power to choose among them. Yet the girls who are the central characters in teen novels have few real choices, fewer prospects, and no real power. The central task of adolescence as Erikson defined it scarcely exists for them: their sex has already determined their identity.

The only approved role model for girls in these novels is that of wife and mother. The single or (worse) divorced aunt who has a career is a sketchy figure at best and often either slightly comic or a little pathetic. The exceedingly rare mother who works full-time at a real career does so offstage and in the shadow of mild disapproval because she does not bake cookies or sew on buttons.[16] If they work at all, fictional mothers work for "extra" money, rather like the teenagers themselves.

Though high school girls sometimes refer to "careers" in these stories, they mean a few years as an airline stewardess or maybe an unspecified something in a publishing house, not a long-term commitment requiring professional training. Standard professions like doctor, lawyer, scientist, or university teacher are never mentioned as possibilities for women. Even the Mary Stolz heroine who says she will become "an archeologist, or a Navy nurse, or a traveling salesman" is not really an exception. As her best friend observes, "You don't want to be all those things because you want to be them. You only want not to be a housewife, which is quite a different matter. Ambition isn't part of it."[17] And sure enough, when Betty meets the right man, she abandons her career notions, probable and otherwise, and plans to marry within a few years. Though few fictional girls actively wish to be housewives, all of them want to marry. Most of them expect to go to college but not because they are searching for intellectual development. Girls see college as a place to meet someone suitable to marry (if they have not already accomplished this) or as a holding pattern for a few years between high school and marriage. It is notable that parents in the fiction never offer a different vision of higher education; quite obviously, college *was* a superior marriage market for the daughters of the middle class.

More striking still than the narrow future held out to girls is the pervasive leveling pressure in these novels. In dozens of ways, implicit and explicit, the literature counsels acquiescence, acceptance, and adjustment to undemanding prospects. Ambition is decidedly not "part of it"; in fact, fictional girls often reduce their already meager choices by adopting further, and self-constructed, boundaries. Cleary's Jean knows that she and her best friend are "salt-of-the-earth types . . . , girls whom no one would ever expect to dance a ballet, fly an airplane, run for Congress." And that is quite all right with Jean, who does not even aspire to cheerleading. " 'I would rather be part of the crowd cheering for the team,' said Jean."[18]

A litany of limitation runs through book after book: Beany Malone "had no illusions about herself," which is to say that she, like her older sister before her, is a "mop-squeezer" who willingly takes on unspectacular domestic duties, at school as at home. Jane Purdy classifies herself, contentedly, as "an ordinary girl," and Morgan Connor's father describes her as "destined, from the start, to be a mother and a wife. Not anything daring or glimmering." Morgan's own reflections not only do not challenge this assessment, they show her resigned to "years of waiting" before her destiny can begin.[19] Even if authors suggest some possibilities outside the domestic, basic priorities are always clear. Whatever else she may consider doing, a girl must conform to conventional ideals of feminine attractiveness and behavior, even if it means putting her own tastes and aspirations aside.[20]

No one can doubt that the emphasis on the value of an average person was kindly meant. Writers wanted to tell their adolescent readers that it was possible to be attractive and worthwhile even if one was not outstanding, to reassure girls who were not "queens" of their high school hierarchy that they were not therefore doomed as outcasts for all time. The ever-audible adult voice in the novels spoke firmly against the shallow values of mere popularity and good looks (though the unspoken messages were more ambiguous) and in support of honesty, loyalty, and simplicity. Be true to yourself and to home-taught values, the stories told their readers, and you will find acceptance and love.

All the same, there is something sad about the persistent damping down of ambition, the rounding of all the sharp corners of life, the denial of conflict and individuality. Change is inevitable for any growing organism, and for the adolescent, it is the very definition of being. And no change is entirely without difficulties; the passage from one stage of life to the next is rarely accomplished without some pain.

The literature admitted this in theory but denied it in fact. Authors consistently minimized the hazards in the road from childhood to young adulthood, refused to acknowledge that real conflicts can arise between parents and their developing children, and, ultimately, trivialized the choices that adolescents confront. Even in protected environments like most of those depicted in the fiction, ethical and moral issues are inescapable for teenagers: sex and alcohol are only the most obvious examples for the postwar period. Yet genuine ethical dilemmas, even on less touchy subjects, are remarkably uncommon in the literature, and when they do come up, it is only to be quickly resolved or dismissed altogether. The adolescent mind revealed in teen fiction is not just nonideological, it is ideologically untouched—like a child's, in fact.

Most novels leave the impression that authors resisted the realities of adolescent change. They were reluctant to withdraw childhood's protection from the developing teenager and more than reluctant to acknowledge the decisions every youngster must sooner or later confront. In this they were representative of many adults for whom the indeterminate quality of postwar adolescence complicated the relationship between parent and child. Teenagers were economically independent as consumers even when they continued to be dependents within the family, which meant that while their parents fed and housed them, teenagers could—and did—buy clothing, cars, and records their parents deplored. Teenagers in the prosperous postwar years could be less responsible in some ways than teens of earlier generations, yet many graduated early into marriage and family responsibilities, while others prolonged their semidependent status in college. The mismatch between adolescent dependence on the one hand and autonomy on the other was an obvious source of conflict in many families.

The teen subculture also had two sides. It could be seen as just young, naive, harmlessly faddy, and a little kooky, something an adult could observe with amused tolerance. But there was a dark side. The contemporary concern with juvenile delinquency, the alarms set off by "zoot-suiters," and "Beats" reflected the anxiety of adults who saw their children moving out of the protective family circle into a dangerous twilight zone. Not yet fully mature, but no longer within the safe realm of childhood, adolescents seemed vulnerable to every threat in the changing culture. And there can be no question that the distaste many Americans felt for some aspects of teen culture—the tight jeans, DA haircuts, rock music, and hot rods, among others—barely masked anxieties about class, sexual morality, and adolescent rebellion against mainstream American culture.[21] Hollywood is rarely prescient, but some 1950s movies caught the tone, as in *Rebel Without a Cause, Blackboard Jungle,* and *Blue Denim.*

Girls' novels, on the other hand, ignored the dark side of adolescent culture in favor of sunny optimism and affectionate tolerance. Madeleine L'Engle sometimes raised questions of delinquency and alienation in the young, usually to supply her answer: loving but authoritarian parents and religious certainty. Most stories, however, were simply cheerful, protective, bland—and full of silences. To compare these novels with Barbara White's findings in her study of adult novels of American girlhood is to see how much of even personal experience was left out of teen fiction. In adult fiction published between 1920 and 1972, White found remarkably consistent themes in women's novels about growing up. Again and again, she observes, "the protagonist is in conflict over her gender role." Adolescent heroines in adult novels have "negative attitudes toward marriage," seeing it as "a . . . kind of dying . . . , [as] identity destroyed." Again and again, the heroines find no adult role models acceptable to them. The girls in Katherine Anne Porter's *Old Mortality* and Sylvia Plath's *The Bell Jar* conclude that there is "no place" for a girl in the world except "serving men"—which they do not want.[22]

This kind of rejection of her social role never occurs to the protagonist of a typical teen novel, nor is there the slightest hint of the physical fears and traumas White found often in adult novels of adolescence. Where adult novels showed their adolescent protagonists repelled by sex, fearful of childbirth, and, often, victims of rape or near-rape, teen novels were far too sanitized to offer even veiled references to such subjects.

Instead, girls found patterns in these books they could as well have found in nineteenth-century literature for girls. Their novels pointed them toward a future that was loving, limited, safe, familiar, and dependent. Obligatory mention of college and career were scarcely convincing, since in the overwhelming majority of the stories no girl evinces the faintest intellectual curiosity or long-range ambition to do or to be anything in particular. College was justified, as it had been justified in the nineteenth century, by the proposition that an educated woman was "better equipped to be a wife and mother."[23] Like adolescent girls for generations before them, young women of postwar America were pressed to trade possibility for security and love. Their literature told them, indirectly but persistently, that there were no other real choices for them.

Hindsight is clearer. Scholars have shown that the postwar years were an aberration in American social history, not a trend.[24] Even as popular magazines, TV sitcoms, and teen fiction sang of early marriage, large families, and lifelong domesticity as every girl's certain destiny, reality was moving in another direction. Though conventional opinion holds that all postwar American wives were in the house, baking cookies and making the linoleum shine, in fact "between 1940 and 1950 the most rapid acceleration in labor force participation occurred among women who were between thirty-five and fifty years old."[25] To be sure, mothers with small children were still mostly at home; nevertheless, the prevailing wind had shifted. Married women no longer believed they had to occupy for life what the nineteenth century had called "a separate sphere." They might work only part-time, they might have jobs rather than careers, but even in the domesticated fifties, women were employed outside their homes in record numbers. By 1960, the marriage age had begun to rise again, the birth rate dropped, and the divorce rate resumed its long climb upward.[26]

The greatly expanded opportunity in the postwar years to go to college also opened new possibilities to girls, even if they did not always pursue them. Many a college-educated woman who had embraced the domestic ideals of the 1950s came to recognize, and regret, the opportunities she had not taken. By the mid-1960s, such women, who found their disillusionment voiced in Betty Friedan's *The Feminine Mystique*, were a strong phalanx in a resurgent women's movement.

It is enlightening to consider the girl who read Beverly Cleary's *Sister of the Bride* in 1963, the year of its publication. She was probably thirteen or fourteen, reading about sixteen-year-old Barbara caught up in the excitement of her eighteen-year-old sister's wedding. Barbara thinks, often, that she herself may be a bride—like Rosemary—in only two years if she can launch her dating career promptly, which she does by the book's end.

In five years, when Cleary's reader is eighteen or nineteen, it will be 1968. Will she—like Rosemary—be going to bridal showers, adapting her grandmother's wedding veil to her own wedding dress, joining a Dames Club as the wife of a graduate student, and earning a "PhT"—Putting Him Through—that is, working to support her husband's graduate study? Maybe. But then again, she might be riding a freedom bus, demonstrating against the Vietnam war on a campus somewhere, or getting her head bloodied at the Democratic Convention in Chicago. Or she might be beginning an academic effort that will lead her eventually to her own professional degree and career. Outside the kindly but closed world of the postwar teen novel, time moved on, and adolescents inevitably moved with it. American culture, it turned out, had not obliterated the social changes wrought by depression and war. Life held more possibilities, even for girls, than the fiction predicted and more revolutions than the authors (or almost anyone else) had guessed. By the middle of the 1960s, political and social changes leaned hard on the crystal cage that had surrounded children's literature for decades. It cracked, and the world flowed in.

American Boys

Bad Boys:
Tom Bailey and Tom Sawyer

><del>€ ></del><

"This is the story of a bad boy. Well, not such a very bad, but a pretty bad boy . . ." So begins Thomas Bailey Aldrich's autobiographical novel of his boyhood years in New Hampshire. No one is meant to believe, of course, that Tom Bailey was really "bad." He was just "a real human boy, such as you may meet anywhere in New England, and no more like the impossible boy in a story-book than a sound orange is like one that has been sucked dry." [1] The self-congratulatory tone is already apparent; this story of boyish escapades is meant to be amusing and nostalgic—no moral edification is intended. It is a tale of American boyhood as it should be, lived by a hero who surely wears Leslie Fiedler's Good Bad Boy label.[2]

So too Mark Twain's *Adventures of Tom Sawyer*. Most of the adventures, Twain says, were really true; they were his or those of his boyhood friends, and Tom combined "the characters of three boys whom I knew." [3] In other words, these two stories, one published in 1869, the other in 1875, both in some degree autobiographical, present the authors' ideas of "real" American boyhood. Their concept of boyhood must have matched that of most Americans, if the popularity of both books then and for a long time afterward is any measure.

The novels differ in tone. Aldrich seems at all times aware of an adult as well as a child audience, while Twain speaks more directly (though by no means exclusively) to a young reader. Aldrich reminisces throughout his book, remembering himself and his exploits with fond amusement, reminding the reader that he is a grown man reflecting on events long past. Twain also steps back from his story from time to time to comment on it, but his presence is more anonymous and less obtrusive than Aldrich's. This difference alone, as Ann Beattie remarks, may account for *Tom Sawyer*'s status as a major classic, while Aldrich's story is "at best, a minor one."[4]

In many respects, the two stories cover a good deal of the same ground, showing their heroes in relation to the social and moral order of their communities, the institutions of church and school, and to a lesser extent, their families. Neither boy's family setting is quite standard. *The Story of a Bad Boy* begins with Tom's parents deciding to take him from their home in New Orleans to Portsmouth, New Hampshire, where he will live with his grandfather and go to school. The Portsmouth household consists of Grandfather Nutter and his sister, Tom's Aunt Abigail; Kitty, housekeeper and maid of all work; and Tom. While Aldrich clearly loved and respected him, his grandfather's presence in the book is more peripheral than central. His word counted: when he put limits on Tom, they were observed, but the limits were not many, and Aldrich's reflections do not suggest that his grandfather exerted much moral influence on him. Aunt Abigail plays no role in Tom's life except as a mild figure of fun.

Tom Sawyer's family consists of his much-tried Aunt Polly, doing her best to raise her dead sister's boy; his half brother, the infamous Sidney, who does everything right and tells on Tom (who does most things wrong), and Mary, an older sister who appears only occasionally. Twain lets his reader know that Tom has a conscience—indeed, without it, the plot would come to a halt at Muff Potter's trial—but it is doubtful that Aunt Polly is its source, since Tom routinely deceives her without suffering much by way of conscientious pangs. Tom feels some affection for his aunt, but the affection has no noticeable restraining influence on him. Sidney has no role in Tom's life except as an irritant; in the book, he is a literary foil for Tom's more authentic boyishness.

Both Toms are schoolboys, but the resemblance ends when that is said. Tom Bailey is outstandingly respectable as a student. In many ways, the academy he attends (probably private) is the center of his life. His friends are all there. He likes and respects his schoolmaster, works reasonably hard at his studies, and does well.

Tom Sawyer's is the village school, open to all boys and girls of school age, and presided over by a schoolmaster who would rather have been a doctor. This beleaguered soul lives in a state of more or less open warfare with his pupils, he flogging them regularly, they resisting as best they can, playing tricks on him, making fun of him, and skipping school as often as possible—which in Tom's case is pretty often. Tom's school is a lot like the one Edward Eggleston described in *The Hoosier Schoolmaster:* "[The scholars] had come to regard the whole world as divided into two classes, the teacher on the one side representing lawful authority, and the pupils on the other in a state of chronic rebellion. To play a trick on the master was in evidence of spirit; to 'lick' the master was to be crowned hero of [the] district."[5] No one licks the schoolmaster in Tom Sawyer—boys big enough to do that do not figure in the story—but the smaller boys get their revenge with a spectacular prank, as funny as it is mean, on Examination Day, when the master is the worse for drink, as they well knew he would be.

Church as an institution does not fare very well in either book. For Tom Sawyer, church, like school, means confinement and boredom. Twain pokes a lot of elaborate, rather adult fun at Sunday school, church and parson, and the fire-and-brimstone sermon that attracts not a fraction of the attention the congregation gives to the meeting between dog and pinch bug in the church aisle. His hero is depressed not by the dark view Presbyterianism takes of his chance for eternal salvation (he is not listening) but only by being shut in from the interesting world outdoors.

Tom Bailey is also afflicted by the weekly loss of freedom, mental as well as physical; even his reading is severely restricted on the Sabbath. Aldrich, however, complains less of boredom than of oppression of spirit, objecting mostly to the gloom that permeated a normally cheerful household on a New England Sunday. He does not suspect the pious of hypocrisy, as Twain does, but in this, as in other matters, Aldrich retreats from Puritan austerity, opting for a more comfortable worship of a more cheerful creed.

In their chronicles of boyhood, Aldrich and Twain consciously repudiated the moralism that dominated children's literature before the Civil War. Both suggested, between the lines at least, that boyhood should be exempt from the stringent moral standards that earlier fiction sought to inculcate. Both denied, in fact, that they were out to inculcate at all. Yet these authors could hardly evade moral and ethical questions altogether in their narratives. The concept of boyhood that shaped their books meant that the protagonists were defined primarily by their relation to the conventional mores of the community. The Toms were "bad boys" because they blithely broke conventional rules; at the same time, the new literary ideal of boyhood assumed their intrinsic goodness, no matter what their mischievous behavior. Both novels, then, say a good deal about the confrontation of their heroes and community ethics, on the one hand, and, on the other, about the essential goodness of "real" boys.

Tom Bailey's scrapes, though many and imaginative, never leave him with a moral balance to pay. Independence Day celebrations in Portsmouth included a midnight bonfire attended by all the boys in town. Tom was eager to go but not sure that his grandfather would give his permission. He solved the problem by not asking. When the household was safely asleep, he went out his bedroom window with the help of a clothesline. The night watchman, however, was indeed watching and collared him. When Tom said he was on his way to the bonfire, he let him go, muttering, "Boys is boys."[6] So far, Tom is well within the latitude allowed to "real human boys." Later, however, when Tom and four of his friends steal a decaying coach and roll it down the hill into the bonfire, they are seized by four policemen and marched to the local lockup. On the advice of one of the jail inmates, they escape through a window before being identified. In the end, they have to pay the owner of the coach (who saw them take it) a more-than-fair price for it. Aldrich admits some fault—"Though the property in question was valueless, we were clearly wrong in destroying it"—but not much: "[The owner] had allowed his property to be destroyed in order that he might realize a large profit."[7] The moral reckoning, such as it is, is in Tom's favor.

The complacency rarely wavers. Tom's fight with the school bully, though against academy rules, is amply justified because he was protecting a younger boy; the tone is entirely self-approving. In a couple of other excursions beyond strict legitimacy, including the very funny episode of the cannons, Tom and his friends go undetected because they run fast and keep their mouths shut. None of them is ever moved to confess unless caught, and none seems to feel any burden of guilt. Even the famous snow fight, which went on for weeks between the boys of the two ends of town and escalated to an exchange of really dangerous missiles, evokes only fond memories from Aldrich. If Portsmouth parents worried when their sons came home "bunged up" by frozen snowballs with marbles in their centers, Aldrich does not say so. It was the selectmen who sent the police, and it took eight constables plus "a numerous body of citizens" to break it up—the boys made common cause to fight off the forces of order. Aldrich takes none of the obvious opportunities to draw moral conclusions.

There is one sad chapter in this otherwise cheerful history, the account of Binny Wallace's drowning after he drifts out to sea in the midst of a storm while his three companions watch helplessly from the shore. Aldrich begins the story of the tragic outing by noting, in a single, throwaway line, that he did not ask permission to take his little boat on the river: "I wonder if Christopher Columbus quietly slipped out of the house without letting his estimable family know what he was up to?"[8] For all the grief that suffuses the rest of this tale, this evasion is never referred to again. If Tom felt any moral responsibility for Binny's death, it goes unspoken. Grief and loss are here in abundance but not guilt.

Tom Sawyer's conscience is a flexible organ. On small matters—skipping school, lying to Aunt Polly, "hooking" doughnuts or sugar—it is silent. On larger matters—taking a whole ham, staying away from home long enough to be mourned as dead, letting an innocent man be condemned to death for a murder he did not commit—it may speak up. What it says, however, is not always ethically crystalline. In the well-known episode in which Tom, Huck, and Joe run away to Jackson Island to take up life as pirates, Tom soon realizes that the village believes that the boys have drowned, and he crosses the river by night, carrying with him a note to Aunt Polly to tell her that they are alive. But then, hidden as he listens to her grief-stricken conversation with Joe's mother, Tom realizes that he and his fellow pirates have a chance to witness their own funeral. The prospect is too thrilling to be resisted; Tom pockets his note again and returns to the island. After the highly satisfying drama of the funeral and the boys' reappearance has been played out, Aunt Polly reproaches Tom for letting her think him dead. He tells her—after a few twists and turns—of his visit, the note, and how he could not bring himself to spoil his plan. Understandably skeptical, she checks the pocket of his pirating jacket for the note. When she finds it, she dissolves in tears, not only willing but grateful to take a weak intention for the deed. Either Twain did not notice the ethical muddiness of this evidence of Tom's goodheartedness or he accepted such shell games as sufficient virtue for a boy.

Tom's other major attack of conscience is also morally ambiguous. Tom and Huck witnessed the murder Muff Potter seems likely to hang for, but they have sworn most solemnly to one another to keep the secret for fear of Injun Joe, who really did it. On the eve of the trial, Tom's conscience overrides his fear and he tells his tale to Potter's lawyer. At the trial the next day, he testifies, naming the real murderer. Only Injun Joe's escape from the courtroom saves Huck from being identified as the second witness. Tom becomes a hero, though an uneasy one, and Muff Potter is naturally grateful to him, but for the objective reader, ethical questions may dim the glory a little. In spite of their pact of silence and although his testimony endangered Huck as much as himself, Tom made his decision without a word to Huck. Twain observes that "Huck's confidence in the human race was well-nigh obliterated" and drops the matter.[9] A boy's most solemn oath must be understood, apparently, as something less than a full commitment.

The two Toms are harbingers of a new era in American writing for children. Gone are the moral lessons that justified the very existence of fiction; gone the ruling concept of character formation through experience. Neither Tom learns—in the old sense—from his adventures. Tom Sawyer is the same boy at the end as at the beginning of his story. Tom Bailey grows up, but his father's death, not his boyhood adventures, brings about the transformation. He crosses from boyhood to maturity in a single step when his circumstances change.

By the time they wrote their chronicles of "real" boyhood, Aldrich and Twain had embraced the kind of romanticism that would change the whole texture of children's fiction in the latter half of the nineteenth century. They set childhood (or, more accurately, boyhood) apart from the rest of human life, seeing it as a territory where rules were different and the judgments lighter than in the grown-up world. In the name of realism (and, not incidentally, for the sake of humor and adventure) these authors accepted, and even glorified, antisocial behavior in boys while insisting that their inherent goodness balanced the ledger.

Such a view led to a blurring of ethical and moral distinctions that would have been unthinkable in earlier literature. Until the Civil War, practically all American children's fiction built on a theme of transgression and expiation, worked out in small, carefully reasoned domestic dramas. Girls' fiction was slower than boys' to relinquish this theme, as two familiar girls' novels of the period demonstrate. *Little Women*, published in 1868, offers many examples, including the ice-skating episode, when Jo must acknowledge how nearly she brought about Amy's death by giving in to anger. In Susan Coolidge's *What Katy Did*, published in 1875, Katy's lighthearted disobedience results in a spinal injury and five years of painful expiation-cum-moral-education. In time, as romanticism took over the literature, girls too benefited from greater tolerance, though it is noteworthy that the faults of most romanticized girls ran to overactive imaginations and excessive candor rather than to lying, destructive pranks, or open resistance to community institutions.

The shift away from moral didacticism that began after the Civil War has generally been hailed as the release of children's literature from bondage, and it is true that romanticism gave authors greater freedom to accept and enjoy children as children. Fiction for children became warmer, more relaxed, and more amusing when authors ceased trying to improve children and undertook instead to celebrate them. Yet, while much was gained in the change (certainly in literary terms), something was also lost, as the Tom books demonstrate. The ethical evasions in Twain's story and the uncertain moral accountability in Aldrich's signaled that moral seriousness was beginning to drain away from children's literature and maybe from childhood, too. To shrug off a child's transgressions against the moral code of his society—"boys is boys"—is doubtless in some degree realistic, but it also trivializes children in relation to their society. Children's literature came into being when adults began to take children seriously as moral beings.[10] *The Story of a Bad Boy* and *The Adventures of Tom Sawyer* mark an early point in the long process by which that attitude was eroded, and American society came to accept a view of childhood that rarely connects the moral capacities of children with its own future.

Good Democrats:
Ragged Dick and
Little Lord Fauntleroy

Ragged Dick and Little Lord Fauntleroy are unlikely kin, being super-
ficially about as much alike as—well, Horatio Alger and Frances
Hodgson Burnett. Yet they are blood brothers in one important respect: each is his creator's idealized version of American boyhood
and, by the same token, a prototype of democratic character. And in
fact, they have more likenesses than one might suppose, but they also
have some signal differences. One boy represents a concept of democracy wholly American, while the other bears traces of a society both
older and more firmly committed to its system of social hierarchy.

Horatio Alger and Frances Hodgson Burnett arrived at their views
of democracy from very different starting places. Alger was American, born and bred in New England, the son of a Unitarian minister
and a failed clergyman himself. After a few false starts as a writer, he
happened onto a highly effective formula for boys' stories, moved to
New York, and settled down to repeat his success by writing essen-

tially the same story over and over for more than thirty years. The formula never varied, nor did the basic character of the boy hero, who was always Alger's idea of democracy embodied.

Burnett was a transplanted Englishwoman whose family had emigrated to the United States from Manchester when she was fifteen years old and whose ties to England remained strong throughout her life. Her writing, like Alger's, belonged to the second half of the nineteenth century, although it began and ended some twenty years later. Burnett was not at all a formula writer; she wrote fewer, and far better, books than Alger, many of them for adults, all of them for a better educated audience than the one Alger normally attracted. Some of Burnett's books are still read, but *Little Lord Fauntleroy* is not among the survivors. Its success—which was enormous—was due mainly to an adult taste for a highly romanticized view of childhood, a taste that has now all but disappeared. Interest in the book today is almost entirely historical; it is viewed as a cultural phenomenon and as the author's one full-length portrait of an American boy.

Horatio Alger's *Ragged Dick* was published in 1868, the first and still the best known of the rags-to-riches tales that were to make Alger's name a byword in American culture. In a clumsy prose style that never improved in a lifetime of writing, Alger tells the story of an uneducated orphan boy who scratches a living as a bootblack on the streets of New York. He is poor but industrious, a street waif but honest and responsive to the right influences when they happen to touch his life. Circumstances bring him to the attention of a Christian businessman who takes an interest in him, encouraging him with a new suit and a great deal of good advice to make an ambitious effort to move up in the world. And in fact, Dick makes some progress on his own. He learns to read, saves his meager wages, and improves his habits of dress and cleanliness. But the decisive turn in his fortunes comes about when he rescues from drowning the child of a wealthy merchant and is rewarded with a clerking job that settles him at last into middle-class respectability.

Ragged Dick is in many ways the standard American exemplar of democracy; certainly that is how Alger saw him. Dick feels, assertively if necessary, that he is as good as anyone around him. Poor though he may be, he is self-respecting, confident, and enterprising—both egalitarian and ambitious. Like every Alger hero he scorns the dandified sons of rich men who think they are superior by virtue of their fathers' money and position. Dick does not care about inherited advantages; all he asks is an opportunity to please an employer and be rewarded fairly for his efforts.

But somehow Dick, again like all Alger's heroes, seems to trade in some of his American independence once he has met the benefactor who can usher him into the middle-class life he craves. At once, he adopts all the employee virtues Alger regularly urged upon his readers, making "his employer's interest his own," taking on the opinions as well as the manners of his betters, and evincing a respect that at least borders on the servile.

Alger's heroes want respectability much more than they want wealth or any particular achievement or position. But acceptance by a respectable middle class requires that these boys, who have been independent, however poor, give up their freedom and take on the coloration of those whose ranks they wish to join. And they do. Not reluctantly but eagerly, these aspiring lads correct their speech, discipline themselves to regular hours, and relinquish their spontaneous and spendthrift ways. They learn to meld, to blend in with the respectable class. Courting middle-class acceptance, they conform to middle-class standards when and where they must. There is not a Natty Bumppo or a Huck Finn among them.

Little Lord Fauntleroy, on the other hand, never alters from the beginning to the end of his story; he is an unwavering democrat throughout. Like Dick he is confident and self-respecting and, though limited by his age (he is seven years old, while Dick is fourteen), enterprising when the opportunity arises. Burnett's novel is as much a success story as Alger's, although it proceeds along very different lines. Cedric, whose nobly born father was disowned for marrying an American, becomes heir apparent to an English earldom, raising the question of how an American boy brought up in a democratic society will acquit himself as a prospective earl. Burnett's answer to this question is compounded of her ideas of democracy, of child nature and child nurture, and of the redemptive power of love.

Cedric takes with him from America to England his open-hearted, loving acceptance of people of whatever social level. Guilelessly, he thinks the best of everyone he meets. If Dick considers himself as good as everyone else, Cedric believes that everyone else is as good—in every sense—as he is himself. Thus armed with grace, Cedric redeems the selfish, embittered old earl, improves life for the tenants of the estate, and eventually heals the breach between his widowed mother and his aristocratic grandfather. All this he does quite unconsciously, simply by acting in accord with his nature and—Burnett is careful to point out—with the conscientious upbringing his American mother has given him.

Cedric is American and democratic, at once an aristocratic and idealized child of the late nineteenth century. Burnett's fond characterization bundles together a variety of notions, not entirely without contradictions. Little Lord Fauntleroy's innocence echoes contemporary European descriptions of American ingenuousness; he has the unwinking trust in self and in world that Europeans often saw as characteristic—and childish—in Americans of all ages. At the same time, his innocence and his faith in the goodness of humankind puts him into the very popular tradition of the Redemptive Child, well represented in earlier decades by such fictional child saints as Little Eva, Elsie Dinsmore, and Pollyanna. Cedric's dignity and modest self-confidence in any company, high or low, is certainly a shining example of a democratic upbringing. Yet Burnett also seems to see Cedric's nature as intrinsic; he is said to be "just like his father," implying that his character is as much inborn as acquired—inherited through blood lines, like his claim to noble estate.

Least ambiguous of Little Lord Fauntleroy's American traits is his attitude toward class: he is simply unaware of social differences. Cedric's dearest American friends are Mr. Hobbs, the grocer, and Dick, a bootblack. His feelings toward these friends do not change when he goes to England to take up life on an earl's estate, and when they come to England, he welcomes them to his ancestral hall without the slightest apprehension that they might not fit in. He does not seem to notice that such difficulties exist: democracy can ask no more.

But this is Cedric, not Burnett. Frances Hodgson Burnett was no democrat at all. She saw acutely the class differences that Cedric does not, and she spent much of the book looking over his head to her readers, asking them to agree with her about how charming Little Lord Fauntleroy is in treating comic underlings as his equals and how amusing it is that he expects his grandfather to do likewise. Most of what humor exists in the novel turns exactly on this point; we are meant to find Cedric's blindness to social distinctions endearing, but we are also meant to smile at his ignorance—one among many clues suggesting that Mrs. Burnett was talking as much to adult readers as to children. After all, if Cedric, at seven, cannot see how low on the social scale his grocer friend is and how hilariously incongruous are Dick and Mr. Hobbs in an earl's drawing room—why would other American children of the same age perceive these things? Surely it was not for democratic children that Mrs. Burnett was writing such scenes but for their parents, and she was assuming that most of those parents were as well aware of class lines as she was.

The fact is that the concept of class is fundamental to the shape and structure of both stories, although the two authors' views of the relationship between class and democracy are at some odds. For Alger the essence of democracy was class mobility. Ragged Dick's passage from street employment to a respectable clerking job was the point of all his efforts and of the novel. Like most Alger tales, *Ragged Dick* recounts a boy's progress toward self-realization, which meant for Alger the successful negotiation of a change in class. Alger's boys were looking not for internal growth but for improved social status; they wanted to "rise in the world." Their measure of success was not inner but outer; they found it in the opinions of others: respectability is, after all, a social judgment.

What Alger saw in democratic society was not a society without class distinctions but one in which the class lines were permeable. His stories said that any American might climb upward from a lowly beginning by ambition, hard work, and moral worthiness, and the books owed much of their popularity to the fact that American readers shared this view of democracy's promise. The stroke of luck that always catapulted an Alger boy across the class gap seems to some modern readers to contradict the author's professed faith in hard work and clean living as the key to success, but I think not. No doubt, in his vague way, Alger recognized occasional difficulties in the work-reward formula. But luck for the deserving was an integral part of the nineteenth-century creed and, besides, was deeply rooted in an older Protestant faith in the intervention of Providence on the side of the worthy. The whole meaning of Alger's phenomenal success, on this point as on others, lies in the accuracy with which he reflected the popular outlook of this time.

Burnett's story is also very much concerned with class but not at all with class mobility. While Cedric acquires both title and wealth in the course of the book, it is a central point that he does not change, does not *need* to change to fit his new position. He is what he is. He is by birth the Earl of Dorincourt's grandson, whatever reversals in fortune may occur. And he is, just as much, American—with an American fearlessness and openness and an American disregard of social hierarchies. The beauty of his character lies in the fact that he is as noble when he is poor as he is democratic when he is rich and titled.

What Cedric experiences, in other words, is a change of circumstance, not of class (just as Sara Crewe does in *A Little Princess*). Nowhere in *Little Lord Fauntleroy* did Burnett suggest that real changes in class are possible. She was sympathetic toward inequalities of condition, and she certainly believed in the obligations of the privileged toward the less fortunate, but class differences themselves she evidently regarded as immutable. Mr. Hobbs, the grocer, in New York becomes Mr. Hobbs, the grocer, in England, as fixed in his sphere as a planet. And while her bootblack is ultimately promised a "solid education" by the Earl of Dorincourt, it is not clear what this might mean to Dick—Burnett did not say. Certainly it is significant that this "education" is a largess bestowed by the earl, not something Dick could do for himself—as Ragged Dick's is. In general, the gaze Burnett turned upon the lower social classes was kindly, even pitiful, but it was not hopeful.

Little Lord Fauntleroy was an extremely popular book on both sides of the Atlantic—evidence that Burnett's social outlook found an audience in America, as Alger's did, although hers differed from his in such crucial ways. And in fact, between them Horatio Alger and Frances Hodgson Burnett encompassed most of the late nineteenth-century attitudes toward class and democracy. Class mobility, as Alger described it, lay at the heart of American democratic pride. The belief that every man might better his lot in life was the bedrock on which American enterprise built and a fundamental element in the popular outlook. Americans pointed with pride to those among them who had risen from humble beginnings; presidential candidates of every sort of origin yearned to claim birth in log cabins. No one in America was supposed to be disadvantaged by class.

And yet: As early as the 1830s, Tocqueville had noted with his usual penetration how the very egalitarianism of American society created a paradoxical sensitivity to the smallest signs of class distinction. Striving Americans looked for ways to assure themselves that they had achieved the success they worked so hard to get. Status symbols were then, as now, of remarkable importance to the Republic.

Frances Hodgson Burnett's class attitudes, formed in her English childhood and overlaid by her later experience in the United States, tapped into just these contradictions in the American social outlook. By the 1880s the amalgam of social ideas that Burnett articulated in *Little Lord Fauntleroy* had found a ready acceptance in the United States, particularly among affluent Americans who were impressed by the elegance of upper-class English society but who had by no means abandoned all pride in their democratic heritage. As a status symbol, an innate aristocracy of character could hardly be bettered (as Annie Fellows Johnston demonstrated in her very successful *Little Colonel* series). Yet it was also pleasing to read of an American child who carried the democratic virtues of an American upbringing into the very lion's den of British aristocracy and won all hearts thereby. *Little Lord Fauntleroy* combined the attractions of class society with a flattering view of the democratic personality and thus appealed greatly to Americans who wanted to believe themselves better than their less successful countrymen, as good as any aristocrat, and equal to anything. Just as Alger's promise of democratic opportunity encouraged the ambitious have-nots of American society, so Burnett's suggestion of inborn superiority warmed those who had arrived.

The immense popular success of both authors is plain evidence that their fiction expressed social attitudes that were shared, contradictions and all, by a great many of their American contemporaries.

Children in Fiction and Fact

Children's Literature
for a New Nation,
1820–1860

※※

The United States in 1820 was a nation still new to nationhood and already caught in a swift tide of change. When Washington Irving, writing in that year, referred to the "great torrent of migration and improvement, which is making such incessant change in . . . this restless country," his description was surely no more than accurate.[1] For with the Peace of 1815, which closed the second British-American war, the country entered upon an era of great economic and physical expansion. The forty years from 1820 to 1860 were a boom time (though punctuated by periodic financial collapses), during which the American population grew by more than 200 percent, national territory increased enormously, and technology transformed the character of the economy. The evolution of an agrarian nation into an industrial and urban society was underway and proceeding at a remarkable pace. In fact, the salient observation to be made about many of the changes of the era has less to do with their nature than with the rate at which they took place. The pace was headlong throughout the antebellum period.

Strain and unrest accompanied change; socially, economically, and politically, Jacksonian society was turbulent. In addition to the growth that affected so many aspects of the new nation, the period was marked by the excitements of evangelical religion, by an astonishing wave of reform movements, and most of all, by the ever more acrimonious debate over slavery, the issue that by 1860 overwhelmed all others and brought the young republic to civil war.

American reaction to the ferment of the time was mixed. On the surface, optimism and a buoyant sense of national pride prevailed. Americans believed energetically in their country; they were proud of its recent past and convinced of the promise of the future. The rhetoric of the period generally celebrated the progress, the prosperity, the democratic spirit, and the opportunity offered by American society.

At the same time, Jacksonian Americans felt the anxieties that inevitably afflict those who live in times of rapid change. Pride in the past and hope for the future were alike tempered by apprehension lest the promise of America be somehow betrayed. Even while they moved with their society, responding vigorously to economic and social opportunity, many Americans also yearned toward the stability of the past, and worried over the direction of the future.

When an American fictional literature for children began to be written, about 1820, it was distinctly a product of its time. It reflected the intense interest in family and childhood that was to mark all of the nineteenth century, and it reflected too the sharpened nationalism so characteristic of the Jacksonian era: imported children's stories, like other foreign influences, Americans now thought inadequate to the needs of a republic. "Foreign books . . . are not to be proscribed," one author conceded, "but it is absurd that they should be made, among our children, the main standard of feeling and thought."[2] By the second quarter of the century, national feeling required that books for American children should be home products.

But it was undoubtedly the American preoccupation with the future that was the strongest impetus behind the development of a nonschool juvenile literature before 1860. The children who were to inherit the republic were increasingly the object of adult attention on that account. As the fiction created for them reveals, they were the repository for much of the optimism of the Jacksonian period and for many of its anxieties as well. Written out of a concern for children and country, the literature could not but embody something of its authors' expectations and apprehensions for the future of both. And so it did: in the hundreds of storybooks published in the United States between 1820 and 1860 is a record of what adults wanted of and for the next generation. Less directly, but just as surely, the books offer insight into what Americans wanted of and for their society.

The connections between this literature and its background are not always immediately obvious, however. To examine in detail the juvenile fiction of antebellum America is to enter a twilight world, a world that seems at first almost wholly sheltered from the robust life around it. The tensions and turmoil of Jacksonian society seem remote, the arguments muted. Although they were produced in a nation experiencing great and rapid change, the children's stories were static and repetitious. There were few departures from conventional opinion, few surprising points of view. Controversy was as rare as genius in the literature.

The focus of the stories was extremely narrow. They were written to teach, and specifically, to teach morality. All Americans of the period agreed that a high level of individual morality was indispensable if the promise of the nation's future was to be fulfilled. The nature of American institutions was settled, they believed; what remained was to make them work, to insure that the republic survived. "It is not now to be made a question whether our political institutions are right or wrong," wrote one early author of children's fiction. "Education is to be conducted with reference to honor and usefulness under these institutions as they are, and to the sentiments on which they depend for permanent support."[3]

It was clear to thoughtful Americans that the permanent support of democratic institutions lay in public virtue and equally clear that public virtue depended upon the character of private citizens. Thus the developing moral character of children was the object of much anxious attention in the period. Education, whether home or school, was primarily *moral* education—in part, of course, for its own sake, but also because only the firm establishment of exemplary character in the rising generation could secure the future of the republic.

Children's fiction before 1860 was written entirely as an adjunct to such moral education. Every other consideration was secondary, if indeed other considerations figured at all. The authors wished to be entertaining, but only just enough to attract child readers, that they might be instructed in morality. They were wary of the "gaudy" allures of "high-wrought wonder," and of the improbabilities of old folk tales. William Cardell spoke for them all when he scornfully discarded "Blue Beard . . . [and] fiddling cats . . . [and] motherly talking goats" in favor of "fidelity to nature, to moral truth; regard to the public good [and] the endearing scenes of domestic life."[4]

All the writers were as earnest. These sober stories, each leading to a moral lesson, were written to provide children with models of virtuous living. Moral didacticism was their sole reason for being, as the authors often told their young readers directly: "When I tell you stories of things that never happened," Samuel Goodrich explained, "my real design is to give you lessons of importance."[5] It would not have occurred to the authors to doubt that fiction could shape character; they believed deeply in their mission. "If one pair of erring feet may be turned into the path of obedience and peace by means of my story," said the author of *Self-Willed Susie,* "the end for which it was written will be accomplished."[6]

No doubt because their purposes were so selective, authors gave scant attention to the settings of their narratives. It would be difficult to construct from the literature a picture of the physical surrounding of the stories, to come away from them with a feeling for the communities, the houses, the schools that made up a child's landscape in the period. There were few homely details of food or dress or common activity to anchor the fiction to a particular time and place; most stories were played out against backgrounds almost abstract in their generality. Unlike the richly detailed, often autobiographical children's fiction of later years, early juvenile tales said little about the daily business of growing up in an American household during the first half of the nineteenth century. The evocation of a way of life that can be found in such books as *Tom Sawyer, Little Women,* Aldrich's

Story of a Bad Boy, or Eggleston's *Hoosier Schoolmaster* simply does not exist in juvenile literature before 1860.

Characterization and plots were purposefully flat. Nineteenth-century theorists of child nurture were tireless in pointing out that children learned much better by example than by precept, and early nineteenth-century authors were equally tireless in their efforts to provide the examples that would edify the young. Since complexity could only have obscured the messages, characterization was simple and it was always easy to identify the good and bad models. Lazy, fretful Louisa was contrasted with her cheerful, industrious cousin, and the story showed how the differences in their temperaments shaped their lives.[7] An honest, temperate youth was seen to thrive, while the deceitful lad who stole his father's rum and so succumbed to drink went from bad to worse and ended wretchedly, in prison.[8] In story after story, good character was contrasted with bad, and appropriate conclusions drawn.

It should be said that the fiction was usually optimistic about the possibility of reforming the bad examples. Though some errant characters proceeded briskly from early mistakes to an untimely end, many more were salvaged, quite often by the good examples, who frequently talked in moral precepts at the same time they demonstrated sound character. One outstanding boy reformed an unpromising acquaintance in a matter of a few weeks, by talking "much and very sensibly" to him.[9] Good children sometimes even led adults to a better way of life in the fiction, though of course in such cases they worked by "the silent power of example alone," since it would hardly have been fitting for a child to lecture an adult, no matter how helpfully.[10]

Narratives were staid, domestic, and predictable. Each tale centered on a child in need of some moral correction; the correction of this or that fault then constituted the whole plot. Since most authors theoretically favored the idea that experience is the best teacher, what small excitement there was in the stories was furnished by the consequences of childish misbehavior. A girl whose fondness for sweets took her into the pantry by night to lick the honey jar managed to burn down the house with the candle she left there. A boy who skated on thin ice against all parental warning fell through and narrowly escaped death by drowning. There was, in fact, a plethora of narrow escapes in the literature, all fitting and frightening results of moral error. But near-disaster was usually close enough. Though wrongdoing always had consequences, preferably vivid and more or less logical, the punishment was not often extreme—just inevitable. The authors, of course, were not really willing to let experience speak for itself, however loudly. They underlined the moral conclusions for their readers, suggesting that while the fictional children learned from painful experience, readers could be forewarned and spared much misery by listening to their elders in the first place.

All juvenile fiction before 1860 was much the same: simple narratives, always pointing to moral, featureless backgrounds, stock characters moving through patterned plots. It is startling to contemplate how much was left out, for all the authors' claims that they wrote about reality.

Except for frequent and pious references to George Washington, the American past was largely ignored. The pioneer struggle against the wilderness, which was to provide material for hundreds of children's books in later times, was never the subject of these early tales. In fact, wilderness was hardly mentioned at all; it would have been impossible to discover from children's stories the enormous expansion to the West that took place in the period. The American Revolution, in its rare appearances, was not an occasion for adventure tales, but for close and earnest reasoning about the moral implications of war in general.

In the same way, slavery was all but invisible in juvenile fiction, though it was the issue that dominated American political debate from 1820, the year of the Missouri Compromise, to 1860, the eve of the Civil War. Even when it was inserted into stories by authors who were dedicated abolitionists, the mention was usually mild and indirect—small clue to the bitter struggle that was to split the nation.

Industrialization and urbanization, both important trends in the period, were equally elusive in the fiction. Most writers of juvenile literature regarded cities with suspicion, if not with outright hostility. They saw them as dangerous, corrupting, and immoral, and rarely made them the background for their narratives. As cities grew, so did the authors' mistrust. By the last decade of the period, though cities were the locale of more stories, they were almost always portrayed as terrible testing grounds for the home-learned morality of fictional heroes and heroines. The best advice in most juvenile books suggested that all Americans were better off in the country, which was both moral and healthy, than in cities.

As for factories, though their role in the economy expanded steadily after 1820, they were given no place at all in most children's books before 1850. Even in the 1850s, there were only a few direct references to industry; most writers continued to idealize the yeoman farmer as the backbone of the nation at a time when it was already becoming apparent that the nation's economic future lay in another direction.

Yet in spite of these and other silences, the juvenile literature of Jacksonian America does speak both of and for its time. In special and frequently oblique ways, it furnishes clues to the feeling life of the society that produced it. Though its recording of factual reality was sketchy and certainly selective, as a chronicle of emotional reaction, it is eloquent. What the fiction speaks of is not so much what happened in the period as what many quite representative middle-class Americans *felt* about what was happening. It tells of their pride in the United States and in its institutions and its recent past, and it says much about their hopes for the future. But pride was accompanied by uneasiness as social change hurtled on, and hope was shaded by anxiety—and the juvenile stories carried doubtful messages as well. When American writers undertook the moral and social instruction of children through fiction, they necessarily documented their own attitudes, both conscious and unconscious, toward childhood and society. If we look at these, and at the historical context in which they were expressed, we can begin to read, in and between the lines of children's fiction, a story more interesting and more moving, in its own way, than any the authors consciously wrote.

Attitudes toward childhood, for example, determined both the form and the tone of juvenile literature. Moral didacticism reflected accurately the prevailing ideas of adults about both the nature of children and the purposes of childhood. The fiction was usually optimistic about child nature. Again and again, the stories tell of children who were "for the most part good," but who were "possessed of one great fault" (or two or three): a mix, in other words, of good and bad; imperfect, but not beyond hope of redemption. Though the old Calvinist concept of infant depravity lingered on in some quarters and was expressed occasionally in some of the children's books published by denominational presses, in general a more benign view dominated by 1830. Without much theoretical struggle, most Americans had by that time adopted the opinion that children came to the world with potential for both good and evil, and that the direction of their lives depended heavily upon the training they received in their years of growing up. Thus the note of optimism that undergirded the steady moralizing of the books. If the nature of children was not evil inborn, but neutral or potential, then character could surely be influenced for the good by wise and conscientious adults. Children could be made Christian, as Horace Bushnell suggested, without the conversion experience, through home training alone.[11] Thus, too, the sense of urgency that made of every childish experience an opportunity for teaching morality. That urgency, and the characteristically sober tone of all the literature, were natural consequences of the authors' view of the purpose of childhood, which was serious in the extreme. Childhood was wholly preparation, entirely a moral training ground for adult life. Frivolity, imaginative play, and uninstructive entertainment were dismissed, not so much because they were sinful as because they wasted the brief, precious time in which a child must learn so much that was so important. The idea of childhood as a period of intrinsic value, full of joy and free of care, was not yet.

The ideals of moral character set out in the children's fiction are also revealing at several levels. The virtues recommended to young readers were many and various, but they fit into a general pattern. All were in the direction of order, restraint, stability, and a strong sense of social responsibility as the age interpreted it. Obedience was the most fundamental virtue for a child to acquire: few stories closed without at least one salute to its importance. Clearly, obedience was paramount because it provided the necessary framework within which all other morality could be taught. Even more important, order within the family, which obedience implied, was a paradigm for order in society: "The obedience of children to their parents is the basis of all government," observed one author,[12] and most writers of juvenile fiction agreed. The inheritors of the American Revolution were anxious indeed to secure social order in their own time.

Besides obedience, always the signal virtue, self-control, usefulness, charity, and a willingness to put the wishes of others above one's own were the character traits most consistently recommended in the literature. All of these emphasized regard for other people, and the books affirmed that commitment in explicit and highly exaggerated terms. To live "for others," children were often told, was the only sure way to contentment. As one fictional mother told her daughter, "You can never be unhappy while you do everything that is in your power for others, without the hope of recompense."[13]

Logically enough, the faults the literature scored most relentlessly were opposites of the virtues it praised. Selfishness was the greatest and most encompassing failing; to look to one's own advantage was always suspect in children's stories. Ambition or any form of competitive spirit was equated with selfishness and equally condemned. Contentment, rather than striving, was idealized. Juvenile fiction frequently advised children to be satisfied with what they had, instead of chasing after the uncertain rewards of fame and fortune. Many stories warned that "restless seeking" could yield no permanent prizes; boys in particular were cautioned against the dangers of leaving home to pursue wealth and advancement. Ambition, symbolized by soldiering and seafaring and city employment, was dangerous; safety and moral certainty were better guides to happiness, according to the fiction.

In short, the idealizations in children's fiction ran directly counter to the prevailing direction of change in Jacksonian society. The moral values set out in the literature were a kind of mirror image of the most apparent realities of the period—and therein, of course, is their connection with that turbulent time. The exuberance of the young United States, its social fluidity, its fiercely competitive spirit, and its mounting tensions rarely appeared directly in juvenile fiction, yet they were all there in the reverse images of order, cooperation, and sober attention to duty and conscience that were repeated in every book. Clearly, the authors were reacting against the alarming tendencies of their society by idealizing virtues that would counterbalance the dangers as they saw them.

Faced with disorder and instability, they valued predictability and order; living with ceaseless change, they idealized certainty. As physical migration separated families and splintered communities, the fiction urged children to stay close to home. As economic life shifted toward cities and factories, stories warned of the spiritual hazards of the city, and extolled the independence and morality of a farmer's life.

Most insistent of all was the drive in the fiction to counter the growing materialism and the rampant competitiveness of American society. Here was the source of the constant admonitions to children to live "for others"; here the reason for the ubiquitous anxious warnings against "selfishness" and the repeated assurances that only care for others could bring happiness. The material ambition that all observers, foreign and American, saw as the hallmark of the Jacksonian age was steadily repudiated in children's fiction: fame was ephemeral, success might be reversed overnight, wealth could never insure contentment. Not the rich but the good were happy, children's stories said, not personal attainment but cooperation and responsibility toward others were worthy goals in human life.

The effort to impart these attitudes to children was always marked with some anxiety. The authors had few illusions that the world beyond resembled their idealized home: as one fictional mother observed, "The principles which wisdom and truth sanction are not those which govern society."[14] If a child was to acquire firm moral principles, he must do so early, in the brief years before he left home.

The aim was independent moral strength. Though the writers constantly pointed out that obedience to parents was the "first law in life" to children, a careful reading of the fiction makes it clear that the real goal of child nurture was not so much to make children amenable to adult authority as to create in them a reliable inner direction as early as possible. It was not at all uncommon for stories about children as young as four or five to record long, grave conversations between parent and child in which the child's moral behavior was meticulously weighed and judged.[15] Such home training was to provide a child with a moral gyroscope, an unshakable center from which his behavior would always proceed, that he might "pass unscathed through the temptations of the world."[16] And though that moral strength might begin in parental direction, it would not remain dependent upon it, nor, indeed, upon any outer authority.

For outer authority was precisely what American life could not be counted on to provide. The freedom of Jacksonian society, however often they praised it, also alarmed many Americans, certainly including many of those who wrote for children. The absence of a fixed social order, the lightness of the law, the fluidity of economic and social life, all threatened to leave individuals without defined relations to one another or to the larger world in which they all must live. Opportunity and ambition unrestrained threatened to reduce American society to a desperate struggle for advantage.

The counter the children's fiction posed to this awesome freedom was an idealized self-control, an inner discipline each person imposed upon himself that would meet the challenge of a changing social order. If the outer world could not be frozen into predictable form, the inner world of moral character might be, provided the effort was made early and earnestly enough. The whole point of childhood training as children's authors saw it—and therefore the whole point of children's fiction as they wrote it—was to develop in children that sensitive conscience, that internalized set of principles that would make them morally self-sufficient. Then, and only then, could American society live with its freedom without descending into social anarchy.

Yet to point out connections between an anxious, unsettled society and a didactic, moralizing literature for children is not to suggest that the literature was nothing more than an effort at "social control." It was that, of course, but it had other qualities as well.

No one can make a claim for the literary merit of this fiction: there was none. But there was a simple dignity and conviction in that it went beyond a certain attempt to control society by indoctrinating children with safe moral values. The attitude the fiction displayed toward its child audience was kindly, on the whole, and in some ways more respectful than it has been in many children's books since. However much they may have overestimated children's interest in ethical questions, the authors took them seriously as moral beings. If we find their attention to matters of childish right and wrong overly solemn and heavy-handed, still we can recognize that it was an attitude more willing to acknowledge a child's human dignity than, say, the sentimental vision that dwelt upon children's charm and innocence, or the condescending view of them as "cute" and amusing to adults.

And surely the virtues the fiction hoped to instill in children were more than trivial. Moral self-reliance, inner independence, kindness, responsibility, and a decent regard for the needs of others—these qualities transcend the limited aims of adult convenience and societal "law and order." Even for us, a century and a half older as a nation and far removed from the simplistic moral outlook of early nineteenth-century juvenile fiction, it may be possible to agree with the authors who thought such virtues sound qualities for the citizens of a republic.

Child and Conscience

※ ※

If these are the feelings that belong to guilt, I wonder
anyone can bear the pain of being wicked.
                    "The Journal," *Parley's Magazine* (1834)

Americans have a long history of fervent aspiration for their children
and about as long a tradition of making those aspirations publicly
known. From the sermons and catechisms of the seventeenth century to the pop psychology of the twentieth, a record of American
hopes for the next generation exists, in detail and in print. In the
early nineteenth century, when the republic was young and national
feeling ran high, concern for the future of the new nation and for the
children who would soon be its active citizens became thoroughly
intertwined. Together, these preoccupations produced a flood of advice literature for parents and instructive fiction for children, most
of which said nearly identical things about ideal child management,
on the one hand, and ideal child behavior, on the other. Both litera-
tures were prescriptive, the fiction no less than the advice books, and
the prescriptions were quite remarkably consistent. The image of the
well-managed child and of the ideal home that was to produce him
or her shine forth everywhere in the admonitory writing of the new
American republic.

How closely reality fit these images is a great deal harder to know.

The experience of children is difficult to penetrate at any time, the more so when it is the experience of a childhood long past. Children leave few accounts of themselves; we must almost always reconstruct their lives and ways from evidence supplied by adults.

Probably the most direct path we can find to a remote childhood is through autobiography, in spite of the fact that it is written by adults. Personal memoirs are no more free of distortion than other sources, of course. Memory is imperfect, and recall of childhood may well be colored by nostalgia, exaggeration, resentment, or any number of other emotions. Adults may remember their youth as harder or harsher than it was, or they may see it through a haze of sentiment that softens or romanticizes past reality. All the same, used with reasonable respect for its limitations, autobiography can be immensely revealing. If patterns appear, if the experience in one account is echoed in others, then it seems fair to assume some reality in what we read.

As it happens, there are many autobiographies of childhood by Americans who grew up in the first fifty or sixty years of the nineteenth century. Alongside the volumes by statesmen and military heroes stand a surprising number of reminiscences by more ordinary people, who dedicated their books to their children or grandchildren and had them privately printed or published by small, local presses, obviously expecting that they would be read mostly by family and friends. Many memoirs of nineteenth-century childhood were written, not because the authors had achieved fame as adults, but because they were conscious of having lived through the formative period of their country's history—because, as one of them said, they wished to "recall and record a vanished civilization." [1]

Not every autobiographer dwelt upon the particulars of childhood. Men whose adult careers had made them prominent figures in national life usually recited their ancestry, brushed past their early years, and settled into detail only when they reached their higher education or first significant position in public or private business. Women, on the other hand, were likely to lead lives that kept them in closer touch with the experience of childhood. As Carol Smith-Rosenberg and Nancy Cott have shown, women usually remained close to their mothers, sisters, and women friends throughout life;

they were much involved in the nurture of their own children and, often, those of other women.[2] Then too, nineteenth-century women were living during a period of great glorification of motherhood. "Circumstances," wrote John S. C. Abbott sententiously in 1834, "are now directing the eyes of the community to the nursery; and the truth is daily coming more distinctly before the public, that the influence which is exerted upon the mind, during the first eight or ten years of existence, in a great degree guides the destinies of that mind for time and eternity." On all sides, American society agreed that a mother's influence on her children was crucial, that it was a matter of grave importance to children and to the nation as well how childhood was managed. A child's character, Abbott (like many others) told mothers, "is . . . in an important sense, in your hands, and you are to form it for good or for evil."[3]

For all these reasons, and because few of them lived much outside the domestic "sphere" conceded to them by nineteenth-century society, women autobiographers were likelier than men to describe childhood in detail, remembering their parents' attitudes, both spoken and unspoken, toward the common relations between parent and child and recalling the emotions of childish experience, sensitive to the meaning of childhood for the adult who lived it. Accounts of this kind (whether by men or women) can help a curious reader of the present day explore what match there was—if any—between prescription and the realities of child nurture. And autobiographies can also suggest some answers to the even more elusive question of how children responded to prescribed methods of child training.

Prescription, of course, includes the children's fiction of the early nineteenth century, which was written never to beguile children but always to teach them. More specifically, children's fiction taught moral values; stories imparted the many lessons a child must learn if he was to become a responsible citizen and a moral human being. Since authors generally agreed on both the values they held and on the literary model (Maria Edgeworth, usually) they followed, their stories sounded much alike.

At the center of each tale was a child character intended as a model for the child reader to emulate. This fictional ideal was generally good, which is to say obedient, industrious, affectionate to parents, and respectful toward authority; yet he or she was not (or at least not usually) a prig. Fictional children had faults and lapses from grace: they sulked or shirked or disobeyed their parents; they lost their tempers and teased their sisters, doubtless like children the authors really knew. What made them models was not their perfection, which did not exist, but their sensitive consciences, which did. The fictional child who did wrong was quick to repent and eager to reform, and of all the qualities the authors tried to implant in children, these were perhaps the most important. Early nineteenth-century children's fiction was too close to eighteenth-century thinking to postulate perfection in human form, especially in children. What could be hoped for and, more to the point, inculcated, was an active conscience capable of correcting inevitable missteps and serving as a steadying guide in a far from perfect world.

"Inculcated" was the operative word. Whatever the fictional child's strengths, they were not his by simple birthright. Though the Calvinist view of children receded after 1820, and so the nineteenth-century child was (generally) absolved of innate depravity, romantic notions of childhood perfection did not reach children's fiction until the latter half of the century. If few antebellum authors looked on children as limbs of Satan, fewer yet saw them as flawless. Quite the contrary, in fact; a major point in early nineteenth-century juvenile books was that the sound moral character of model children was a product, not a natural endowment. A good child represented the triumph of wise and loving parental guidance.

In fact, most children's stories were didactic in two directions. On the one hand, they instructed the child reader in the value of goodness and the doleful consequences of disobedience, carelessness, pride, and a host of other moral failings. At the same time, they offered models of correct child nurture for parents. Most early nineteenth-century children's fiction reflected the transforming influence of Rousseau and Locke, who had taught that experience, rather than admonition, was the most effective teacher. Children's authors endorsed this philosophy wholeheartedly. They advised parents to forbid and warn as little as possible, in favor of allowing children to learn from the consequences of their own decisions, and they designed stories to show the method in practice.

In fiction, therefore, children discovered the error of their ways through the sad experience that inevitably followed wrongdoing in the books. Eight-year-old Sophia Morton, for example, hated sewing, and said so. Her rational mother did not argue or demand but quietly locked up Sophia's workbasket until she should ask for it again. It is only fair to record that Sophia's was not a simple case of laziness. With the time she gained by giving up sewing, Sophia turned her mind to learning Greek and catching up with her brother in Latin, and very happy she was, at first, without her seams to stitch. But the day inevitably came when Sophia began to be tired of "looking like a slut." Then events moved swiftly, as they always do in these stories. Sophia was invited to a dance, where she overheard the other children criticize her roundly for her "shabby" and "sluttish" dress. As the philosophers had promised, experience spoke and Sophia heard: "How foolishly, how wrong, I have acted! said Sophia," enlightened at last. It is typical of the literature, however, that Sophia's own conclusions were firmly reinforced by her mother: "You will one of these days, my daughter, become a woman; and you will then discern . . . how happy you were to have been taught . . . when you were young, all those things which every woman ought to know. . . . Let her be ever so learned or so wise, she will always be laughed at, if she is found to be ignorant of them."[4]

Since Providence did not always oblige with suitable as well as timely punishment, parents also had to discipline children. But discipline was to be rational, combining love and firmness in judicious proportion. Lydia Maria Child recommended gentleness toward children in *The Mother's Book:* "It's effects are beyond calculation, both on the affections and the understanding." But, she added, "that is not all; there should be united with [gentleness] firmness—great firmness."[5] Affection and reason were the twin pillars of family management, in children's books as in advice literature, both of which assumed that children were rational as well as affectionate by nature. Authors counseled that quiet meditation was more effective than punishment, since it allowed a child's own powers of reasoning to bring about reform; many a fictional child improved his character by solitary contemplation of his sins. While lonely reflection was usually imposed by parents, it could also be self-administered. In one of the numerous "contrast" stories of the time, a bad boy, "hooted" by the other boys in the village, retires alone to seek the cause. "He . . . confined himself to his room, for some days. There he reasoned with himself on the cause that could produce such treatment. . . . 'For what reason,' said he to himself, 'could my little neighbors . . . hoot me?' . . . On comparing the good boy's behavior with his own, he very soon discovered the reason. To become sensible of our errors is half the work of reformation."[6]

Catherine Sedgwick's *Home* draws the thinnest of fictional veils over detailed instruction on the subject of family government. In an early chapter of this rather solemn story, Wallace Barclay, a ten-year-old lad with a terrible temper, kills his sister's kitten in a fit of rage. Father despairs of his son's character ("the boy is hopeless!"). Though Mother is more optimistic ("my dear husband! Hopeless at ten?"), she agrees that it is time for stern measures. " 'Go to your own room,' Mr. Barclay tells Wallace, 'You have forfeited your right to a place among us.' "

Wallace spends the next two weeks in silence: "[He] went to school as usual, and returned to his solitude, without speaking or being spoken to." When his aunt protests because he is "mewed up" so long, his mother explains the family philosophy: "We do not keep him mewed up . . . nor does he continue mewed up, for a single flash of temper; but because, with all his good resolutions, his passionate temper is constantly getting the better of him. There is no easy cure for such a fault. If Wallace had the seeds of consumption, you would think it the extreme of folly not to submit to a few weeks' confinement, . . . and how much worse than a consumption is a moral disease!"[7]

Most of the assumptions and all of the purposes of these stories can be found many times over in children's fiction of the period. Writers pressed parents to take the moral lapses of their children seriously yet they also urged them to treat children as rational beings. They condemned physical punishment and constant reproach as useless— or worse, as Lydia Maria Child observed: "Constant reproof may lead a child to conceal faults; but it seldom leads one to overcome them."[8] And if harsh words were a mistake, still less helpful was harsh physical punishment. Jacob Abbott, one of the most influential children's authors of his time, remarked many times in his stories on the evil effects of overseverity. The "wild and reckless character" of a boy in one of Abbott's *Franconia* tales is explained as "partly his father's fault, who never gave him any kind and friendly instruction, and always treated him with a great degree of sternness and severity."[9] A child badly reared, wrote another author, "had so much to unlearn; so much of hardness and unkindness, falsehood and indolence, that he did not know where to begin."[10]

Better than "hardness," the writers counseled, was the "law of love." "The only right way to govern any one is by giving them confidence in your kindly feelings toward them—by love."[11] Sedgwick's Mr. Barclay brought the two halves of the philosophy together: "[He] held whipping on a par with such nostrums in medicine as peppermint and lavender, which suspend the manifestation of the disease, without conducing to its cure. He believed the only effectual and lasting government—the only one that touches the springs of action, and in all circumstances controls them, is *self*-government. It was this he labored to teach his children. The process was slow but sure. It required judgement, and gentleness, and above all, patience on the part of parents, but every inch of ground gained was kept. The children might not appear so orderly as they whose parents are like drill-sergeants . . . but; deprived of external aid or restraint, the self-regulating machine shows its superiority."[12]

What the stories said was said again, and at length, in the many advice books on child management. As stern admonitions about "breaking a child's will" early in life gave way to kinder assumptions about child nature, a less rigorous—and less anxious—form of nurture became possible. If it was no longer necessary to see childish misbehavior as evidence of inborn evil, then correction of it could be milder and, doubtless, more optimistic. "What we call a natural love of mischief," said *The Mother's Book,* "is, in fact, nothing but activity. . . . If [children] are not furnished with what is useful or innocent, they will do mischief."[13] With some rock-hard exceptions, child nurture authors agreed with fiction writers that the true source of obedience was love, rather than fear, and that the soundest family order built upon affection and respect between parent and child. Throughout the first half of the nineteenth century, orthodox and reform writers alike counseled parents that "environment, persuasion, example, precept and carefully formed habits" were the best instruments of home training.[14] "The most efficient family government may be almost entirely administered by affection," according to John S. C. Abbott, "if it be distinctly understood that disobedience cannot pass unpunished. . . . It is ruinous to the disposition of a child, exclusively to control him by [fear.]"[15] When Lyman Cobb published a book called "The Evil Tendencies of Corporal Punishment" in 1847, he was not breaking new ground but summarizing several decades of advice literature.

To authors of children's books and advice literature, the advantage of self-regulation was as apparent as it was to Mr. Barclay, and the best possible argument for firm but gentle parenting. Harsh training might produce a child—and ultimately an adult—obedient to *external* restraint, but external restraints were few in nineteenth-century American society. An upbringing that produced a sensitive conscience, on the other hand, made for *internal* control; independent, individual, and reliable. Nineteenth-century parents would not have understood the twentieth-century dread of guilty feelings; to them guilt was the signal that conscience was at work. "Guilt fixes . . . the sting of remorse within the bosom," and remorse, most nineteenth-century Americans believed, would spur improvement.[16]

Didactic fiction and admonitory advice literature are easy to dismiss as tracts whose examples are idealized beyond any connection with reality. It is certainly true that the children who emerge from autobiography are not much like either the pattern children of fiction or the exemplary models of advice literature. If nothing else, their mischief was more creative than the feeble pranks that didactic authors invented for their characters. The children of autobiography did not sin and learn in equal measure; indeed, they often created havoc without necessarily supplying a moral text for their mentors. The enterprising children of Samuel Gridley and Julia Ward Howe were immortalized in two autobiographies by Laura E. [Howe] Richards, one for children, one for adults. Richards tells of being upended in a horse trough at age four by her brother Harry, age six, who felt no malice toward her; he only wanted to know what would happen. True, scientific curiosity also moved Harry to drop wet sponges down the stairwell of the tall Boston house where the Howes lived onto the bald heads of his father's distinguished visitors. Years later, when he was a celebrated scientist, Harry sighed a little because he could afford orchestra seats at the opera, which offered less scope than the balcony for experimentation.[17] It is hard to find the moral here. In fact, few of the Howe children's many and varied escapades (Flossy and Julia drinking train oil under the impression it was syrup, Laura falling into the sugar barrel while trying to satisfy her sweet tooth) seems to have promoted much moral reflection.[18]

Jeanette Gilder's memoirs are a lively catalog of her childhood scrapes, only a few of which improved her character noticeably. She certainly felt remorse from time to time; however, as neither she nor anyone else knew what she might do next time, her education by experience proceeded slowly. When she ran away (at nine) to join the Union army, the colonel of her chosen regiment hastily sent her back to her family, but she was not discouraged. "I was marched promptly off to bed, but I made a tent of my sheets, and with a broom for a musket, drilled myself till I was so tired that I fell asleep."[19] Autobiography is full of such rowdy, inventive, scapegrace children, girls and boys alike, who were not always preoccupied with the pursuit of goodness.

Nevertheless, the fiction is not altogether misleading and the advice writers not entirely unvindicated. There is plenty of evidence in autobiography that American child nurture was often as mild and as reasonable as the experts recommended and as effective in developing a child's conscience as the fiction promised. Many American parents took their family obligations as seriously as any advice writer could wish. Alice Kingsbury's parents did not send their children away to school, because they "believed that their influence over us, their companionship, was more important in our development than that of strangers, and they consciously exerted themselves to provide what they considered the right influence to be true companions." In Kingsbury's memory, this approach was a success: "As a family, we were great comrades, great talkers, great laughers."[20] William Dean Howells remembered a home "serenely bright with a father's reason and warm with a mother's love."[21]

Frequent or severe physical punishment seems to have been rare, whether the family was rich or not, country or city, pioneer or settled gentility, northern or southern. Autobiographers remarked often on their parents' tolerance, sometimes with an air of faint surprise. If young Harry nearly drowned his little sister, even in a scientific spirit, he needed correction, but Julia Ward Howe was as rational and restrained as any fictional model. "We were almost never whipped, " wrote Richards, "but for this misdeed Harry was put to bed at once, and our mother, sitting beside him, gave him . . . a 'talking to' which he did not soon forget."[22]

Adela Orpen, child of pioneer Kansas, observed that "such a thing as father being unkind to his child was unheard of, and was in fact non-existent. No father was unkind, the children were too few and too precious."[23] There must have been exceptions, but they are hard to find in autobiography. In quite a different setting, Cornelia Morse Raymond's father, who was president of Vassar College in the 1860s, had plenty of children—nine, in fact, who rocketed in and out of his study at will. Yet he, too, was patient and kind. When a visitor asked (cautiously) whether the noise bothered him, he said, "Good noise never bothers me." Raymond recorded that her father "never scolded" and "always understood," just as Laura Richards said that her father, though "absorbed in high works," was "never out of patience" with his children.[24] Caroline Creevey defused her own vivid imaginings of the Judgement Day by hoping that God was as forebearing as her mother: "God might be very like my mother who did not scold or punish severely, even when deeply offended. I could, generally, make her smile when she reproved me."[25]

Indeed, the limits of parental tolerance could be quite surprisingly elastic. Eleanor Abbott and her sister, Madeline, granddaughters of the sage and famous Jacob, grew up in Cambridge, Massachusetts, where they were known in the neighborhood as "The Fighting Abbotts." "Our technique was simple. I caught and tripped the victim. Madeline sat on him. And we both pounded him. Most always it was only boys that we fought. I don't know just why." After one especially stirring encounter, the fighting Abbotts returned home somewhat damaged. Their father met them at the gate "with rather a grave mouth but a twinkle in his eye. 'One might almost infer,' he said, 'that there has been an accident.' 'There was!' I said, 'But we won it!'" The Abbotts, of course, knew everyone of intellectual consequence in Cambridge, and it is satisfying, somehow, to learn that enterprising Eleanor and her brother put a toad in James Russell Lowell's mailbox.[26]

Tradition often holds that boys were punished more sternly than girls, but the memoirs furnish little evidence of it. James Weldon Johnson recorded that his mother spanked him sometimes (though "the force applied was never excessive") but his father never did so. "My Richmond grandmother's advice . . . about not sparing the rod and spoiling the child had no effect on him; not once in his life did he lay a finger in punishment on me or my brother."[27] "There was never any scolding or punishing by my parents," wrote Ulysses S. Grant, "no objection to rational enjoyments, such as fishing, [or] going to the creek. . . . I have no recollection of ever being punished at home, either by scolding or by the rod."[28] William Dean Howells's father admonished his sons when they had done wrong and "then ended the matter, as he often did, by saying 'Boys, consider yourselves soundly thrashed.'"[29]

None of this meant that children lived their lives outside adult control. Though they so often called their childhood years "happy," "indulgent," or "carefree," autobiographers also remembered discipline. Of his father, Johnson wrote, "By firmness and sometimes by sternness, he did exercise strong control over us."[30] Isabella Alden's parents were gentle and understanding but not all flaccid: "My mother was by no means given to changing her mind; having once spoken firmly, I had not the slightest hope of getting [what I wanted.]"[31] As fiction and advice literature recommended, the discipline recorded in most autobiography aimed at the inner control of conscience, not the obedience of fear. "Mother never locked us in the closet for our misdeeds," observed Henrietta Skinner, "but she would say, 'Go upstairs to my bedroom, take a chair into the closet and sit there half an hour. You may leave the door open six inches for light and air." It was never *said* that we were to take neither books nor toys to amuse ourselves . . . but it was 'understood.' We were *trusted,* and so it became impossible to do anything but carry out our punishment in its implied spirit."[32]

The "law of love" *was* powerful: though her father never scolded, Cornelia Raymond recalled that "one word from [him] . . . always sank into my mind to become a moral principle influencing my whole life."[33] Virginia Terhune Van de Water was an extremely sensitive child, painfully vulnerable to ridicule or thoughtless criticism. Her parents protected her when they could and themselves treated her with great gentleness. Affection gave them all the authority they needed over her. "To a loving child," her memoirs observe, "a parent's unhappiness means more than that parent's anger. . . . Love and faith had greater restraining power over me than had anger and fear."[34] Una Hunt also admitted that her parents' loving, rational rule was successful, if not always welcome. "The matter was always explained to us and left to our better natures to decide—how I detested my Better Nature!"[35]

Autobiography suggests that the longer-range results of this approach were all the moralists hoped for. Children did indeed develop tender consciences at an early age. Looking back, adults often remembered with dramatic clarity the first time they knowingly violated the moral standards they had learned from birth and experienced the pangs of a conscience they had not quite known they had. Lucy Larcom, who grew up in early nineteenth-century New England, recorded this memory:

> I suppose I was five or six years old. I had begun to be trusted with errands; one of them was to go to a farm-house for a quart of milk every morning, to purchase which I went always to the money-drawer in the shop and took out four cents. We were allowed to take a . . . biscuit, or a date or a fig, . . . but we well understood that we could not help ourselves to money.
>
> Now there was a little painted sugar equestrian in a shop window downtown, which I had seen and set my heart upon. I had learned that its price was two cents; and one morning as I passed around the counter with my tin pail, I made up my mind to possess myself of that amount. My father's back was turned; he was busy at his desk. . . . I counted out four cents aloud, but took six, and started on my errand. . . .
>
> When I was fairly through the bars that led into the farmer's field, and nobody was in sight, I took out my purloined pennies, and looked at them as they lay in my palm.

Then a strange thing happened. It was a bright morning, but it seemed to me as if the sky grew suddenly dark; and those two pennies began to burn my hand, to scorch me, as if they were red hot, to my very soul. It was agony to hold them. I laid them down under a tuft of grass in the footpath, and ran as if I had left a demon behind me. . . . I did my errand, and returning, I looked about in the grass for the two cents, wondering if they make me feel so badly again. . . . I should have been a much happier child if I had confessed, for I had to carry about with me for weeks and months a heavy burden of shame.

I thought of myself as a thief, and used to dream of being carried off to jail and condemned to the gallows for my offense; one of my storybooks told about a boy who was hanged at Tyburn for stealing, and how was I better than he?

Whatever naughtiness I was guilty of afterwards, I never again wanted to take what belonged to another, whether in the family or out of it.[36]

There is nothing unique or even uniquely New England in this story; a Hoosier upbringing produced just as tender a conscience in another little girl. Rachel Butz told a story remarkably like Larcom's in her memoirs: Rachel and her mother were visiting with Aunt Margaret, and Rachel had been left alone with her supper. She found four apples in a box. "The temptation proved too great. . . . I took one, shut the box and ran out into the yard to eat the coveted fruit." Guilt spoiled her pleasure immediately. "I choked on the fruit"; it lay "like a heavy burden on my heart." Aunt Margaret wondered out loud who could have taken the apple and ended by deciding that the hired man must have been the culprit. "But I had not read the story of George Washington and his Little Hatchet in vain," wrote Butz. "I made full confession of my sin . . . sobbing meanwhile." Aunt Margaret offered to give the repentant sinner another apple, but "I had enough for that time, and ever since then have I had the slightest inclination to take what was not my own."[37]

James Weldon Johnson, raised in Florida, remembered that "one evening after dark [when] I and my brother, being in possession of a few pennies, conspired to run around the corner to Mrs. Handy's grocery store and buy two "prize" boxes of candy. We went without giving notice or asking permission. On starting back I became immediately aware of the gravity of the situation. With each step homeward my foreboding increased. . . . When I entered the house it was with as heavy a sense of sin as any infant conscience could carry." [38]

Conscientious children were full of good resolutions, but they found perfect virtue hard to sustain. William Dean Howells and his brother read a boy's story in the *New York Mirror* that showed "how at many important moments the hero had been balked of fortune by his habit of lying. They took counsel together, and pledged themselves not to tell the smallest lie, upon any occasion whatever. It was a frightful slavery, for there are a great many times in a boy's life when it seems as if the truth really could *not* serve him. . . . My boy and his brother groaned under this good resolution, I do not know how long, but the day came when they could bear it no longer, though I cannot give just the time or the terms of their backsliding." [39]

That memoirs often mention children's fiction in their accounts of moral crisis is not, I think, incidental. Didactic fiction repeated to children the same values they learned at church, at home, and at school. For most American children, the moral universe presented to them by adults was, at least in theory, coherent to a degree we would scarcely recognize. No one would argue that adult society always lived up to the moral code found in children's books; for that matter, neither the fiction or advice literature ever pretended it did. Literature was rife with warnings to children that the world was full of temptation and downright wickedness. But whatever its lapses in action, society endorsed the code in precept: honesty, industry, charity, self-control—such standard virtues received universal lip service. If children's fiction was not often unflinchingly realistic, neither was it wholly unconnected with its society. The family life it described was highly idealized, to be sure, but it was an ideal many American families acknowledged and some achieved.

Nor was advice literature just an abstraction, though it must have seemed irrelevant at some parental moments. The dominant Protestant, middle-class culture of the early United States took it as given that self-regulated citizens formed the basis of social order and that self-control, a commitment to the work ethic, and a reasonable concern for the good of the community were virtues indispensable to the young Republic. That these values were best instilled in children by rational means was a conviction that had taken root in the broad and varied American middle class of the late eighteenth century, planted, assuredly, by Locke and Rousseau but cultivated by the didactic children's stories of Maria Edgeworth and Hannah More. Henrietta Skinner wrote that her mother "had been brought up on the ideas of . . . Maria Edgeworth and . . . Hannah More, that children should be educated mentally and morally through lessons drawn pleasantly and easily from the practical things of life."[40] If so, she was typical of many American parents whose mode of child rearing at least approximated the ideal set out in both books of advice and children's fiction, and whose success at creating self-regulated children acutely sensitive to the rule of conscience is recorded in many American memoirs of the early nineteenth century.

Children, Adults, and Reading
at the Turn of the Century

¥€ ¥€

Turn-of-the-century society is associated in the American mind with high decorum, large families, and lots of reading. The decorum may be exaggerated—it is always easy to believe that people behaved better in the past than they do now—and the large family is something of a myth; in fact, family size declined in the course of the nineteenth century. But there is plenty of evidence to support the belief about reading. Americans of the late nineteenth and early twentieth centuries did read prodigiously as children, as adults, and as families; quite often, they read the same books. Families read together much as families today might watch television together and for the same reason: reading was then, as television is today, by far the most available form of entertainment for most Americans. "Long evenings my mother read aloud," wrote Harvey Fergusson in his memoirs. "Before I could read myself I went down the great river with Huck Finn and fought Indians with Leatherstocking. . . . I walked in lace with Little Lord Fauntleroy."[1] Mary Ellen Chase recalled that her mother "somehow found time for reading to us, although how she did it remains a mystery. She liked to choose books which all of us from sixteen to six could enjoy . . . Lamb's *Tales from Shakespeare* . . . *The Swiss Family Robinson* . . . the poems of Whittier. When she read for an hour in the evening, my father always listened with us, the book mattering little to him."[2]

Mary Ellen Chase grew up in Maine in the 1890s. It was not an affluent family nor a leisurely household, but it was fervently literate. Her father, Chase said, was "never without a book. My father's love for books and study [was] the consuming passion of his life." Her mother was just as intellectually inclined, managing to combine the care of a large family with supervision of their schoolwork, with special affection for Latin studies. To the evening homework session, she brought "her enormous mending basket, heaped with underwear and stockings . . . and her own Caesar, Cicero and Virgil." When the Latin learners struggled to translate *The Gallic Wars*, "she was unsparing in her criticism of our clumsy construings, our laborious English renderings. . . . 'Orgetorix,' said my mother, holding a pair of worn red flannel drawers to the light, 'would turn over in his grave could he hear your translation!'" Chase's study of Greek was supervised by her father. "In the matter of accents and breathings, he gave no quarter, being as ruthless as one of the Homeric gods. . . . Once I had reached the . . . more thrilling labours of translation, we held together for two years high and delighted converse with the mighty dead."[3]

Chase saw nothing unusual about such home evenings in an American rural community: "Hundreds of other Maine families in the nineties . . . believed and behaved in precisely the same manner." As an example she cited the case of one Sarah Alden Ripley, found by a caller at home "rocking the baby's cradle . . . , shelling peas . . . , teaching Calculus to one Harvard student . . . , [and] correcting a translation of Sophocles made by another Harvard student." America, Chase observed, "once saw no dissimilarity between a milking-stool and a love of Shakespeare, between a plough and the thoughts above Tintern Abbey, between the Gallic Wars and a pair of red flannel drawers."[4]

Whether that was so or not outside of the state of Maine, it was certainly true that American children of every region and of all sorts of backgrounds read with passion. "My reading," reminisced one child of the nineties, "was not just a pastime or a pleasure. It was the world in which I lived, and everything else around me turned into shadow." H. L. Mencken at about eleven "began to inhabit a world that was two-thirds letterpress and only one-third trees, fields, streets and people." "We did not merely read . . . books, we lived them," wrote Una Hunt in her autobiography.[5]

What they read was a great grab bag of material, good, bad, and mediocre, adult and juvenile, books and magazines. Children of the time read, as reading children always do, whatever they could put their hands on, mixing levels and qualities entirely without prejudice. Edna Ferber, for example: "Our reading was undirected, haphazard. . . . By the time I was nine I had read all of Dickens, but I also adored the Five Little Pepper books, the St. Nicholas magazine, all of Louisa May Alcott, and the bound copies of Harper's Bazaar, *Hans Brinker and the Silver Skates*, the novels of The Duchess [a popular romance writer of the day]. . . . Good and bad, adult or infantile, I read all the books in the house, all the books in the store stock, all the books in the very inadequate public library." Another avid reader found her way into the public library stacks. "I went through the juveniles in a few weeks and started on the adult books. I began neatly with A. . . . I read all of Thomas Bailey Aldrich, and through a lot of A's to the B's and started with Cousin Bette. . . . the head librarian called on Mama to see what should be done."[6]

The list of authors grows familiar: Shakespeare, Thackeray, George Eliot, Alcott, Dickens and the Brontës, Hawthorne, Cooper, and Robert Louis Stevenson. So does the eclectic approach: "I do not remember," wrote Mary Ellen Chase, "that I was conscious of any difference in treatment between *Bleak House* and *Little Women*, between George Eliot and Sophie May, that I regarded one as duller than the other [or] more difficult to 'get into.' They were all stories. If they took me into a different world . . . I gloried in the . . . transference; if they related experiences I had had, I felt a . . . sense of companionship and sympathy."[7]

Open-minded as they were, they had preferences. Fergusson may have walked with Little Lord Fauntleroy, but he considered the little Lord's life "boring." On her own, Una Hunt read Andersen (whose tales made her cry), *Pilgrim's Progress, Water Babies,* Hawthorne's

Wonder Book, The Last of the Mohicans. When she was about seven, her mother read *Robinson Crusoe* and *Swiss Family Robinson* to her, but Una was "a good deal bored by them." Ferber accepted much uncritically, but not Elsie Dinsmore: "I loathed the Elsie Dinsmore books and found the lachrymose Elsie a bloody bore." Heavy sentiment and transparent moralizing did not sit well. Sunday school books, the irritatingly didactic Thomas Day, and awful Elsie were all scorned; one boy dismissed Andersen's stories as sentimental, preferring the stronger flavor of the Grimm tales. On the other hand, even books well loved in childhood were not necessarily approved in retrospect. Helen Woodward loved Dickens, Thackeray, Scott, and Louisa May Alcott (she, too, had "no patience with Elsie Dinsmore") but as an adult, she deplored Alcott's considerable influence on her. "The sweet and gentle benignity of her books did me a good deal of harm. They gave me preposterous ideas about kindness, and worse ones about the value of gentility."[8]

It is not difficult to know why children read adult books. They read them because they were there to be read, because they told stories, because they opened windows on a world of fact and fantasy that transcended daily life—all the reasons people read in any time. That so many adults read children's books, not just to children but for their own pleasure, is more surprising. To understand the widespread adult interest in children's literature one must look at the cultural mood of the late nineteenth century, when that interest was one part of a more general view of child and adult life.

The era was the high point in American romanticization of childhood. Conventional opinion idealized childhood as a free, golden period when children were close to God and nature, when "the real business of life . . . [was] play."[9] At the popular level, the romantic outlook was sentimental, dwelling on children's beauty and innocence. At the aesthetic level, romanticism went farther, surrounding childhood with an aura of myth, seeing in children the elemental qualities of nature unspoiled.

The view of adult life was darker. The twilight of Victorianism found many Americans weary of unbridled materialism and political corruption. The affluent classes feared that their cushioned lives insulated them from "real" experience and that the strictures of Victorian mores flattened emotional life. They hated industrial ugliness. Even more; in spite of exuberant economic success, late nineteenth-century America was beset by social strains: poverty, slums, exploited labor, destitute children, urban crime, and growing class conflict. By the 1890s, consciousness of all these ills was high. Reaction and reform efforts marked American society to the eve of World War I.

Reaction included a cultural outlook widely shared in the middle and upper classes that has been characterized by one historian as "antimodernism," by others as anti-Victorianism.[10] Either term suggests the rising criticism of American society, a criticism that had much to do with shaping cultural tastes in the late nineteenth century. Edith Wharton's autobiography speaks of the "impoverished emotional atmosphere" of old New York. "The average well-to-do New Yorker of my childhood," she wrote, "was . . . starved for a sight of the high gods. Beauty, passion and danger were automatically excluded from . . . life."[11] In search of "beauty, passion and danger," American literary taste turned from the present to the distant past, from complexity to simplicity. Readers deserted domestic realism for myth, folktale, and historical romance, where they hoped to find "the childhood of the race." They admired heroic action, moral grandeur, and emotional openness. Blackmore's *Lorna Doone* was an example, recommended for what one critic called its "manly hero . . . of brawn and heart equally well tempered."[12] Medievalism had a great vogue as late Victorians, looking for the virtues they believed lost in their own time, constructed a highly idealized (and highly inaccurate) idea of medieval society as simple and direct, childlike in its robust emotions and love of action. Medieval myth and legend, reshaped to nineteenth-century sensibilities, came in floods: *The Song of Roland, Robin Hood, King Arthur, Tristan and Isolde;* as epic poetry in *Idylls of the King,* as opera in Wagner's *Ring Cycle,* as children's fare in Howard Pyle's buoyant versions of Malory and the Robin Hood legends, and Sidney Lanier's *Boys' King Arthur,* dense with Victorian renderings of medieval English. "Damsel, as for to tell thee my name, I take no great force: truly, my name is Sir Lancelot du Lake."[13] A good many critics suggested that such literature had a therapeutic effect. G. Stanley Hall, the psychologist often credited with "inventing" adolescence, believed that medieval legends and folk literature would elevate the adolescent imagination. To those who thought modern life tepid, Sir Walter Scott's romanticized versions of clan warfare seemed the ideal literary model. *Century Magazine* published in 1899 a verse calling for a return to Scott's vigor:

> Rhymers and writers of our day,
> Too much of melancholy!
> Give us the old heroic lay;
> A whiff of wholesome folly;
> The escapade, the dance;
> A touch of wild romance.
> Wake from this self-conscious fit;
> Give us again Sir Walter's wit;
> His love of earth, of sky, of life;
> His ringing page with humor rife;
> His never-weary pen;
> His love of men! [14]

Families could read together because different generations enjoyed the same literature; they shared an aesthetic. For a decade or so on either side of the turn of the century, there was a community of literary tastes among adults and children greater than ever before or since. Adults and children alike took pleasure in strong narratives, romantic characters, high adventure, and an idealized picture of the world, both contemporary and historical. Many of the best-known authors of the time wrote for both adults and children. The *St. Nicholas Magazine*, a spectacularly successful periodical for children, asked for and got contributions from the most respected writers of the period: Kipling, Twain, Burnett, and Cable, to name but a few.

A romantic view of childhood made adults susceptible to books about children as well. Adults willingly read novels with children as main characters if the children were lovable and the story sentimental. *Rebecca of Sunnybrook Farm, Little Lord Fauntleroy,* and *Captain January* were as familiar to adults as to children. It was surely adult taste that raised *Little Lord Fauntleroy* to the status of a classic; the Burnett book that passed from child to child, now as then, is not *Fauntleroy* but *The Secret Garden.* No doubt children—some children, anyway—enjoyed *Peter Pan,* but it was adults who flocked to the theaters to see the play (with children, of course, but also without them), and it was adults who thought it said something true about childhood. When the play was first produced in London, in 1904, the *Daily Telegraph* proclaimed it "so true, so natural, so touching that it brought the audience to the writer's feet." The response, like much of the literature, was entirely transatlantic. When the play reached America, there was an equal outburst of enthusiasm. The American magazine, *Outlook,* called *Peter Pan* "a breath of fresh air . . . by the writer who . . . has most truly kept the heart and mind of a child." [15]

The *Outlook*'s words go to the core of late nineteenth-century feeling about childhood. In a better world, the crystalline qualities of childhood would not disappear with maturity; adults would be as spontaneous and as innocently joyful as children. It is not easy to imagine Robin Hood in nineteenth-century dress, but he represented the ideal: a boyish heart and mind in manly form. The romantic view held, not only that the best adults retained much of the child in them, but that the truest literary taste was interchangeable with a child's; the best books for children were also good for adults. "Older people," wrote Kate Douglas Wiggin, "can always read with pleasure the best children's books. . . . It would not bore you . . . to be shut up for a day or two with nothing but *Robinson Crusoe, Aesop's Fables, Arabian Nights,* Kingsley's *Water Babies, Alice in Wonderland,* Hawthorne's *Wonder Book* and *Tanglewood Tales,* Andersen's and Grimm's Fairy Tales, *Two Years Before the Mast* . . . the simpler poems of Scott, Lowell, Whittier, or Longfellow, and a sheaf of songs from the Elizabethan poets. If, indeed, you would be dreadfully bored, it is conceivable that you are a bit pedantic, stiff, and academic in your tastes, or a bit given to literary game of very high and 'gamy' flavor, so that French 'made dishes' have spoiled you for Anglo-Saxon roast beef." [16] Like her list of titles, Wiggin's sentiments in this passage are characteristic of her time and class, including the preference for hearty, Anglo-Saxon influences and the slight scorn for those who could not share the tastes of childhood.

Wiggin was speaking, of course, of mainstream, genteel, on-the-recommended-lists and in-the-library literature. The version of the *Arabian Nights* she had in mind was certainly not Sir Richard Burton's but Andrew Lang's or her own; in any case, collections from which were removed those parts suitable only, as Lang said, for "Arabs and very old gentlemen."

Outside the mainstream, there was another kind of reading, not as "gamy" as the unexpurgated *Arabian Nights,* though surely not acceptable in family circles either, but a form of literature widely indulged by the young all the same. The latter half of the nineteenth century produced an immense amount of popular "trash" literature in the form of series books, rags-to-riches tales, sensational "boys' papers," westerns, and dime and crime novels. Some of this was ignored in its early days; some was even accepted. The early trash, from about 1860 to 1880, preposterous and badly written as it was, had a kind of innocence. It was wildly melodramatic and its style affronted the sensitive reader, but it was staunchly moral. All fights were over matters of high principle, and fisticuffs, not guns, upheld the right. Nearer the end of the century, however, the morality evaporated, leaving only an ever-increasing sensationalism. Daniel Boone and Kit Carson were replaced as heroes by hard-drinking desperadoes called Deadshot Dave or the Black Avenger, characters likelier to shoot the Sheriff and rob a train than defend the law.[17]

Tolerance soon gave way to a reformist commitment to protect children from the pernicious influence of such stuff. Within the highly successful public library movement, the also successful drive to establish specialized services for children was equally a crusade to direct children's reading to "the best." The "best" excluded lowbrow trash, of course; it also ruled out undistinguished "juveniles" of all kinds. Children's literature experts insisted that early reading habits influenced a child's entire future as a reader. "If you find a twelve-year-old boy addicted to juveniles," said Kate Douglas Wiggin in 1901, "you may as well give the poor little creature up. . . . His ears will be deaf to the music of St. Paul's Epistles and the Book of Job; he will never know the Faerie Queene or the Red Cross Knight, Don Quixote, Hector or Ajax; Dante and Goethe will be sealed oracles to him until the end of time. . . . He drank too long and too deeply of nursery pap, and his literary appetite and digestion are both weakened beyond cure." Two years later, a reviewer for the *Atlantic Monthly* echoed Wiggin's disdain for mediocre children's books and went on: "One of the dangerous things about giving children unguided indulgence in child-books is that they are prepared to relish . . . such inferior stuff. . . . All stories are grist to the mill of infancy but it is true, nevertheless, that very few of them are worth grinding." "A child's reading," said yet another commentator, "should be chosen with the sole view of developing breadth and strength and health of character. . . . it should be like a magical broom . . . sweeping away the cobwebs of moodiness and broodiness and listlessness from heart and soul. . . . Dreamy-eyed children MUST be given literature . . . that will teach the blessedness of action. . . . Dreamy children, left to themselves . . . are almost certain to become morbid men and women." [18]

These writers (and many others) urged that children's reading be guided by knowledgeable adults, and in the twentieth century, that guidance was increasingly available. A whole industry grew up around children's books, professionalized by trained children's librarians, children's book editors, and children's book reviewing services. Children's book experts were idealistic, in keeping with the spirit of the public library movement. They hoped to educate the masses, uplift the lowly, and guide the immigrant child into the mainstream, while also seeing to it that middle-class children never fell prey to the low sensationalism of trash literature or the mediocrity of most series books. The tide of dime novels had ebbed by 1890, but series books flourished, to the growing distress of librarians, who deplored "juvenile series of the . . . ranting, canting, hypocritical sort." [19] They fought to cast out Horatio Alger; Martha Finley, guilty of *Elsie Dinsmore* and its terrible sequels; Frank Baum, producer of endless Oz books; and the octopus empire of Edward Stratemeyer, pouring forth the Rover Boys, Bobbsey Twins, Tom Swifts, and who could name what else. In many public library systems they succeeded, for many decades.

Children's book people were a strong-minded lot who were certain that they knew what was good in books and good for children. What they looked for in children's books can be gleaned from the language of book reviews, critical commentary, and recommended book lists. The most basic tenet of their philosophy was the single standard to be applied to all literature, whether child's or adult. "There is . . . no separate standard of taste by which to determine the value of books written for children. To be of permanent use, they must possess literary quality, that is, they must be whole-souled, broad, mature in temper, however simple they may need to be in theme or manner."[20]

The whole profession subscribed to statements like that; everyone agreed that literary quality admitted books to libraries, while lack of it kept them out. The precisions of literary quality were less obvious: "whole-souled" and "mature in temper" were abstract, to say the least.[21] Reviews were slightly more clarifying though not about the nature of literary quality. What reviewers revealed best were their tastes in moral tone, social values, and child character. Even as they criticized low literary quality, their remarks often suggest that they really meant something else. In 1907, the superintendent of school libraries in New York spoke of popular boys' books unwelcome in libraries in spite of their "lively style": "The books are not immoral, but they are poorly written, their heroes are too often of the 'cheap and smart' variety, and their ideals are not always the best." There was, he went on to say, plenty of other material "just as interesting and of a much higher tone [to] replace this cheap literature."[22]

Reviewers liked "healthy, true and sensible stories"—Alcott's, for example, or Jean Webster's, whose *Patty* stories were "the kind of book[s] to give our girls—clean, wholesome, and refreshing." They looked for something similar in child character. Henry James admired Stevenson's Jim Hawkins, who had "a delightful, rosy good-boyishness, and a conscious, modest liability to error." While Henry James was hardly the standard critic of children's writers, in this case his attitude was not unusual. Reviewers warmed to cheerful, unsophisticated fictional children without secrets or resentment; children like Fauntleroy and Rebecca of Sunnybrook Farm and Laura Richards's well-bred Hildegard, whose ideals were certainly "the best." They favored stories about "lovable, mischievous, wholesome" fun so long as it was understood that whatever "harmless mischief" there was would "always end in the proper manner."[23]

Specialists shaped children's literary experiences (as of course they meant to) because they chose books for libraries and schools, but children's preferences also influenced the ever-expanding body of literature written for them. Grammar school children consulted in 1907 were definite about what they liked in books: action, illustration, and conversation, they said, but not long description or digression. "I like it very much because there is so much asking and telling in it," explained one child. "I do not like it very much because it has no conversation in it," said another. *The Rose and the Ring* was chosen because "the book is thick, but the writing is large, and you can finish it in a short while."[24] Publishers of children's books heard and responded to the views of both the experts and the child readers. The specialists got the wholesomeness they wanted; the children got large print, illustration, and "lots of conversation."

By 1910, children's and adult literature had begun to diverge again; the era of shared reading was coming to an end. One reason was the professionalization of children's literature, which had a gradual but profound effect on children's reading. As specialists trained their attention on books for children, they redefined the literature in accord with the requirements of its readers as they saw them. Reading, like teaching, became more and more specifically geared to age and grade. Adult books were dropped not because they were deemed morally unsuitable for children, at least not those by Dickens, Scott, Cooper, or Defoe, but because they were too long or too complex for this or that child reader. Starting about the turn of the century, lists of recommended books, whether compiled by librarians or by publishers, showed a rising proportion of titles written for children and a slow but steady decline of adult titles. *Robinson Crusoe* and *Pilgrim's Progress,* if included at all, were often in abridged editions. Dickens and Scott persisted, though ever more selectively, but Thackeray, George Eliot, and the Brontës little by little disappeared. A 1912 purchase list of 550 children's books for public libraries included few adult titles, and those few were retellings of such classics as *Don Quixote* and Irving's *Rip Van Winkle.*[25] Professionals, after all, were enthusiastically engaged not only in selecting books for children but in encouraging their publication and in choosing, editing, and reviewing literature written especially for the young. With so many good children's books available, books that were wholesome, easy to read, and fun, specialists steered children to children's books, sure that they would be enjoyed and certain that that enjoyment would encourage a lifetime of worthwhile reading.

At the same time, another wedge was being driven between children's reading and that of adults in the twentieth century. Adult tastes had begun to shift from romanticism toward realism. The change was complex and gradual, of course, as cultural change is. Realistic fiction was not a twentieth-century invention; it had been written and read since at least the 1870s. Mark Twain, Stephen Crane, Henry James, and William Dean Howells all rank as realistic writers. But genteel and popular audiences alike before 1910 resisted strongly realistic literature, in particular, sexual frankness and "sordidness." Dreiser's *Sister Carrie* and Kate Chopin's *The Awakening*, both published in 1900 and both shockingly frank by nineteenth-century standards, were rejected by most of the reading public. Still, the literary argument between romanticism and realism went on, and after 1910, it was increasingly apparent that mainstream adult literature was moving decisively in the direction of realism.

Children's literature did not follow. The books flowing into the children's market were still romantic historical novels; wholesome (and idealized) girls' stories and equally wholesome adventure stories for boys; and new, beautifully illustrated editions of myths and legends and of folk and fairy tales. This is not to say that the field was in the doldrums; far from it, in fact. Supported by a prosperous economy, the expansion of the children's book business continued at a brisk pace. Publishing houses created special departments for children's books, run by editors trained in children's literature. Specialists reviewed new books as they came out; the *Horn Book*, devoted entirely to children's books, began publication in 1924. The 1920s also saw a burst of creativity applied to bookmaking for children. New illustrators worked out fresh concepts for picture books; visually, children's books reflected the best of the age.

Nevertheless, children's literature became an enclave. All the creative activity, all the knowledgeable producing and reviewing and purveying of children's books, took place a little apart from the larger world of literature. By about 1920, children's literature was a garden, lovingly tended by those who cared about it but isolated as well as protected by the cultural walls that surrounded it. The common aesthetic of the late nineteenth century was gone; adults and children read different authors, different books. Adults read Sinclair Lewis, Ernest Hemingway, and F. Scott Fitzgerald; children read Alcott,

Kipling, Burnett, and Andersen. Less and less frequently were children's books read or reviewed by adults not professionally involved in some way with children's literature.

The separation was never absolute, of course. Adults still read to their children, guided sometimes by the experts, sometimes by their memories of their own childhood reading. And children still borrowed from adult fare if it suited them; indeed, they eventually made of Jack London, that avatar of social realism, a writer now firmly associated with the young. Autobiography still records the eclectic tastes of childhood, mixing Emily Dickinson and Campfire Girls, Tom Swift and Ben Hur. But the days of reading in the family circle were, for all practical purposes, over. The old mutual enjoyment of *Oliver Twist* and *King Arthur* belonged to the past; reading had divided along generational lines. It was to be a long time before adults found reason again to look over the wall into the secret garden of children's literature.

Images: American Children in the Early Nineteenth Century

✂

Like all children's literature, early nineteenth-century juvenile fiction created an image of the ideal child. There is usually no telling how this model looks: rosy cheeks and golden ringlets came later. Authors before 1850 tended to concentrate on inner character and on the outward behavior that revealed the state of the inner self. The children whom authors admired in fiction were conscientious, self-disciplined, and obedient, not because they were trained in fear, but because they understood that their parents and teachers gave them rational direction for their own good. They were thoughtfully responsive to the gentle but tireless moral assessments that surrounded them on every side.[1]

Ideal did not mean perfect: fictional children made mistakes, losing their tempers or shirking their duties or worse. Most authors depicted such lapses seriously, but not catastrophically. They wrote, after all, to improve and to correct. With some stern exceptions, then, fictional consequences of mistaken judgment (there were always consequences) were instructive rather than fatal. When the lesson to be

127

drawn was pointed out to fictional children (as it always was), the children tried earnestly to improve. The characteristic story in early nineteenth-century children's books is of a well-intentioned child who is learning, through precept and experience, to be good.

Though no one except a few scholars reads these stories now, the image of the Good Child of nineteenth-century juvenile literature persists and has even acquired a certain reality in many minds. Influenced by what early nineteenth-century adults said they wanted from their children, we tend to assume they got it. Conventional opinion often describes the real children of that era as dutiful, quietly obedient, and more than a little repressed: "seen but not heard" is a common description of early nineteenth-century children.

But were they? Was the tractable, conscience-ridden child of fiction a reflection, even if exaggerated, of reality? Were the young citizens of the new republic docile, decorous, and dutiful? Of course, there is no way to answer such a question with certainty, but the comments of contemporary observers, particularly those of visitors to the country, are interesting on the point. They are also plentiful. In the first half of the nineteenth century, the United States were the object of a great interest to foreign visitors, many of them Britishers who retained a lively interest in their former colonies. They came to see the young republic in action, to observe its curious democratic ways, and they frequently recorded and published their observations. A remarkable number of these published travel reports included comments on the children of the republican experiment.[2] While the foreign travelers' descriptions of American children can hardly be taken as unbiased fact, they do offer a counterbalance to the idealized images of didactic fiction.

If there was one thing the foreign visitors agreed upon, it was that the American child was not repressed—not nearly repressed enough, most of them thought. "There is seldom any very great restraint imposed upon the youth of America," wrote Francis Wyse. "[Their] precocious intellect, brought forth and exercised at an early . . . age, and otherwise encouraged under the republican institutions of the country, has generally made them impatient of parental authority."[3]

That was a mild statement. Even friendly observers found American children "independent"; less sympathetic commentators called them rude, impertinent, shockingly undisciplined. "Their infant lips utter smart sayings, and baby oaths are too often encouraged . . . even by their parents, whose counsel and restraint they quickly learn wholly to despise."[4] The visitors did not hesitate to place the blame for these unruly children. American parents did not demand, and American children therefore did not give, the respect that should inform a child's behavior toward his mother and father. Far from it, in fact: visitors regularly accused Americans of encouraging their children to defy authority. Doubtless the best-known story on the subject is Captain Marryat's account of a dialogue between a three-year-old American and his parents:

"Johnny, my dear, come here," says his mama.
"I won't," cries Johnny.
"You must, my love, you are all wet, and you'll catch cold."
"I won't," replies Johnny.
"Come, my sweet, and I've something for you."
"I won't."
"Oh, Mr. ——— , do, pray make Johnny come in."
"Come in Johnny," says his father.
"I won't."
"I tell you, come in directly, sir—do you hear?"
"I won't," replies the urchin, taking to his heels.
"A sturdy republican, sir," says the father to me, smiling at the boy's resolute disobedience.[5]

Foreigners apparently never met the docile and obedient child who was the central image in children's stories. On the contrary, one English visitor found that "the child in the full sense of that word in England—a child with rosy cheeks and bright laugh, its docile obedience and simplicity, its healthful play and disciplined work, is a being almost unknown in America." The commonest observation was that American children were not children at all: "Little America," wrote Lady Emmeline Stuart-Wortley, "is, unhappily, generally grown-up America seen through a telescope turned the wrong [way]. . . . there are no childlike children here." "[They] are plagues," said Edward Abdy.[6]

In fact, the American child as foreign visitors described him was not just unlike the model child of fiction, he was the very mirror image of that idealized being. Exactly those characteristics so insistently ascribed to the good fictional child were reversed in the children the travelers complained of. The fictional child was obedient, respectful, thoughtful, and docile; the real American child, visitors claimed, was arrogant, disrespectful, and undisciplined. The children of juvenile stories were thoroughly locked into family life, sensitive to parental approval, aware of adult opinion. Not so the children the visitors described, who were careless of their parents' wishes, heedless of adult disapproval, who operated in the outer world as "diminutive men and women." The fictional child was inwardly turned; he weighed his own motives and judged his own character; he was anxious to improve. The child of the travelers' reports was breezy and confident, not given to self-examination, not apparently doubtful of his right to do whatever he wanted.

For all their differences, however, these two images of the American child were closely related: one was the other turned inside out. Both reflected the concern of authors for authority and deference, within families and, by analogy, within society. Attitudes toward the future of democratic society colored both images; there was a preoccupation with the child as a potential citizen of a new kind of society, and an implicit formula for the kind of citizen who could make that society succeed. He must have the "just disposition, virtuous habits and . . . rational self-governing character" the juvenile books sought to foster if democratic society was to survive.[7] The good child was the hope of the future; the wayward child was the potential destroyer of the social order. American authors were optimistic that moral education could guarantee good citizens; foreign visitors usually implied that the cause was already lost in American children.

In either version, some important realities of children's lives seem missing, obscured by a welter of adult concerns. Whichever they were, introverted and conscientious or extroverted and overconfident, real children surely had more aspects than the literary portraits allowed. A child is more than a potential adult, more than an apprentice to the future. Children are also present beings, living a daily life and participating in their own time. When we speculate about the children of the past, we want to know something about their practical lives; we want to understand something of the part they played in their own world.

The autobiographies of Americans who grew up in the years before the Civil War are sources for such insights. With some exceptions, they record the lives of children in circumstances quite like those of the children in juvenile fiction and probably not unlike those of most of the children foreign visitors met in their travels. The writers were mostly sons and daughters of farmers, small business owners, clergymen, or other people of modest means; neither rich nor poor, they and their families usually belonged to that large and flexible category of Americans considered middle-class. But where the literary sources concentrated on the middle-class child primarily as a future citizen, the autobiographies introduce us to children who were already contributing to their society in substantial ways well before they left childhood. Though they vary in setting and substance, these personal accounts are remarkably consistent in recording a central reality of a nineteenth-century childhood: children of that time were more often than not working members of their families and communities. They were social and moral entities certainly, as the literary sources claimed, but they were also a necessary part of the economic life of the country.

In a new nation, predominantly agricultural and expanding at a rapid rate, farm labor was chronically scarce. Most families had no choice but to depend heavily on their children to help with the constant work, in fields and house alike, that kept a family farm going. Field work was heavy and hard in the days before mechanization, and it began early for the boys of the family. John Muir, who was to become one of America's most distinguished naturalists, came to this country from Scotland when he was eleven years old, pioneering with his family on a backwoods farm in Wisconsin. In his autobiography, Muir described the long labors of his boyhood on the farm: "I was put to the plough at the age of twelve, when my head reached but little above the handles, and for many years I had to do the greatest part of the ploughing. It was hard work for so small a boy; nevertheless, as good ploughing was exacted from me if I were a man." Indeed, the early portion of this autobiography is a litany of the endless work that, in Muir's words, "stopped my growth and earned for me the title 'runt of the family.'"[8]

Muir conceded that the Scottish immigrants drove themselves unnecessarily hard; nevertheless, his experience was not unique. Hamlin Garland took over the plowing the fall he was ten, proud at first to do a man's job. "Alas! my sense of elation did not last long. To guide a team for a few minutes . . . was one thing—to plow all day . . . was another. . . . It meant moving to and fro hour after hour, day after day, with no one to talk to but the horses. It meant trudging eight or nine miles in the forenoon and as many more in the afternoon, with less than one hour off. . . . The work would have been quite tolerable had it not been so long drawn out. Ten hours of it even on a fine day made about twice too many for a boy." But many a nineteenth-century farm boy put in such long days of work well before he reached his full growth; the United States census began its count of farm workers at ten years old.[9]

American custom frowned on permitting women or girls to work in the fields, but their portion of the daily work was still demanding. Women clothed and fed their families, often starting with only the most basic of raw materials, and they early taught their children to help. Even little children could perform such tasks as "quilling"— that is, winding thread on spools. In his recollections of a "hard-scrabble boyhood" in upstate New York, Henry Conklin told of the many hours he spent quilling before he was old enough to go to school. He could not have been more than four or five years old. When he was six, his older sisters went out to work, so their work became his: "sweeping, washing dishes, and helping mother to wash [clothes]."[10]

Cooking was the responsibility of the women of a farm household. If an adult woman was not present, the role usually passed on to the next available girl even if she was still quite young. Adela Orpen pioneered with her father and an aunt on a farm in Kansas in the early 1860s. When her aunt was called away for several months, Adela, who was then eight years old, took over the household duties:

> I had to keep house for [my father and his helper], feed them and myself, and still look after my hens and chickens. Feeding

men meant baking all the bread, frying all the meat they required, milking and churning. I could do all this quite well with Auntie at hand. . . . It was very different when I had to keep track myself of the time when each duty came to its appointed moment. Breakfast was 5 a.m. There was cold cornbread ready, of course, . . . but mush had to be cooked. . . . After that came flapjacks like unto the sands of the sea for a multitude. . . . A working man will eat two dozen and smilingly ask for more. Imagine a small child standing over a very hot stove, flap-jacking for dear life at 5 a.m.[11]

Dinner was midday, according to farm custom, and this little girl usually produced chicken pot pie, sweet potatoes, and cornbread. Supper, mercifully, was what was left over from dinner, served cold.

Farm and domestic work were the dominant occupations in the early nineteenth century, for children as for adult Americans, but children also worked at a variety of other employments. While the system of trade apprenticeship was breaking down in this period, some boys still spent years learning such skills as cabinetmaking, bricklaying, printing, smithing, and so on, earning their keep and their instruction by their labor. Boys also went to sea as cabin boys and apprentice sailors, sometimes as young as eleven, often by fourteen. Whaling ships took on boys of thirteen, fourteen, and fifteen for voyages that lasted at least two years and frequently twice that long.[12]

By the 1830s, as manufacturing expanded in the United States, growing numbers of children were employed in factories. At first, children were hired mainly by the textile mills of the Northeast, where they tended the looms, changing bobbins and doing other simple, repetitive work. As time went on, glass, iron, shoe, printing, and dyeing manufactories also began to employ children. They worked a ten- to twelve-hour day, usually, and were paid, on the average, twenty-five to fifty cents a day. William Matthews, who worked from the age of twelve to nineteen in a New England woolen mill, calculated first wages as he wrote his memoirs: "The mill owning, side-whiskered gentleman who lived in a big, white, lawn-surrounded house on the very top of the hill had computed my worth as a harness cleaner in his mill at the rate of a little less than four cents an hour."

Matthews did very well, at least by comparison with another boy who worked as a bobbin boy in a Rhode Island mill in 1835. "For my services I was allowed forty-two cents per week, which, being analyzed, was seven cents per day, or one-half cent per hour."[13]

There were great variations, both in pay and in work conditions. The Lowell mills, of Lowell, Massachusetts, were model factories of their time, known the world over for the careful treatment given the girls they employed. Harriet Robinson was ten years old when she started work in a Lowell mill in 1835:

> I worked first in the spinning-room as a "doffer." The doffers were the very youngest girls, whose work was to doff, or take off, the full bobbins, and replace them with the empty ones. I can see myself now, racing down the alley, between the spinning frames, carrying in front of me a bobbin-box bigger than I was. These mites had to be very swift in their movements, so as not to keep the spinning-frames stopped long, and they worked only about fifteen minutes in every hour. The rest of the time was their own, and when the overseer was kind they were allowed to read, knit, or even to go outside the mill-yard to play. . . . The working hours of all girls extended from five o'clock in the morning until seven in the evening, with one-half hour for breakfast and for dinner. Even the doffers were forced to be on duty nearly fourteen hours a day, and this was the greatest hardship in the lives of these children. For it was not until 1842 that the hours of labor for children under twelve-years-of-age were limited to ten per day.[14]

The point the autobiographies make unambiguously is that children were a significant part of the labor force in the United States in the early nineteenth century. It was taken for granted that children would work; their labor was an integral part of the economic pattern of their families and, by extension, of their communities and of the nation. Farm children of all but the wealthiest families worked on the family farm and in their own homes, doing not just minor chores but essential work and sometimes fully as much of it as an adult. As hired labor, children, like women, represented a fall-back resource for families in time of financial trouble. They went into the labor market when the wages they could earn became essential to the family's survival—which usually meant when the father of the family was dead or out of work. Their stay at the labor market was not necessarily permanent; some children moved in and out of factories as family needs dictated. Unfortunately, here, as in so many other aspects of these children's lives, firm statistical data are impossible to come by.

Far more ambiguous and complex is the role that work played in the lives of the children of the period. That it robbed some children of an education, as Horace Mann pointed out in 1840, is unquestionable, and in many cases it robbed children of childhood.[15] The hours were long, in factories and often at home as well, and the labor was sometimes cruelly demanding of a child's limited strength. Yet the picture of child labor before 1850 is not quite comparable with that of the later nineteenth and early twentieth century, when the horror tales of children stunted and maimed by their labor in factories, mines, and sweatshops eventually helped to bring about effective child labor laws. Some textile mills (by far the largest employers of children in the antebellum period) were relatively benign places of work in the early decades. Lucy Larcom, who worked in the Lowell mills in the 1840s, found the work mild and easy—"almost like play." As her account and Robinson's suggest, it was the long hours that were the most arduous feature for the young; the tasks themselves were light and intermittent. After 1848, when the work "speed-up" began, Robinson records, the pressure and pace of work in the mills became oppressive and far more dangerous.[16]

Any assessment of the place of work in children's lives must take account of the pride that many felt in their labors. Early nineteenth-century Americans lived in a society in which nearly everyone worked. Children's work, whatever its costs, gave children value in that society, and they knew it. Pride in their skills and their accomplishments, and particularly pride in their contribution to the family economy, runs as a theme through many autobiographical accounts of childhood. "I was proud of my skill," said John Muir of his back-breaking labors. And Robinson wrote of her feelings on payday: "We were paid two dollars a week; and how proud I was when my turn came to stand up on the bobbin box, and write my name in the paymaster's book."[17] The same note sounds many times over in other memoirs. The working child often had a keen sense of independence and self-esteem.

This felt independence, this autonomous sense of self, brings together the three images discussed here. Autonomy is the characteristic shared by the moral child of early children's fiction, the assertive child of the foreigner's accounts, and the working child of the autobiographies. The otherwise disparate images begin to merge when we recognize that autonomy stands at the very center of each.

If the working child's autonomy is the most overt, the others nevertheless demonstrate in their own way the same characteristic. Foreign visitors, when they called American children "diminutive adults," were testifying directly on the point. If American children did not conform to their ideas of childhood, it was precisely the quality of independence, the lack of deference toward authority, and the ease American children felt in adult company, together with their confident expression of will, that so many foreigners found unsettling in them. The authors of these entertaining travel accounts came mostly from the upper layers of their own societies; they were accustomed to hierarchical arrangements that placed children, like servants, well down on the deferential scale. For most of them, therefore, the relative equity that prevailed in American families between adult and child was more than startling; it was a disruption of "natural order." Even those who did not pass judgment made the observation: "The Yankee child astonishes the European with his boldness, his crafty prudence, and his knowledge of life at ten years of age," observed President Sarmiento of Argentina. "From the earliest period of his life," wrote Frances Grund, "a young American is accustomed to rely upon himself as the principal artificer of his fortune. . . . The most characteristic feature of American children, whether male or female, is . . . an early development of the understanding, and a certain untimely intelligence seldom to be found in Europe."[18] Whether they deplored or admired or only remarked, foreign observers, if they took note at all of American childhood, invariably called attention to its autonomous quality.

The autonomous character of the ideal child of didactic fiction is somewhat obscured by the exaggerated conscientiousness of the children portrayed in the stories and by the authors' steady harping on the importance of obedience to parental authority. At first glance, it may seem that children's stories aimed at creating docile puppets for adults to command rather than independent human beings. Yet a careful reading of early nineteenth-century juvenile literature makes it clear that the real hope of its authors was to establish moral autonomy in children. The stories furnished endless examples of children who learned very early to take responsibility for their own moral characters. They were taught morality, of course, by conscientious parents. But the point of the teaching was always to transfer the code of values wholly to the children, to create in them a moral balance wheel that would function independently of parental authority. However often the authors extolled obedience in the stories they wrote for children, and whatever rhetoric they lavished on the attractions of hearth and home, they understood well enough that American children moved quickly away from all such strictures. They saw early moral autonomy as democracy's best hope for a reliable citizenry, and they made it the central goal of their writing for children. The climactic episode of nearly every didactic tale showed a child making a correct moral decision *independently,* having internalized the moral values of his parents.

From three very different angles, then, autonomy emerges as a salient feature of American childhood before 1865. It was the most particularly American characteristic of those children, the one that seemed to all observers, friendly or doubtful, to be a direct consequence of the democratic nature of American society. The looseness of hierarchical lines, the passion of the young nation for equality, and the constant need for every hand, young or old, to do the nation's work—these influences shaped childhood as they did adult life. "Children, even at home," wrote Henry Bradshaw Fearon, "are perfectly independent." [19] When Tocqueville explored the relationship between democratic society and family governance, he found, like other foreign visitors, that "the general principle that it is good and lawful to judge of all things for oneself" was extended to the children of American families. In the United States, he observed, "A species of equality prevails around the domestic hearth." Unlike many visitors, Tocqueville found the resulting family relationships an improvement over those of aristocratic society: "In proportion as manners and laws become more democratic, the relation of father and son becomes more intimate and more affectionate; rules and authority are less talked of; confidence and tenderness are oftentimes increased, and it would seem that the natural bond is drawn closer in proportion as the social bond is loosened."[20]

Tocqueville gave most of his attention to the relations between father and son, but when he turned to the education of American girls, he saw a degree of autonomy that paralleled that of boys, though its focus in the girls' case was moral. What he described was a system of nurture directed toward exactly the kind of early moral independence that juvenile fiction fostered. Americans, Tocqueville said, recognized that "in a democracy the independence of individuals cannot fail to be ,very great, tastes ill-restrained, customs fleeting . . . [and] paternal authority weak." The firm social structures that controlled the activities of girls in European society did not exist in America. Consequently, if a young woman's virtue was to be protected, another way had to be found. Americans, Tocqueville observed, relied upon a strong inner character developed early. "They . . . seek to enhance her confidence in her own strength of character. . . . They make the most vigorous efforts to bring individual independence to exercise a proper control over itself."[21] Even if the purpose of such "individual independence" was ultimately restraint, it was a self-imposed restraint, an internalization, like the fictional children's, of the society's moral standards. And it meant that, for girls as much as boys, a confident independence was a common attribute in a democratic society.

What autonomy meant to the children of the young United States is, of course, hard to assess. Only the autobiographical accounts give any glimpse, and there the evidence is more often implicit than explicit. What it did *not* mean was psychological or emotional separation from family and community. On the contrary, children who knew that they contributed in an important way to their world quite obviously felt near the center of things. They could measure their own worth at least partly in the same terms by which the adults of their time measured theirs and so could count themselves an integral, rather than a separate, part of their society. In many autobiographies, this sense of connection lies between the lines, but Lucy Larcom, recalling her work in the Lowell mill, expressed it directly: "I enjoyed even the unremitting clatter of the mill because it indicated something was going on. I liked to feel the people around me, even those whom I did not know, as a wave may like to feel the surrounding waves urging forward, with or against its own will. I felt that I belonged to the world, that there was something for me to do in it, though I had not yet found out what. Something to do; it might be very little, but it would still be my own work."[22]

They "belonged to the world." That was the visible quality in these children that made them startling to the foreigners, that caused the authors of their literature to be anxious for their moral well-being, and that makes them seem, even now, distinctly different from children who are held away from the workings of their own world by barriers of age. And their sense of belonging, their conviction of having "something to do" that made them part of their busy, striving society at an early age, was both cause and effect of the confident independence that characterized so often the sturdy, outspoken, autonomous children of a new republic.

A World Apart

The Children of
Children's Literature
in the Nineteenth Century

>£ >£

In the course of the nineteenth century, American children's literature made a momentous journey, from eighteenth-century rationalism to nineteenth-century romanticism. When the journey was complete, the children of children's fiction, rational, sober, and imperfect at the beginning of the century, had become innocent, charming, and perfect: the rational child had become the romantic child. The change in children's literature was by no means even or steady, or predictably linked to changes in adult literature. In fact, for half the century, children's fiction was all but static in form and content. When the break came, at about 1850, it was brought about by social change; the literature was reshaped and pressed into service as social protest in a changing society.

Early nineteenth-century American fiction for children followed eighteenth-century English models; in particular, the models provided by Maria Edgeworth's lively, but improving stories. Maria Edgeworth was the daughter of Richard Lovell Edgeworth—the "portentous bore," Virginia Woolf called him—and was, like her father, a philosophic disciple of Jean-Jacques Rousseau. Richard had eighteen living children by four wives, most of whom were raised, for all practical purposes, by Maria. She approached this task with the Rousseauesque conviction that children were reasonable creatures who learned best from experience and affectionate, rational teaching. She also wrote, among other works, a number of very successful stories for children embodying this same outlook, published around the turn of the nineteenth century and widely read on both sides of the Atlantic. In writing for the young, as she said in one preface for parents, she did not intend to give children knowledge of the world, "which ought not, cannot be given prematurely," but "some control of their own minds . . . [which] cannot be given too early and is in the power of all to attain, even before they are called into the active scenes of life."[1]

To this end, her stories told of mildly wayward children learning rationally from their mistakes, aided, invariably, by the serene moralizing of their parents. The underlying attitude captured the essence of eighteenth-century rationalism, conceding the imperfection of human nature while arranging for its improvement. It was optimism well laced with realism. The characteristic tone was struck in one Edgeworth tale when a father tells his erring daughter, "If you have sense enough to see your own mistakes, and can afterwards avoid them, you will never be a fool."[2]

Edgeworth's work was much admired in America; many children, both before and after the turn of the nineteenth century, read her books with pleasure, apparently absorbing their reasonable messages without objection. It is not surprising, then, that in the early decades of the nineteenth century, when American authors took up writing for American children, Maria Edgeworth's fiction furnished the major pattern for their work. Americans turned out hundreds of imitations of Edgeworth's tales, less lively by half, but every bit as dedicated to rational child nurture and the lessons of experience.

Which is to say that American children's fiction before 1850 told plain and sober stories of rather nice children making rather ordinary childish errors of judgment and learning appropriately from the consequences. The plots of early juvenile fiction were not designed to surprise, but to encourage children to learn that "control of their own minds" that Edgeworth recommended and that American authors agreed was the proper end of fiction. Fictional children learned to moderate quick tempers and restrain greediness, to think of others before themselves, to find happiness in duty and self-control. And authors arranged that these useful lessons followed relentlessly from practical experience.

But early nineteenth-century Americans never considered children self-sufficient; the parents' role as moral instructor was crucial. Like Emile's tireless tutor, parents in juvenile fiction were ever-present, to draw the moral and reinforce the connection between mistake and consequence. The tone of these inevitable conversations was mild and affectionate. "You see, my dear child . . ." they typically began, and went on to explain how happiness resulted from obedience and selflessness and how miserable was the child who was self-indulgent, ill-tempered or resistant to God's benign rule. Goodness and happiness went hand-in-hand, always. As one little sinner learned, "That which we obtain by improper means, seldom contributes to our happiness; but often renders us miserable."[3]

Discipline followed the same reasonable course. Fictional parents were never angry with their children. They approached childish failings calmly, explaining rather than punishing, urging children to meditate upon their behavior in order to perceive for themselves the better course of action. When five-year-old Rollo wants to go out to play, his mother asks if he had read his lesson for the morning. He says he forgot it, and his mother tells him he may not go out until he has read it. "Rollo was sadly disappointed, and also a little displeased. He turned away, hung down his head, and began to cry. 'Come here my son,' said his mother. Rollo came to his mother, and she said to him kindly, 'You have done wrong now twice, this morning. . . . it is my duty not to yield to such feelings as you have now, but to punish them.' Rollo stood silent for a minute—he perceived that he had done wrong, and was sorry."[4] And so they mostly were, these rational fictional children, when they did wrong. Told kindly of their errors, they obligingly saw their faults in a new light and set about at once to correct them.

To put it briefly, children's fiction in the early nineteenth century idealized children without sentimentalizing them. The tone was matter-of-fact and reasonable; the picture of children was affectionate but not "enthusiastic," in the eighteenth-century sense of emotionally extravagant. These books neither praised the innate perfection of children, nor did they wax eloquent about their redemptive powers. Fictional children did not correct or convert their elders in this period unless by silent example, and even that was rare. Mostly, children were pupils to the wisdom of adults.

The structure of the literature rested upon the concept of the child as a rational but unfinished being. By the nineteenth century, the Calvinist doctrine of innate depravity had faded from all but a few books published by sectarian presses; on the whole the literature showed children in a more optimistic light. Most authors looked on children as bundles of possibilities, some good, some evil; they thought them well-meaning, usually, but in need of plenty of instruction. If they were not sinful by nature, neither were they naturally perfect. Though they expected children to have an earnest concern for their own moral development, authors saw them as apprentices to moral perfection, not examples of it.

This picture held steady in children's fiction until about the middle of the century when the homogeneity of the literature began to break up. New writers introduced literary extravagance into a heretofore sober literature, and sentimentality, already rife in popular writing for adults, invaded the fiction written for children. By the 1850s, authors were harnessing children's literature to the cause of social protest, using sentimentality toward children to rouse public concern for the child victims of what they saw as a crisis in American urban society.

Fundamentally, the changes in children's literature followed (though at a little distance) the nineteenth-century adult taste for romantic and sentimental literature. But the change began when and how it did for social reasons; sentiment in children's literature was borne in on a wave of social concern for the children of the urban poor.

Poverty exploded in American cities during the 1840s and 1850s; port cities especially were overwhelmed by thousands of increasingly destitute immigrants. Between 1845 and 1855, the proportion of foreign-born in New York increased from one-third to one-half.[5] Unlike earlier immigrants, who fanned out into the country seeking land and work, many of those who arrived around mid-century had no means to move on, or to buy land, and few skills that would support them. Most of the Irish who came to Boston, Oscar Handlin writes, "were completely immobilized; the circumstances that brought them to Boston compelled them to remain there, to struggle on as best they could."[6] The poorest and least skilled immigrants stayed where they landed, living in murky slums and often sending their children into the streets to earn, beg, or steal a few pennies each day, that the family might buy bread—or whiskey.

The children pierced the public consciousness. They were inescapable, after all, living and working as they did in the city streets. "No one can walk the length of Broadway without meeting some hideous troop of ragged girls, from twelve years old down, brutalized already beyond redemption by premature vice, clad in filthy refuse of the ragpicker's collections, obscene of speech, the stamp of childhood gone from their faces, hurrying along with harsh laughter and foulness on their lips that some of them have learned by rote, yet too young to understand it; with thief written in their cunning eyes and whore on their depraved faces."[7] New York's Chief of Police estimated in 1850 that 3,000 vagrant children lived in the streets, scavenging a living one way or another.[8] They could be seen everywhere, "on the streets and the docks and the woodpiles," Charles Loring Brace wrote, "naturally enough," he added, since their homes were too wretched to bear.[9] Mayor Kingsland in 1852 pointed out the menace of these children. "A great majority are apt pupils in the school of vice, licentiousness and theft, who, if permitted to grow up, will constitute a large portion of the inmates of our prisons."[10]

By the late 1840s, these children of the urban poor began to appear in children's stories, sometimes in books, sometimes in such periodicals as different as the staid *Youth's Companion* magazine, on the one hand, and the lively *New York Ledger* on the other, in the popular column written by "Fanny Fern" (Sara Parton).[11] The *Youth's Companion* described "little blue-lipped and barefooted children on the pavements" of New York, poor children "with no one to care for them,

[who] spend their lives in the street, or in comfortless sheds and outbuildings, where you would think no human being could live." Fanny Fern told her "dear little readers" how the poor "live huddled together in garrets and cellars, half-starved, half-naked, and dirty and wretched beyond what you . . . ever could dream of." [12]

These pitiful children shared no qualities with their rational predecessors in juvenile fiction. They were neither models for character development nor examples of rational child nurture, but vehicles for social protest; their stories were told to move the public mind. Authors dwelt upon children's innocence and helplessness to underscore the wrongs in a social system that not only did not help them, but allowed their corruption. Like the Mayor, Parton warned that children in New York's slums learned vice early. Far from being protected by their parents, they were "taught to be wicked . . . whipped, and beaten for *not* being wicked." A street boy might be "a boy in years, but a man in vicious knowledge." [13]

Obviously, this kind of writing was directed at least as much toward adults as toward children. After all, even when she addressed her pathetic tales to "dear little readers," Parton often published them first in her newspaper column, which she wrote primarily for adults. Like many a social critic, Parton knew that sentimentality about children caught the adult attention as chilly statistics never would. She, and other children's writers as well, borrowed from Dickens the weapons of sentiment to expose social injustice. To show the suffering of the little victims of poverty, on the one hand, and the wickedness they learned in their slums, on the other, spoke to both sides of American reaction to the urban poor; that is, to compassion and to fear. Hearts too hard to be moved by children's misery might yet quail at Charles Loring Brace's vision of the slums as "nests in which the young fledglings of misfortune and vice begin their flight." The children of the slums, he pointed out, grow up to be "the dangerous classes." [14] If sympathy was not available, then self-interest might be. Either way, some attention might be paid; something might be done.

The Civil War, when it came, quickly overshadowed the acute concern of the 1850s for both the adult victims of urban poverty and the lost children of American cities. And when the war was over and a brisk economic expansion blessed the United States everywhere but in the devastated South, most Americans were willing to enjoy the prosperity and to consign social problems to organized benevolent institutions. The issue all but disappeared from children's literature.

The changes introduced into the fiction during the uneasy 1850s, however, stayed and multiplied. Children's literature diversified rapidly in the postwar years. Most authors abandoned the patterns of Edgeworthian didacticism and moved into forms already familiar in adult popular fiction. At the genteel middle-class level, children's literature found models in the evangelical fiction and the domestic novels enormously popular in adult literature about mid-century. Less genteel publications adapted the sensational tale to a whole genre of adventure fiction aimed at boys of the working class. The lurid, improbable "dime novel" started a long and successful career in the 1860s, as did the "rags-to-riches" story, which made Horatio Alger famous in American popular culture. At all levels, a new sentimentality toward children more and more colored the literature written for them.

Three well-known American children's novels, all published in the 1860s, give a sense of how quickly the literature was leaving behind the formulas of the early nineteenth century, and how various were the paths the authors took into the new era. Closest in some ways to prewar fiction, curiously enough, was the novel that has survived longest into the alien culture of the twentieth century, Louisa May Alcott's *Little Women*.

In *Little Women*—indeed, in all of Alcott's children's novels—the children are rounded versions of the flat characters in earlier fiction. Like the fictional children before them, Alcott's children are basically good and well intentioned, but they are always less than perfect. Any reader of *Little Women* can name the March girls' characteristic faults: Jo's temper, Amy's selfishness, Meg's false pride, Beth's shyness. And every reader remembers their struggles to overcome these flaws, to learn self-control, and to acquire the strong sense of duty that was the hallmark of admirable character in early nineteenth-century society.

The family system in which they learn these lessons surrounds them with love and reason. Marmee is the model rational parent, who believes, at least theoretically, in letting experience be the teacher. The well-known episode near the beginning of the novel where Marmee allows her grumbling daughters to take a holiday from their usual household chores is better told and more believable than innumerable didactic stories written earlier, but the premises are exactly the same. The girls learn that no happiness can come of neglecting the simple duties of domesticity. They find themselves bored and fretful, and they miss the order of their usual home life. At the end of the experiment, they admit their mistake, but Marmee, like all the model parents before her, spells out the lesson anyway: "I wanted you to see how the comfort of all depends on each doing her share faithfully. . . . Work is wholesome, and there is plenty for every one; it keeps us from . . . mischief, is good for health and spirits, and gives us a sense of power and independence better than money or fashion." [15]

Alcott's protagonists were not yet romantic children whose inborn perfection would give them a mission to redeem adults. Her fictional children still achieved moral character gradually, with effort and lapses, and under the careful tutelage of adults. Even Beth, whose failing was as gentle as her nature, must try to overcome it. She is, of course, an ideal of unassuming goodness for her sisters, but she is also doomed to die before she grows up. Her role as a model is mainly an effect of her death.

In *An Old Fashioned Girl*, Alcott allows her heroine to reform a misguided family, but she stays within the old formulas to do it. Over the course of her visit to the city, Polly transforms a "fashionable" household, though it is no purpose of hers to do so. She simply follows the teachings of her own wholesome, country upbringing, which have made her happy, healthy, and "useful to others," and her unconscious example changes the lives of those who have lost touch with such basic values. Alcott addressed questions of child nurture in all her children's books—*Eight Cousins* is the most overt example—and left no doubt about her opinions on the subject. Her views on children and family place her firmly in the preromantic period of children's literature.

Yet, in some important ways, Alcott's work heralded the new age. Her first book for children, *Little Women*, was semiautobiographical, and her subsequent work never altogether lost the particularity of real experience. Alcott's characterizations conveyed personality and individuality, rather than ideal types, and, while her stories were fully as "moral" as those of earlier authors, she made the effort to "be good" come alive because, remembering, she made it personal and subjective. She admitted that it was hard to overcome a fault, not abstractly (as even early fiction sometimes did) but concretely. She showed her major characters trying, and failing, and trying again. Marmee preached, as all good mothers preached in early nineteenth-century fiction, but readers forget that. What they remember is Jo struggling with her temper, her conscience, her overwhelming grief for Beth. They remember the passage in which Marmee tells Jo that she, too, has wrestled with a quick temper all her life. Very likely they also remember that even idealized Mrs. March has never altogether defeated her own natural temperament, but only learned to control it. While it is true that *Little Women*, which stayed closest to Alcott's own experience, was the best and the most felt of all her children's books, the less successful stories, in which the message gained the upper hand and the action was mechanical, still had personality and humor and a specificity that set them apart from antebellum fiction for the young. Those qualities, together with Alcott's capacity for portraying children as genuine people, not just patterns for her readers, went far to move children's fiction from the instructive abstractions of earlier decades toward romantic particularity.

At first glance, it seems odd to connect Horatio Alger's "rags-to-riches" stories to romanticism. But Alger's books, if not themselves "romantic," did in their own way contribute to the creation of a literature for children that was romantic about children. Alger's heroes were the street workers who had drawn so much attention in the 1850s. Bootblacks, match boys, newsboys, peddlers—all the young-sters who worked on the street, on their own, living an independent, catch-as-catch-can kind of life, were his protagonists. His plots took these boys from their lowly occupations into respectability, by way of good character, hard work, luck, and the intervention of Christian businessmen. Contrary to legend, it was not usually riches his heroes achieved, but something more modest. The title of one of his books says it all: *Slow and Sure; or, From the Street to the Shop.* Alger wanted his fictional boys, and the real boys they represented, to move from independent poverty to regular employment.

To make his stories attractive and persuasive, Alger had to make his characters attractive, and to do that, he had to blink at the worst possibilities of the lives of street workers, their moral corruption. Alger met the difficulty with sentimentality. He conceded some of the hazards of street life, admitting that boys might take to smoking or gambling or begging, but he evaded the "vicious knowledge" Sara Parton had pointed to. *Ragged Dick,* his first great success, published in 1868, was the story of a bootblack who lived in rags and slept in a box. Dick was "not a model boy in all respects," Alger admitted, but his sins were no more than bad habits. "His nature was a noble one, and had saved him from all mean faults."[16] Alger insisted that "noble natures" were plentiful under the tattered coats of his boys, to assure readers not only that a powerful person might take an interest in a bootblack, but also that the boy deserved his good fortune. And Alger's tales blandly assumed that the innate goodness of his heroes would triumph over the degrading influence of their street lives and work—a romantic notion very much at odds with the environmentalism of the antebellum period.

Alger's sentimentality, like that of some 1850s authors, was partly an effort to create sympathy for an underclass. The effectiveness of the approach was shown by his 1871 book, *Phil, the Fiddler,* which exposed the abuses of a contract labor system then operating in New York. Boys brought from Calabria to beg in the American streets were not only exploited, but so badly abused by their masters that many of them died. When Alger's story described the system and the wrongs suffered by the helpless youngsters caught in it, the public responded vigorously. There were meetings and protests, and eventually, a court case on behalf of one brutally mistreated child. In 1874, the New York legislature passed a law to prevent cruelty to children, the first of its kind in the United States.[17] If Alger's boys were not quite romantic children, they were nevertheless pure enough, likable enough, and sometimes pathetic enough to mobilize a growing American sentimentality toward children.

Elsie Dinsmore, by Martha Finley [Farquarson], was published in 1868. The novel owes a good deal to the adult Christian evangelical school of fiction and therefore belongs partly to pre–Civil War tradition. But the overdrawn sentiment of Finley's story, and her insistence on both the innocent purity of her heroine and on her power to redeem others, place the book within the developing romantic strain in children's fiction.

Finley's model was surely Susan Warner's best-selling 1850 evangelical novel, *Wide, Wide World*. In that lachrymose tale, the young heroine, Ellen Montgomery, weeps and sighs and strives for Christian humility for well over 500 pages. Elsie Dinsmore does much the same, though in fewer pages. Yet the novels are fundamentally different because the relations between the child protagonists and the adults around them are fundamentally different. Where Warner's protagonist seeks and finds a series of adult mentors to help her understand and follow Christ's teaching, Finley's Elsie is confident that she knows what a Christian should do. And why not? Elsie, Finley tells us, had a "very clear and correct view on almost every subject connected with her duty to God and her neighbor." [18] This eight-year-old is not only able, but eager to instruct adults, including her father, on *their* duty to God.

A famous scene in the novel has Mr. Dinsmore demanding that Elsie play the piano to entertain his guests. Alas, it is Sunday, and Elsie knows that to play the piano on Sunday would be wicked. So she refuses. Mr. Dinsmore insists, saying that she will sit in front of the piano until she agrees to play. Elsie (by now becomingly bathed in the light of martyrdom) sits and refuses and sits, until at last she topples from the stool in a faint, bashing her head and causing her father's friends to exclaim, "Dinsmore, you're a brute." [19] In other words, Elsie shames her father, but in time (it takes two books) she also redeems him, thus reversing what an earlier generation of children's writers presented as the natural order. Adult authority yields to the incandescent power of childhood purity; the child becomes mentor to the adult.

Elsie Dinsmore is a dreadful creation, whose incestuously emotional relations between father and daughter appall the post-Freudian reader, but it is interesting for its peculiarly radical mix of old and new in children's literature. The religious intensity of the story is old-fashioned, particularly the pages of unadorned preaching, and so is

Finley's insistence on Elsie's submissiveness, not as child so much as Christian. Yet the overriding fact of the novel is that Elsie is the clear winner in every contest between child and adult, even (or especially) when the adult is her parent. Finley made high moral drama of parent-child relations, with the child at the center, and ascendent. It was a giant step in the direction of romanticizing childhood.

These novels of the 1860s foreshadowed the romantic child who reached full flower in the children's literature of the last decades of the nineteenth century. Frances Hodgson Burnett's *Little Lord Fauntleroy* is probably the best-known romantic novel of childhood that passed as a novel for children. Burnett folds into Cedric's character every element of the romantic idea of children: physical beauty, innocence, personality, nobility of spirit, and the power of redemption. Her extravagant portrait of childish perfection has survived mostly as a byword for the excesses of Victorian romanticism.

Lord Fauntleroy's perfections were paralleled by other, now long forgotten, romantic fictional children. Laura Richards's very popular *Captain January,* published in 1890, concerns a ten-year-old child of "almost startling beauty. Her hair floated like a cloud of pale gold about her shoulders, her eyes were blue . . . violet, wonderful eyes, shaded by long, curved lashes of deepest black, which fell on the soft, rose-and-ivory tinted cheek."[20] This passionately fond description introduces Star Bright, who was rescued from a shipwreck by old Captain January ten years before the story opens. The narrative is unimportant except as a vehicle for Richards's romantic notions of childhood. Captain January is a stock rustic character who speaks in a Maine dialect. He dotes on Star Bright (he named her), describing her to a neighbor as "a picture . . . of health, and pootiness, and goodness."[21] He refuses to send her to school, teaching her himself out of only two books, the Bible and Shakespeare, which accounts for a certain quaintness in her language (but which doesn't explain why she lacks any trace of the Captain's dialect, though they are one another's only company for weeks on end).

Like Little Lord Fauntleroy and like romantic children generally, Star Bright is a redemptive force, bringing not just happiness but virtue to a lost soul. Captain January had years before become a lighthouse keeper because he could no longer bear the company of other people. Into his bleak and lonely life, the orphaned child came as a gift from God: She is, he tells her, "My light and my joy . . . a light from heaven to shine in a dark place, and the Lord's message to a sinful man."[22]

And shine she does, as Elsie Dinsmore did before her, but with winning differences from Elsie. Star has no need for either Elsie's submissiveness or her incessant preaching; full-blown romantic children redeem simply by being. Star's personality is quite like Rebecca of Sunnybrook Farm's and Anne of Green Gables's: volatile, quick-tempered, sympathetic, and loving. As Richards describes her, she is a combination of fairy and housewife (Richards always had a high regard for competent housekeeping).

She is also dramatic, like Anne and Rebecca, but to more purpose. An unlikely series of events brings her near her aunt, who instantly recognizes that she must be her sister's child and tries to claim her, that she may be properly educated. "You cannot grow to womanhood in a place like this. You must be with your own people." Captain January readily concedes the class argument. "I always told ye, ye remember, that ye was the child of gentlefolks. . . . you should have gentle raisin' by them as is your flesh and blood." But Star Bright will have none of it. "'You may kill me,' said the child, 'and take my body away, if you like. I will not go while I am alive.'"[23] She wins, and life resumes its idyllic round of nature watching, reading, and homely duty until the Captain's death at the end of the book. The sequel, published in 1927, takes up the rest of the story—and incidentally demonstrates the difficulties of turning a romantic child into a plausible adult.

Everything about the romantic novel of childhood stands in startling contrast to early nineteenth-century children's fiction. The emotional language, the sentimental view of life, the lingering delight in children's beauty, and, most of all, the assumption that children were by nature good as well as innocent, and that their God-given moral purity could redeem fallen or strayed adults—all these combined to create an image that is nearly as remote as it is possible to be from the sober rationality of earlier literature. Except that their creators approved of them, Jacob Abbott's Rollo and Burnett's Little Lord Fauntleroy had almost nothing in common.

The change was more than literary; it recorded some profound changes in the way Americans regarded children and their place in society. It is unlikely that late nineteenth-century American parents wholly embraced the notion that children were perfect, but it is certain that their view of childhood differed fundamentally from that of earlier generations. Early nineteenth-century adults looked on childhood almost entirely as a time of preparation for adult life. They loved and valued their children, to be sure, but they saw childishness as a condition to be outgrown and the irrational aspects of youth as qualities to be replaced as soon as possible by reasoned behavior.

By the last decades of the century, childhood had acquired value in and of itself. Children's innocence, emotionality, and imagination became qualities to be preserved rather than overcome; a child's sojourn in childhood was to be protected, not hastened. By implication, romantic literature made childhood the high point of life. The road to maturity was not an upward progress, but a descent.

It is hard to overstate how much a romantic attitude toward childhood influenced American thinking about children, socially, politically, and personally. It helped to extend childhood and compulsory schooling; it provided a framework for a strong political movement for laws to protect children against exploitation as workers; it widened class differences between those who could keep their children off the labor market and those who could not. Subtly but pervasively, romanticism altered relations between children and adults in every aspect of life, well into the twentieth century. Even now, when so little of the romantic survives in American attitudes toward childhood, something lingers; some residue of the romantic response to children persists, and perhaps accounts for contemporary uneasiness with the enormous changes in children's books, in children's lives.

Family Stories, 1920–1940

>E 3<

By American standards, from 1920 to 1940 is a long stretch of social history. The year 1920 came only eleven months beyond the end of World War I, a war that, it is a truism to say, closed an era in Western culture. By 1940, the country was within two years of entering the Second World War, which had already rolled over Europe, England, and the Far East. The twenty years bracketed by these catastrophic events saw the United States plunge from a hectic prosperity into a depression that lifted only when the country began to mobilize for war. In other words, these two decades were a period of vivid social change, in a country for which social change has been a norm rather than an exception.

Children's books of this period took the impress of the cultural changes around them. It would certainly not be possible to construct an accurate record of the social, political, or economic developments of this nation between 1920 and 1940 from the evidence in children's stories—this one cannot do in any period. Yet the shifts in cultural attitudes are there, recorded in the indirect way in which children's literature always documents its time and expressed in the values the books held out to young readers. Especially in the domestic fiction written for children, it is possible to trace lingering ties with pre–World War I society as they stretched ever more thinly through the

1920s until they virtually disappeared in the changed world of the Great Depression. And it is possible, too, to see how the family story of the 1930s consolidated an idea of childhood that dominated children's literature for the next thirty-five years, a fusion of realism and idealization of childhood and American family life that has altered fundamentally only in the past twenty to twenty-five years.

The 1920s were halcyon years for children's literature as a profession and as a publishing enterprise. Trained librarians, editors, and reviewers, experts with wide experience of children's books, dominated the field. Publishing houses could and did hire knowledgeable editors to oversee the production of children's books and profited from the strong lists of folk literature, fairy tales, and historical fiction these specialists created. In a booming economy, sales of handsomely designed and illustrated books for children flourished.

The domestic story for children of family and everyday life, however, lagged a little behind these developments. Domestic fiction, so expressive of contemporary attitudes toward childhood and family life, and of the values the adult generation hopes to pass along to children, was in transition. Relatively few family stories appeared in the 1920s, and most of those that did were deeply rooted in an earlier era. Though settings and events were contemporary, the social concepts were often those of turn-of-the-century fiction and in some respects belonged to the whole post–Civil War period. The basic view was sentimental, and the recurrent themes were of striving and achieving in a competitive society. Simple moralities and sentimental solutions to unsentimental problems still framed stories in which luck and personal benevolence overcame poverty, injustice, and class disadvantage.

Certainly the idealized children of 1920s books owed a great deal to their turn-of-the-century counterparts. Romantic children were still popular. As emissaries from a better world, they transformed the lives of joyless adults exactly as they had a generation before. Laura Richards's *Star Bright,* a sequel to *Captain January* published thirty-six years after that highly romanticized story, was still, in 1927, a perfect example of the late nineteenth-century idealization of childhood. Like Anne of Green Gables and Rebecca of Sunnybrook Farm, Star Bright is a quintessential romantic child: imaginative, affectionate, responsive to beauty, especially nature's beauties, and of a dramatic, literary turn of mind. Even after she becomes a woman, she retains a childlike impetuosity and egocentricity. Indeed, this child-woman expresses her deepest feelings in obscure Shakespearean quotes—which gives her conversation a very odd flavor—and is generally about twice as fey as Anne or Rebecca. Fundamentally, however, her character and her role in the lives of others are much like theirs.

Boys were idealized, too, but their qualities were different because their destinies were tied firmly to the outer world. Where a girl was encouraged to brighten the corner where she was and to preserve the charms of childhood as long as possible, boys had a larger sphere to grow into. A boy's character and actions always pointed toward adult life, and fiction often allowed a boy to take a hand in adult affairs. *St. David Walks Again* is exemplary. This 1928 novel is both a portrait of an idealized boy and a round of applause for American enterprise. Though less gracefully written, it is in some ways an interesting parallel with *Little Lord Fauntleroy*, published nearly two generations earlier.

The story concerns two American children, David and Felicity, who go to Cornwall to live with their aristocratic grandfather after the death of their parents. The children's situation is complicated by estrangement, just as Little Lord Fauntleroy's was; their English grandfather of the ancient family never forgave his son for marrying an American, and he is also convinced that David, when he inherits the family seat, Hoblyn House, will promptly turn it into a hotel. David, at twelve, is described as "a very manly little boy. No fiddle-faddle about David. He looked like a man, . . . his chin had a man-jut, and his shoulders were man-set."[1]

The children find Hoblyn House and the fishing village around it asleep like the castle in Sleeping Beauty. Grandfather hates the twentieth century and lives as much as possible as though it were 200 years earlier, using candlelight, wearing eighteenth-century small clothes, and so on. The economy of the village is paralyzed: the fish no longer come, and no one has the energy or enterprise to do anything new. The people look for miracles or an authority to initiate changes. Such passivity is anathema to David: "He was a bold fellow. . . . the history of the Hoblyns and the pluck of American pioneers had gone into the making of David. . . . From his American mother he inherited new, gay, courageous ways of looking at old problems, fresh ways of solving them."[2]

But the discerning eye will note that when David solves the problems of Hoblyn House (as, of course, he does), his methods have little in them that is new, fresh, or twentieth century. Though he cries out against his grandfather's rejection of the present ("It's wicked! . . . yesterday is yesterday. . . . you can't have it over again"), he restores local prosperity by reviving the villagers' belief in the ghost of St. David who brings luck to fishermen. And though he says, "there aren't any miracles . . . unless PEOPLE did them," the fish miraculously return on their own and the economy revives without the introduction of any new industry.[3] Like Grandfather, the author seems to want the past retrieved more or less intact.

However muddled its message, *St. David* is interesting for its attempt to weigh the merits of the Old and the New worlds and for its conclusion that history and noble tradition are worthless without New World pluck and enterprise. The theme was a favorite in children's books of the post–Civil War era and had not yet, in the 1920s, exhausted its attractions. Even with its aristocratic ruffles and flourishes, and in spite of its refusal to accept the realities of twentieth-century economic change, *St. David Walks Again* is recognizable as one more celebration of American "get up and git."

The point of most American enterprise was, of course, to get ahead, to "rise in the world," as Horatio Alger always put it. And just behind the eager wish to get ahead was a general preoccupation with class and wealth, pervasive in the post–Civil War society and still highly visible in children's books of the 1920s. If Alger's wooden simplicities were less convincing after World War I, Frances Hodgson Burnett's curiously combined admiration for both democratic character and aristocratic privilege lived on, still representative of a common American attitude, as the *St. David* story testifies.

The most popular nineteenth-century model, however, seems to have been Margaret Sidney's *Five Little Peppers* series, usually with mother left out. The story of poor but worthy "naturally genteel" children adopted or befriended by affluent gentlefolk was a favorite in the 1920s. Such a plot offered useful scope to the author, who could first show children bravely struggling with hardship and then deliver them to a better life with money, protection, and education. It was also wonderfully revealing of an author's attitudes toward poverty, character, class, and material wealth.

As one would expect, these attitudes were mixed in the 1920s, as they have been in most of American history. Convention insisted that poverty carried no stigma; at the same time, improvement of one's lot was all but mandatory for an American. To be born in a log cabin was an asset to many a career, but to rise above such humble beginnings was the real point in the American credo.

The climb from a lower to a higher economic level, however, involved more than finances: class and culture had to be considered. Authors of mainstream children's books endorsed the genteel tradition that linked wealth with cultivation. It would never do to bestow real affluence on a lower-class child who had neither manners nor finer feelings, who felt no response to beauty and art, or who was, worse yet, vicious and depraved.

Yet the lower classes obviously bred some such offspring, who posed some thorny questions. Were they entirely redeemable by a change of environment? If so, then were class differences wholly circumstantial—the luck of the draw? And if not, then was not the social mobility at the heart of the American dream a threat to a genteel class already faced with waves of Silas Laphams, rich but hopelessly vulgar? These were vexing questions for authors who were not, after all, social philosophers, and the plot devices they chose to handle the awkwardness were usually clumsy. The particular machinery varied, but the basic solution of the problem always involved the notion of inborn quality—a "natural" gentility that qualified certain children to move gracefully into a higher class.

This, too, was an old idea. Most nineteenth-century rags-to-riches stories leaned on the concept of inborn character to make class shifts palatable to the middle classes. Even Alger's heroes, whose rise on the social scale was often more modest than spectacular, were always distinguished from their nonrising street fellows by unusual decency and manners, characteristics generally attributed to genteel forebears who had fallen into poverty but not before bequeathing good character to their children.

Whatever the source, sterling inner character was essential if a child was to make the move from a lower class to a higher one. Fortunately, those in a position to help were always able to spot the sterling beneath the dross. *John and Susanne* is the story of an orphaned brother and sister adopted by an outstandingly genteel family. When the children run away from a ghastly asylum in New York, fate delivers them to the well-to-do Fairleys, who live an affluent and admirably cultivated life in the Connecticut countryside. The Fairleys already have three ideal children, but they add the waifs to their ménage without missing a beat. John, at five, is bursting with artistic talent, which is immediately recognized by the father, fortuitously an artist himself. More important, both children brim with inner worth, as the mother easily discerns: she "looked very straight into their eyes [and] found something very good back there."[4] There are reliable signals of their worthiness throughout: Susanne responds to natural beauty, finding religious meaning in the glories of nature, while John's artistic genius and straightforward honesty more than justify his adoption. As a girl, Susanne is never suspected of any particular genius, but she makes a place for herself by gratitude, a feeling for beauty, and—not least—practical usefulness. Both children strive to overcome the vile grammar of their beginnings, thus taking a giant step toward gentility.

As the family absorbs the orphans into its daily life, a reader gets a detailed picture of an ideal family's activities. There are art lessons for John, home dramatics and reading aloud, toys, space, and a riding horse freely shared; most important, the parents always have time to be with the children. Lest the reader should mistake all this as an inevitable consequence of wealth, the author supplies an episode that throws clear light on the value system that distinguishes gentility from mere affluence. A "fashionable" family comes to visit, bringing its "over-fed and over-dressed" children. Both parents and children are snobbish; they scorn John and Susanne, openly wondering at the place they are given in the Fairley family. Though the adopted waifs feel the slights, Susanne returns good for evil in the best moral tradition by saving overfed Myrtle from a runaway horse. Once the visitors leave, Mrs. Fairley draws the lesson for Susanne, telling her that "ladies" are defined, not by wealth, but by "the way they feel inside."[5] Genteel sensibility was very much alive in 1920s fiction, even if it dwelt side by side with a crasser taste for material well-being.

The value system in most fiction included the doctrine of hard work as well as the comforts of affluence; thus, many a fictional child worked first and found comfort afterward. In yet another orphan story, a sister and brother struggle for months to avoid the Poor Farm by picking apples, fishing for lobster, and growing their own food. It is a heroic effort, but without real hope of success, since, even if they manage to live, they cannot possibly also go to school and "amount to something," as the older sister recognizes. Given the worthiness of these children, it is only a matter of time before a responsible adult steps in to restore their fortunes and take on the role of guardian until they come of age. Yet the experience of hard work has had its value, as Betsey reflects when it is all over: "the hardship, the struggle fused into a shining steel bar which somehow ran through her and made her strong."[6]

Clearly, the 1920s were a period of transition in American attitudes toward the benefits of learning to work, on the one hand, and a child's right to a protected, carefree childhood, on the other. In a 1926 novel, when an adult remarks, "I don't believe it hurts a boy to work a little," he quickly adds, "but I'd hate to see a boy work so hard that he didn't have a good time."[7] The effort to encompass both value systems (without resort to orphans) is apparent in *Dan's Boy,* a novel with a clear debt to *Captains Courageous* and a strong message about how a boy should be brought up. The central character is Alden, the cosseted seven-year-old son of affluent, overprotective parents. A series of unlikely events brings Alden to the forest cabin of old Dan, an odd-jobs man and one of Nature's noblemen. For several months, Dan believes that Alden is his own son (explaining this plot is out of the question) and treats him accordingly—meaning that he kindly but firmly instills his own values in the boy. Alden learns to work, both at home, as part of the household, and away, to earn money. He also learns cleanliness, self-discipline, competitiveness, and how to get along with other boys, which includes fighting when necessary. This education gives him the pride he must have to succeed in a competitive society: "Pride that makes us lift our chins and work a little more is the pride that wins the prize." By the time he returns to his real home, "tough and tanned and freckled," Alden is fit to resume a life of privilege without being spoiled by it.[8]

The values this book promotes—a healthy toughness of body, the will to compete, self-discipline, and a measure of both humility and manly stoicism—were all staples in books for and about boys in the 1920s. And as the educational benefits of hard work or hard knocks were less and less relevant to a middle-class childhood, the job of passing these values along to boys became more and more the responsibility of schools; school stories aimed at an affluent middle class multiplied. Arthur Pier's ten prep school novels, published between 1919 and 1931, use sports as a vehicle for teaching manly character to boys, particularly to those boys whose homes were wealthy but short on gentility. Quite typically, a teacher in one of Pier's novels deplores the "influences prevailing in the homes of some of our excessively solvent citizens."[9] Obviously, the schools—all private in Pier's novels—were to provide the civilizing influences such homes did not.

Ideals for girls were neither identical with those for boys nor as unambiguous. A girl might or might not be encouraged to develop a strong, healthy body; by the end of the decade, she might be urged to be competitive, though only in a girl's sport or a feminine pursuit like canning or quilting contests at a state fair. Assuredly, she would not be encouraged to compete with boys; "tomboys" (always identified) who did had to learn more acceptable ways of using their energies. Work might or might not be an important part of a girl's upbringing; if it was, it was usually work close to home. Of all the ambiguities in attitudes toward girls, the greatest surrounded the authors' feelings about feminine independence. Young girls in 1920s fiction were quite often spirited creatures. Some were practical and enterprising, like the various orphans who fended for themselves and their younger brothers or sisters until help arrived. Some were sturdy tomboys, determined to do anything a boy could do and usually successful at it. Some were free spirits of the *Rebecca of Sunnybrook Farm* kind: they dared things and assumed leadership because they had more imagination than anyone else around.

But while a boy's path ran more or less straight from boyhood to manhood, with the strengths of one phase of life appropriate for the next, the same was not true for girls. Every story that took a girl into adolescence tacitly acknowledged that a young woman was going to have to accept more restrictions on her life than did a preadolescent girl, and that independence of mind was at best an uncomfortable trait in a woman. Whether or not the authors agreed with these conventions, their books did not set out to break them. Adolescent heroines ultimately accepted—without rebellion—their secondary roles, no matter how triumphantly independent they had been as children. Only the consistent authorial enthusiasm for a prolonged childhood for girls (but not for boys) suggests their regret for the metamorphosis their heroines must undergo; the transition itself was usually fogged over by a cloud of romance.

A 1924 novel titled *A Girl of the Plains Country* represents the type. In this oddly fascinating novel, an orphaned girl is raised by her guardian, manager of the ranch she will inherit, with the idea that she will assume control of the operation when she comes of age. As a young girl, she is active, sometimes daring, occasionally outspoken. When she reaches her midteens, still "slim and undeveloped," adults take to warning her against early marriage, and the reader begins to expect that she will in fact become ranch manager in her own right. But toward the end of the book, the direction shifts completely. Suddenly, when she is a mere seventeen, this heroine finds her romantic mate, a noble, courageous youth; all at once it is apparent that she will marry—early—and never manage the ranch on her own after all. It is an absolutely characteristic mixed message: again and again, authors showed young girls fully capable of both the spirit and the physical skills routinely attributed to boys, but they always drew back at the implications of such equality for adult life. Here, as elsewhere, books of the twenties tried for a compromise between change and tradition.

Over time, the success theme diminished in the children's fiction, or at least moved closer to homely reality. From adoptions by well-to-do gentry or discoveries of long-lost mortgages, authors turned to blue ribbons at the fair and first prize in the school race. Yet dreams of striving and winning, of prizes and advancement and a shining future ruled the fiction—until circumstance changed the rules.

The calamitous end to the 1920s boom and the swift decline into a devastating economic depression affected every part of American culture, including mainstream children's literature. Changes came unevenly, of course, but overall there is no mistaking the difference the 1930s made in the world depicted in children's books. It was in many respects a more realistic world. Romanticism faded, and the sentimentality that had clung to 1920s fiction all but disappeared. By 1930, author Grace Carroll saw a need for more realistic reading for adolescent girls. "Light historical fiction, gay stories of upright girls at boarding school, and good, clean accounts of young adventure are not enough." It was time, she said, to discard "heroines who think and speak and live, not as a normal girl *does*, but as the adults' Ideal Girl would."[10] She got some, though hardly all, of her wish. Change came with a new crop of writers who looked at their society differently. They idealized some of what they saw, certainly, but they saw differently, aspired differently, and abandoned once and for all the most sentimental of the literary conventions of the nineteenth century.

Essentially, 1930s writers shifted the focus of children's fiction. Where authors of the 1920s tended to look toward the future, putting achievement, social mobility, and material affluence at the center of their stories, 1930s authors turned their attention from future to present, and from status in society to relationships within families. The characteristic children's book of the 1930s was the family story, in which relations between children and parents, children and children, and children and community constituted the plot, while childhood itself furnished the major theme.[11] Even the time span of the stories contracted; stories of the 1920s often took their young protagonists within sight of adult life, but 1930s fiction was more likely to stay firmly within childhood, focusing on a single year, a few months, or one summer. Plots were episodic and small-gauged as authors tried to recreate the experiences and the feelings of childhood.

To a remarkable degree, the fiction shared a common outlook. Taken together, the work of such prominent authors as Eleanor Estes, Elizabeth Enright, Doris Gates, Rachel Field, and Elizabeth Coatsworth created a coherent concept of children, family, and childhood that shaped the family story for decades. If that concept was mildly idealized (as it surely was), it was an ideal widely shared in middle-class America. If family life was not always just like the fictional model (and doubtless it was not), most Americans would have agreed that it should be.

The ideal began and ended with security, love, and protection for the young. Children were integral parts of their families, yet a child lived at a little distance from the serious concerns of adult life. By the time these authors were growing up, middle-class American culture had reached a consensus about childhood, seeing it as a time for growing and learning under adult protection, a time, above all, for happiness—a season in the sun before the shadow of adult responsibility fell.

The patterns of family life in 1930s fiction reflected the consensus. Children and adults lived together in mutual affection and responsibility, with the weight of responsibility solidly on the adult side. Since love between parent and child was fundamental to the concept of family life in the books, the children had to be lovable, and they always were. Fictional children were good-natured, good-hearted, and childlike; they neither aped nor challenged adults. Though they took responsibility appropriate to their age, it was for adults to make the serious decisions, to nurture and direct children, and—most important—to provide the emotional security on which childhood depended absolutely.

The clear line between adult and child roles neither separated the generations nor made for authoritarian rule at home. On the contrary: in children's fiction, relations between child and adult were almost always warm and easy. Children had ready access to their parents, and parents were sensitive and responsive to children's needs. Adults, in fact, sometimes crossed over from their own sphere into a child's, joining in with children's pleasures. In Coatsworth's *Alice-All-by-Herself*, Alice and her mother and father create a special room in the attic for rainy days. Here is the scene when they first use it: "Alice's father and mother were already there, popping corn over the stove and pouring it into a yellow kitchen bowl with a big pat of butter on a dish and a salt cellar beside it. There was a giant basket of apples, too, and a sweet-smelling bouquet of herbs and the candles lighted. You could hear the rain falling so lightly and steadily on the roof, and the whisper and furling of the flames and the gay dancing and popping of the corn. There was a little chair waiting . . . beside the row of old bound St. Nicholases." [12] The whole genteel wish for a child's world is in that passage.

The adult domain, on the other hand, was not child's territory, particularly in time of trouble, though children were sometimes aware of family problems. In Enright's *Thimble Summer*, nine-year-old Garnet understands that the drought worries her farmer father: "Tonight her father would sit late in the kitchen, worried and silent, doing sums on a piece of paper. Long after everyone else had gone to bed, the lamp would burn and he would be there by himself." [13] But Garnet is never drawn into her father's troubles nor asked to share his fears; such matters belonged to the grown-up world.

I do not want to give the impression that hard reality was consistently filtered out of children's literature in this period: that is not the case. I have said that 1930s fiction was more realistic than that of the preceding decade, and it was. The fairy-tale plots in which fictional characters moved from misery to bliss by way of sudden luck had given way to stories much closer to the experience of ordinary people. The Ideal Girl had been set aside for heroines closer to the "normal girl" Mrs. Carroll hoped for; a few novels for older girls conceded that hardship and uncertainty created tensions within families. [14]

But the 1930s view of children, both as protagonists and audience, kept literary realism within bounds, with the line of demarcation falling, usually, between people and circumstance. Writers were willing to tell children that life was not always perfect, but generally, they chose to identify trouble with impersonal forces, like nature or economics. Personal malevolence, violence, hatred, and despair had little place in their concept of what was appropriate for children.

As one might expect, the commonest misfortune in the stories was poverty, but it was not a very grinding form of poverty the fiction described. It caused neither bitterness nor severe deprivation, and it rarely set the poorer children apart in any important way from those who were better off. Only the migrant workers of *Blue Willow* were painfully poor, and even here, Gates avoided acknowledging the worst social consequences of real poverty. Estes's Moffat family stories were more typical: though the Moffats were poor enough to receive some haphazard charity from their neighbors, it made no difference socially. The Moffats' rented house backed up to the garden of Janey's best friend, whose family was well off enough to enjoy polished floors, thick rugs, and luncheons served by a maid. Yet the sizable economic gap put no social distance between the two little girls, nor was there any difference in the families' standards, values, or manners. The Moffats' poverty was accidental and superficial; it did not characterize them nor drive a class wedge between them and their neighbors. Authors of the 1930s discarded the edgy class consciousness of the 1920s to emphasize the common ground among people.

On the whole, the outer world as pictured in children's fiction was benign, an extension of home kindness toward children. Stories encouraged children to move outward and become acquainted with their communities; indeed, a child's exploration of the world beyond home made up the plot of many a 1930s book. That children must establish a connection with the larger society was fundamental to the philosophy that shaped the literature, as one author of the period explained: "A fully rounded life," she wrote in 1935, "must not be egocentric, but must be centered in the society of which that individual is a part." [15] A child's growing up must include knowing and trusting the community and its people, and learning to look beyond superficial differences to the common humanity that lay beneath.

Most family fiction centered on children of about nine to fourteen —in other words, on children past early childhood and old enough to expand their knowledge of a larger society. The typical narrative pattern took a young protagonist from home into the community, then back to home and family to ponder the lessons learned. Such excursions were both literally and figuratively a child's quest for experience, an initiation into the possibilities of life, and an introduction to the varieties of human personality. In contrast to the essential but shadowy parents, the adults children met on these forays into the world were often vivid characters. One remembers Mrs. Oliphant, of *The Saturdays*, with her furs, necklaces, and generous wealth, far better than the Melendy children's kindly but indistinct father; the oldest inhabitant Janey Moffat befriends is a sharper portrait than

Mrs. Moffat. Clearly, their difference from the familiar was part of the point.

The conclusions a child was led to draw from these encounters were optimistic. Stories encouraged children to look past an unfamiliar or even an unpromising surface to find value in the people they met. Courage, kindness, and enterprise, the books said, come in every kind of package; children must seek the truth about human beings before judging them. "Sometimes people are not the way they look," Mona Melendy observes after her first unaccompanied visit to the city. "It was a great surprise."[16]

Children also learned to be easy with community authority, as they were with the authority of home and parents. Ten-year-old Janey Moffat's conversation with the chief of police dispels her fear that she might go to jail for a childish prank: "Little girl" [says the chief], "don't be afraid of a policeman any more or of anything. Remember this. A policeman is for your protection. He's nothing to be scared of."[17]

"Nothing to be scared of" was the message, spoken and unspoken, about the world, the future, and human character. Life outside the home held some hazards, to be sure, but on balance, the good very much outweighed the bad. Children need not fear the world. Even when troubles came there were decent people around to see that justice and kindness prevailed.

In its own way, then, children's literature recorded and responded to cultural change over two momentous decades. Some of the new directions of the 1930s can be attributed to new authors, who were often better writers than their 1920s predecessors and who had both a more coherent, more socially idealistic, less stereotyped vision to convey and more developed literary skills with which to express it. But the changes in children's fiction, and the particular directions they took, also recorded real shifts in the American outlook over twenty changing years. Looking at them now, some seem no more than logical. The 1920s preoccupation with striving and achieving was obviously out of step with an economy in severe decline. In the face of an economic collapse of the magnitude of the Great Depression, it is not surprising that fiction for the young turned away from dreams of material gain and upward mobility to center on the plainer comforts of home and family. For Americans, home had always been idealized as a haven from the rigors of a competitive society; now it was shelter against the cold winds of economic fear and future uncertainty. If the social order was manifestly insecure, then security must be located in family and community; if everything else was in flux, if the future was clouded, then human love must be the fixed point, and joy must be in the here and now.

What *is* surprising, I think, is the calm serenity of the 1930s stories, the faith in human nature that pervaded them all, the optimism that survived a massive fracture of the social system. A literature that might well have been anxious or bitter or despairing was none of these, not at any level; the stream ran clear and steady, with no fearful undercurrents.

This fictional picture should not be dismissed as pure myth manufactured for children, or as a peculiar unworldliness on the part of the authors. There is truth as well as wish in these stories. Families of the 1930s could and often did function as the stories said: closely integrated yet psychologically separated along generational lines. For all that times were hard and families strained to meet daily needs, many children did grow up at some protective remove from adult concerns; they knew and did not know at the same time. Russell Baker's memoir of his 1930s childhood says it well: "The occasional outbursts of passion that flickered across my childhood were like summer storms. The sky clouded suddenly, thunder rumbled, lightening flashed, and I trembled a few moments, then just as swiftly the sky turned blue again and I was basking contentedly in the peace of innocence." [18]

Baker also confirms that the temperate mood of the stories had its counterpart in reality. Listening to adults talk night after night around the kitchen table, he was, he writes, "receiving an education in the world and how to think about it. What I absorbed most deeply was not information but attitudes, ways of looking at the world that were to stay with me for many years. Sometimes their talk about the Depression was shaded with anger, but its dominant tones were good humor and civility. The anger was never edged with bitterness or self-pity." [19] So the children's books told the truth, as they mostly do. It was not the whole truth; it never is, in this, or perhaps in any, literature, but it is the kind of truth difficult to extract from more objectively complete histories. Whatever surface messages children's books send out, they also transmit the emotional tone of their culture. Books of the 1920s conveyed the nervous energy of a society eager for success and achievement in the material world, while 1930s fiction spoke of a society hunkered down to wait out hard times, returning for reassurance to family and community, taking what comfort it could in human warmth, and enduring, on the whole, with tolerance and good humor.

In retrospect, I suppose one could ask—someone usually does—whether these books were "good for children." In a society that went from boom to bust, from a heedless postwar gala to a second world war, were authors justified in telling children that people were basically good, that society was essentially decent, and that children could grow up to find a place in a rational world? Were children steadied by their season in the sun and armed against the sea of troubles that awaited them? Or were they crippled by their innocence and paralyzed by an inability to recognize evil before it overwhelmed them?

Obviously, the answers to such questions involve the most basic convictions about the meaning and purpose of childhood. It is just these convictions that change with changing times and that determine how adults construct and conduct childhood for children and, most certainly, how they write for children. Whatever the answers, it is worth observing that more recent literature for children suggests that American attitudes toward childhood, society, the world, and the future have moved miles and miles and years and years away from the 1920s and 1930s—but that is a whole other story.

Censorship and Children's Literature

>€ ¾<

The major arguments against censorship of books for adults have been familiar for a long time. Most of them were well expressed in John Milton's *Areopagitica,* published more than 300 years ago. Milton's notion of a free marketplace of ideas where intellectual wares are available for comparison, his insistence on the right of free adults to choose for themselves their moral and intellectual fare, his arguments on the impossibility of suppressing ideas successfully in a free society and on the dangerous weapon that censorship can become in the hands of authority—all these are still basic to the case for uncensored access by adults to printed material. To them most be added another argument, common in modern (though not in Milton's) discussion: that in any case, it does not much matter, that the written word is but one of many influences on an individual and by no means the most decisive. This attitude was perhaps most succinctly stated by a former mayor of New York, Jimmy Walker, in a long-ago legal fight over the restriction of pornographic literature. "Well," the Mayor is said to have remarked in laconic defense of liberty, "no girl was ever ruined by a book."

At a time of serious controversy over whether children's reading should or should not be subjected to some kind of restriction, the question arises whether these same arguments are applicable to children and to children's books. Do children have the same intellectual rights that adults have? Or, to put it more basically, are children free citizens of a free society in the same sense that adults are? Should children be encouraged to make comparisons among intellectual and moral concepts freely available to them? Can children be assumed to be as capable as adults of making reasoned choices among ideas? Is the "harmlessness" argument appropriate—that is, should children's books be free of censorship, if for no other reason than because they are a relatively unimportant influence in children's lives? Do the dangers of restricting children's access to the full range of moral, social, and political attitudes outweigh the dangers of exposing the young to pernicious ideas—or is it the other way around? In short, is the concept of intellectual freedom applicable to children? Is that concept, in fact, even compatible with the concept of childhood?

Even to raise the issue suggests that we are in the midst of a historical shift in our thinking about children and childhood. For a long time, certainly for well over 200 years, most adults in Western society would have given an unhesitant no to any and all of these questions. Until quite recently, there existed in our society a general agreement that the rules on moral and intellectual matters applicable to children belonged to a category altogether separate from those applied to adults. Adults considered that children were beings different from adults intellectually, emotionally, and socially, as well as physically, whose proper development required that they be insulated from certain kinds of knowledge and influences, shielded for their own good, from too direct contact with the full range of adult activity.[1]

The idea of childhood as a distinct and, ideally at least, protected period of life has become so familiar as to seem "natural," perhaps even inherent in the human outlook. It is worth remembering, however, that such a view of childhood is neither eternal nor universal. It has a historical beginning and development and, like any other cultural attitude, it is subject to change.

Historians of childhood differentiate between modern concepts of childhood and those that preceded them. Philippe Aries, whose

Centuries of Childhood was a seminal work in the field, locates the beginning of modern childhood in the early seventeenth century.[2] According to Aries, medieval culture separated children from adult life only through the period of infancy, which ended at about the age of seven. After that, children moved into the adult world, living and working alongside adults, hearing, saying, and seeing what adults heard, said, and saw. Ancient and medieval culture made few efforts to protect children from contact with violence, sex, coarse humor, vulgarity, and brutality of various kinds. All these elements of adult life, which later generations excluded from the category of knowledge suitable for children, were an accepted part of a child's experience once he had left the primary care of mother or nurse.

The rise of the middle class, dating, roughly, from the end of the sixteenth century, brought about fundamental changes in attitudes toward family life in general and toward childhood in particular. Aries describes a steady in-drawing of the family from that time, a separation of family from the larger world beyond; he sees the extended relationships of medieval society narrowing, and the old, rather careless, attitude toward children giving way to a more anxious and demanding view. Increasingly, middle-class people came to regard childhood as a period of preparation for adult life, and, increasingly, preparation became identified with education. As their concern for the education of their children grew, the middle classes steadily lengthened the period they called childhood. School became the central task of a child's life. In school, children were at a remove from adult life for longer than they had ever been in medieval society—"quarantined" is Aries's term.

Whether or not they follow Aries in all respects, most historians of childhood agree that attitudes toward children began to change in important ways around the turn of the seventeenth century. They generally agree, too, that the change was closely connected with the expansion of the middle classes, and with all the economic and social changes that that expansion implied. Because they were not dependent upon the labor of their children for survival, middle-class families could assign their children to the unproductive (in the immediate economic sense) pursuit of formal education for ever-lengthening periods of time—a process that has continued into the present. Because they increasingly tended to regard children as incomplete or unformed until their education was finished, middle-class parents also tended to emphasize the differences between child and adult, to see childhood as a distinct phase of human life and children as distinctly different from adults.

This is not to say that a single view toward children has prevailed since the seventeenth century. On the contrary: while all "modern" views insist on the differences between childhood and adulthood, there have been important shifts in how adults characterize the nature of children themselves. Over the past several centuries a number of ideas, each quite different from the other, have at various times seemed inseparable from the idea of childhood. In some periods, adults have viewed children as depraved from birth, marked by original sin, in need of most stringent spiritual training to prepare them for salvation; at other times, they have seen children as innocent creatures, better than adults, whose innocence must be protected as long as possible from the inroads of sordid reality. Adults have sometimes looked on children as a mixture of good and bad, whose goodness must be nurtured and badness suppressed, whose character must be formed and firmed before it was exposed to a corrupt world. At other times, they have thought of children as blank slates, whose characters were written by adults during the childhood years. More recently, adults have tended to see children primarily in psychological terms, to judge influences on children by their psychological rather than their moral effects, and to be concerned for children's mental health more than for their character.

These examples by no means exhaust the list; the adult view of children has been changed, sometimes drastically, sometimes subtly, many times over the past 300 or so years. Whatever their differences, however, there are two assumptions common to all modern views of childhood. The first is that children need to be separated to some degree from adult life until they have been educated or ripened in some important way. The second is that adults have something of value to teach children, so that the very concept of childhood in modern history is closely associated with that of the nurture, training, and conscious education of the child by responsible adults.

What these assumptions have meant in practical terms is that modern middle-class childhood is managed, directed, organized, and defined by adults, for the good of the child and for the good of society, as adults see both. And management of childhood implies restriction of children, usually by separating them from some aspects of society and by curtailing their access to some kinds of knowledge, experience, and resources—including books.

A managing approach to childhood reached a high point in the nineteenth century and is closely allied with the whole genesis of a separate literature for children. Ideally, if not always actually, nineteenth-century parents regulated their children's lives fully, certainly including their reading. It is scarcely coincidental that the concept of children's books as a special genre found a congenial home in the nineteenth century and flourished accordingly. Nor is it surprising that adults of the period were at least as concerned with the moral content of children's books as with their literary quality. Nearly all books for children before midcentury were more or less frankly moral tracts, and even when authors set about to write what they were pleased to call "entertaining" stories for children, they often had in view obliterating the folk and fairy tales of which they heartily disapproved. Samuel Goodrich, the "Peter Parley" of early nineteenth-century fame, based a long and busy career on his fervent opposition to fairy tales. Even in the second half of the century, when entertainment and literary merit found a place in children's books, adult concern with the moral content of the literature remained high. The movement that created special collections of children's books, housed in separate children's rooms in public libraries and super vised by specially trained librarians, was very much part of the effort to meet the dangerous challenge of trash literature, to provide an attractive alternative to the lurid nickel and dime juveniles so popular in the latter nineteenth century.[3] The idea of selecting children's books for their suitability as moral influences on children was built into library service to children from the beginning.

There is, then, an enormous lot of historical baggage to be sorted through when the question of censorship of children's reading is raised today—as it is with great frequency. Attitudes toward children and childhood have undoubtedly changed in the second half of the twentieth century, as have attitudes toward books and morals. Yet the intensity of current arguments over restriction of children's reading, ringing through journals, meetings, and associations, is ample evidence that the changes have not followed a single direction, nor proceeded at the same pace. The discussion that follows attempts to describe today's situation, together with its background in the first half of the twentieth century, in broadest outline. It cannot detail, though it does try to suggest, the immense intricacies that lie behind today's passionate debates over censorship in children's books. Adult attitudes toward children's books, as toward childhood, are, in any period, an amalgam of personal, social, and sometimes political convictions. The mix has rarely been so complex or so explosive as it is today.

The first half of the present century was a burgeoning season for children's books. Publishers built on the successes of the late nineteenth century, adding luster to an already golden period in children's book production. As the market for children's books expanded, more and more publishing houses created separate children's book divisions, presided over by editors who specialized in the genre. By 1900, children's rooms were an established part of many public libraries; later, and more slowly, libraries began to be added to public schools as well. By 1915, most library schools and teachers' colleges offered courses in children's literature; children's librarians became specialists in their field. The specializing trend also affected writers of children's books. Unlike authors of the nineteenth century, who frequently turned their hands to both adult and children's books, those of the twentieth century usually chose between the two audiences, reflecting and reinforcing the increasingly firm line drawn between the adult and the juvenile fields.

Throughout this time, and indeed until the fateful decade of the 1960s, the issue of censorship within the mainstream of the children's book field was virtually quiescent. While there were sporadic assaults on the evils of comic books and other "trashy" material read by children, the major products of the children's book business, the trade books published by standard, respectable publishing houses and bought by libraries, were pretty much exempt from criticism, or even scrutiny. Libraries generally refused to buy cheap series books—Nancy Drew and Hardy Boys books and such—but the decision was rarely challenged as an act of censorship. If children were disappointed not to find those perennial potboilers in their local library, few adults chose to raise the banner of intellectual freedom on their behalf.

In fact, the concept of intellectual freedom had little place in most discussions of children's reading in this period. The peace that prevailed was grounded in the common set of values shared by the adults who dealt, whether personally or professionally, with children's books. Those values had evolved since the nineteenth century, but not so far as to make intellectual freedom an issue where children were concerned. Childhood was still considered a stage of life in need of adult protection, a time in which restriction of children, and of the influences on them, was considered a natural duty of adults toward children. The moral preoccupation of the nineteenth century lingered, too, though in far less insistent and preachy form. While authors, publishers, and reviewers of children's books all rejected the openly moral lessons that had dominated books of the past, they had by no means lost interest in what they now called "values" in children's literature—by which they meant moral and social values. Children's books were written, published, reviewed, and purchased in accordance with a remarkably consistent point of view about what was suitable reading for children. The community of adults engaged in bringing children and literature together endorsed, apparently without much real dissension, an implicit code of values which was observed virtually unbroken in thousands of children's books published between 1900 and 1965.

The code is most easily described in the negative, by its taboos. The list is long and often has more to do with how a subject was treated in a book for children than with what the subject was. Violence, for example, was not—as many have assumed—entirely absent from children's books before 1965. Given the plethora of pioneer and frontier stories in children's literature, that would hardly have been possible. What was taboo was a lingering on the details of violence and, even more, the depiction of a child, or even someone near and dear to a child, as the object of serious violence. Neither was death the absolute taboo that many present-day commentators insist it was. But the sentimental death scenes of the nineteenth century were certainly out of favor in the twentieth century, and it is clear that children's book people were concerned that the subject might be harrowing to children unless carefully handled. For this reason, children rarely died in children's books, and the death of parents, if it occurred at all, took place offstage or in the past; death and grief were rarely central issues in children's stories. That, in fact, was the general approach to such painful topics as were given space in children's books: they were peripheral, rather than central, to the narrative; acknowledged, but not dwelt upon.

A more absolute blackout applied to problems classed as purely adult. Divorce, mental breakdown, alcoholism, rape, drug dependence, suicide, prostitution, sexual deviance—it would never have occurred to most writers of children's books, let alone their editors, that these were suitable topics for the young. Crime, except for an occasional and relatively innocuous theft, was rare. Even Nancy Drew, whose repetitive adventures usually involved some crime, encountered only the most ludicrously harmless and klutzy thieves. She was often knocked on the head, but never beaten, raped, or murdered. Racial conflict was touched upon gently and gingerly in a few—very few—books for children before the middle 1960s. Florence Cranall Means, Jerrold Beim, and Frank Bonham were among the early writers on the subject. They wrote honestly but with constraint in a field where most publishers feared to tread.

Most obvious to today's observer was the taboo on the subject of sexuality in books for the young. Not only was prepubescent sexuality unacknowledged in children's books—it was hardly widely acknowledged elsewhere in the culture, either—but even the sexual awareness of teenagers found only restrained, oblique recognition. "Romance" was handled nearly as gingerly as race where the young were concerned. One has but to read Maureen Daly's famous *Seventeenth Summer* (published in 1942) to catch a glimpse. The book was written for older teenagers and, at the time, its portrayal of first love was considered reasonably frank. Today, when it is read at all, it is by eleven- or twelve-year-olds, and to any reader its narrow morality, acute anxieties, and personal naivete must make it seem a period piece easily as remote from modern experience as *Little Women*.

While these (and other) taboos did not altogether preclude literary realism in children's books, they did ensure that a protective attitude dominated. Reality was tempered and selective for young audiences. Pain and fear were kept at some distance from child protagonists, wrongs were righted, injustice redressed; things generally turned out well at the end. The same protective optimism applied to the child characters the books portrayed. The extreme idealization of the latter nineteenth century had largely disappeared. In twentieth-century stories, children had faults, made mistakes, and strayed (mildly) from the paths of righteousness. But the books insisted that children lived universally within a firm and supportive social and familial system. Parents or other wise adults were always on hand in children's books to correct the wayward child, gently but effectively, and to assert the claims of the community. The message of the books was that American society operated according to a single moral code; that adults were reliable sources of wisdom, justice, and caring; that childhood and children were sheltered under the protection of responsible adults in a responsible society.

It should be emphasized again that the code I have described was not explicit, was not an iron set of rules to which writers pledged obedience, was not the result of a conspiracy between book editors and librarians or anyone else. Nor was it imposed, in most instances, by conscious censorship, or against any fervent opposition. In the first sixty years of the twentieth century, the issue of censorship in children's books simply did not arise very often, for two reasons. First, the community of adults involved in the production and purchase of books for children was relatively small and relatively homogeneous. Broadly speaking, librarians, teachers, authors, and editors of children's books were the same kind of people, members of a community that shared the general point of view that the code expressed. The rule was one of consensus, rather than coercion.

Second, the children's book field was something of an island in the larger culture. Few adults not professionally involved in children's literature read much or widely in it. Whether the reason was indifference, confidence in the selection processes of public and school libraries, lack of information or misinformation, or the conviction that what children read was unimportant so long as they read—whether it was some of these or all of them, the fact is that until quite recently, most adults, including parents, paid little attention to the content of children's books. Children's literature was sheltered by neglect.

Both consensus and complacency began to break up about the middle of the 1960s. Social upheaval in such manifestations as the civil rights movement, the women's movement, the bitter dissensions of the Vietnam era, and the changing mores and altered family structures of a new era raised questions about the world traditionally pictured in children's books. Belatedly, but inexorably, the winds of change sweeping through American society reached children's books, scattering indifference and consensus once and for all. Every group working for social and political change suddenly discovered what the nineteenth century had so often proclaimed: that children's reading is a potentially powerful influence on society. The closed world of children's book production was opened to newcomers who held no brief for the agreed-upon code of the near past. Peace shattered as hundreds of new voices demanded to be heard; unity gave way to a passionate diversity of views. By the late 1960s, children's books had become a battleground for the personal, social, and political forces of a changing society.

Again, looked at broadly, the struggle can be seen to have proceeded along two quite contradictory lines. On the one hand, there was a strong movement to loosen the strictures on subject matter in children's books. Slowly at first, then with ever-increasing speed, children's books began to reflect the liberalized moral code and the changing family structures of contemporary society. The old insistence that every American family was intact unless broken by death gave way to facts; divorce was soon nearly as common in children's books as it was in reality. By 1972, Norma Klein could even write of a one-parent family in which the mother had simply chosen not to marry the man who had fathered her child.[4] Teenage sexuality, including homosexuality, became a commonplace topic, discussed with varying degrees of explicitness by such writers as Paul Zindel, John Donovan, Isabelle Holland, and Sandra Scoppettone. Judy Blume casually broke dozens of traditional barriers with her flat-footed but frank stories admitting the interest that even fairly young children had in their own bodies.[5] The so-called "problem novel," dealing with such matters as alcoholism, drug dependency, and a staggering variety of other personal and family troubles, became the major staple of the teen reading market.

There was, to be sure, some shock and some resistance to these books as they came to the hands of traditional selectors of books for the young. But the trend was unstoppable. Times had changed, social attitudes had altered, writers and publishers responded eagerly to new demands for "realism"—and the books were, moreover, an undoubted success with their intended audience. Judy Blume's books sold by the thousands in paperback; libraries that refused to buy her novels lost patrons to drugstores. Besides, there was strong, if not unanimous, sentiment within libraries and schools for greater frankness with children. Most teachers recognized that their students' lives were not so sheltered; most librarians were uncomfortable with the role of censor. Those who wanted to maintain protective barriers found themselves at odds with a highly visible, highly vocal liberal-radical coalition that argued forcefully for applying the same standards of intellectual freedom to children's literature as to any other.

Ironically, the concomitant movement ran directly counter to the concept of intellectual freedom. An aroused social consciousness had brought about, at last, an examination of the underlying messages in children's books, and many adults were startled to see what these books did and did not say about race, social responsibility, and the social conditioning of girls or the children of minorities. In the name of social justice long delayed, critics in many quarters began to demand that libraries remove from the shelves books that they, the critics, characterized as racist or sexist. The Council on Interracial Books for Children, founded in 1966, became a powerful voice pronouncing judgment on books for their racial or sexual biases.

Thus, by the latter 1960s, the children's book profession found itself confronting two quite contradictory sets of demands. On the one hand, there was enormous pressure to liberalize children's books, to open them and the collections that housed them to every aspect of reality, so that they might better reflect the pluralism of contemporary American society. At the same time, from the other side of a curious equation came an equally strong pressure on writers, publishers, reviewers, and selectors of children's books to rid the literature of racism and sexism. While a raised social consciousness might accomplish this task for present and future books, the only answer to those already written, according to many social critics, was to remove the offending volumes from children's access. Libraries were pressed to review their children's collections for racist or sexist literature and to discard what they found. (The critics, of course, identified many books they wanted removed from the shelves.) It is one of the many ironies of the time that more than a few liberals and radicals found themselves with a foot in each camp, demanding freedom in one cause, censorship in another. Just as remarkable was the fact that many libraries managed to comply with both of these apparently contradictory demands, defending Blume, Klein, and Zindel in their children's collections while retiring *Little Black Sambo, Mary Poppins,* and *Dr. Doolittle.*

Whatever the differences of direction, change there surely was: the distance traversed in just over fifteen years is nothing short of astonishing. Its measure may be taken from the books themselves: from Betty Cavanna's prom-centered teen romances of the 1950s and early 1960s to Judy Blume's *Forever,* that 1975 how-to manual of teenage sex; from Frank Bonhan's *Durango Street,* which managed to depict (with commendable realism for its 1965 date) slum gangs without mentioning drugs, lethal weapons, or death, to *Headman* (1975) in which the main character dies with a corkscrew in his stomach. Or it may be taken by adult reactions to the books; from the furor over *Harriet the Spy* (1964) because an adult told a child that it was sometimes necessary to lie, to the silent acceptance of such novels as *Steffie Can't Come Out to Play* (teenage prostitution), *Are You in the House Alone?* (rape), or any of Lois Duncan's sour tales of high school "life."

However one measures, it is clear that adult attitudes toward children's reading have undergone some major changes during the turbulent years just past. The wide (though not universal) acceptance of a greatly broadened content in children's books seems to stem from the conviction that children should learn as soon as possible the realities of the world they live in—even the hardest and most unsavory realities. The rationale behind the conviction varies: some books are accepted as awful warnings (*Steffie,* surely); some because adults reason that if children's lives are not protected, it is pointless to restrict their reading. And, of course, some adults are morally neutral toward the content of children's books, simply endorsing the concept of intellectual freedom for children, as for adults.

At the same time, the arguments for restriction of literature for children have moved to new ground. Barriers of the past were meant to protect the innocence of childhood. Today, it is the good of society that is invoked in favor of censorship more often than children's innocence, and this is true whether the call for censorship comes from the right or from the left.

Liberal censors arguing for the reform of what they call a racist society see no possibility for neutrality if social change is to be effected: "In the end, a failure to work for change actually supports the status quo. . . . At this point in history, directly or indirectly, one serves either the racist past or a humanistic future."[6] Essentially the same argument is made about sexism in children's books: if society is to change, the books cannot be neutral. If they are not liberating, they are by definition damaging. Those who see the issues this way are willing to call for censorship, by libraries, by schools, by authors, editors, and publishers, to bring about social change.

Conservative censors have also cast their arguments primarily in social terms. They too want to reform society by eliminating harmful influences in children's books: their target is those books they consider "biased toward increasing the centralized power of a secular humanistic state, [books that] will ultimately destroy the family, decent social standards, and basic principles of decentralized government that safeguard every American's individual freedom."[7] In both camps, the ascendant value is social morality.

At the beginning of the 1980s, censorship of children's books continues to be a lively issue. The prospects for peace restored soon to the field of children's reading are, to say the least, dim. Only if all parties to the arguments of the past decade and a half should suddenly agree to agree or, as suddenly, lose all interest in the questions now vigorously debated, could the quiet of earlier years be restored. Neither seems likely.

Nor is it likely that anyone can predict with confidence what the arguments will be or even who the antagonists will be. We are seeing a conservative reaction against the liberalism of the 1960s and 1970s.

The *Newsletter on Intellectual Freedom* anticipates that the trend will continue, encouraging "would-be censors" to "step up efforts to impose their own moral and social values on library patrons." In the early 1980s, Judith Krug, Director of the Office for Intellectual Freedom, American Library Association, saw the conservative movement well under way: "All of the pressures that were just below the surface are now coming out, pressures to remove those materials that people object to on moral grounds or because they believe the materials do not reflect 'traditional American values.'"[8] The apparent ascendance of such groups as the Moral Majority lends weight to liberal fears of increased pressure to restrict the content of children's books and to roll back some of the changes of recent years, as do the growing number of attempts to restrict both text and trade books in schools across the country.

But the changes in the literature over the past decade and a half are far-reaching, and many of them grew out of fundamental movements within the society. Reaction may modify how these social transformations are reflected in children's books, but it is unlikely that it can return the literature to the codes of the past. Children's books have been opened to a wider range of influences, as well as to a wider scrutiny since the mid 1960s. Inevitably, they reflect, directly and indirectly, the changing society that produced them. The present situation is neither static nor predictable. The only certainty is that children's books themselves and the debate about children's reading will continue to reflect the shifts and seasons of the American view of childhood, society, and truth.

The End of Innocence

Ice Axes: Robert Cormier and the Adolescent Novel

$$\times f \, \times$$

Robert Cormier is a conspicuous oddity in his chosen field. Writing for the adolescent reader, he has departed from standard models and broken some of the most fundamental taboos of that vocation. Each of his hard-edged novels for the young goes considerably beyond the standard limits of "contemporary realism" to describe a world of painful harshness, where choices are few and consequences desperate. Moreover, his novels are unequivocally downbeat; all three violate the unwritten rule that fiction for the young, however sternly realistic the narrative material, must offer some portion of hope, must end at least with some affirmative message. Affirmation is hard to find in Cormier's work, and conventional hopefulness is quite irrelevant to it.

But while these sharp breaks with accepted practice have been much noted by reviewers, and have furnished Cormier's reputation for bleakness, curiously little notice has been taken of another, and to my mind equally interesting, departure from the norm in his novels. Quite aside from his attitudes and conclusions, Cormier is a maverick in the field of adolescent literature because he is writing what are, at bottom, political novels. George Orwell once claimed that there is no such thing as a "genuinely nonpolitical literature," but the dictum seems to me inapplicable to most writing for young adults.[1] A consistent feature of almost the whole body of adolescent literature is its isolation from the political and societal, its nearly total preoccupation with personality. The typical adolescent novel is wrapped tightly around the individual and the personal; questions of psychological development and personal morality dominate the genre. In fact, most authors of adolescent literature seem to take for their model adolescents themselves, with their paramount interest in self, individual morality, interior change, and personality.

Cormier, on the other hand, is far more interested in the systems by which a society operates than he is in individuals. His novels center on the interplay between individuals and their context, between the needs and demands of the system and the needs and rights of individuals—in other words, on the political context in which his characters, like all of us, must live. He is, obviously, concerned with moral questions, but the morality involved is of a wholly different order from the purely personal moral concerns of most teen novels.

Cormier's political cast of mind explains the relative unimportance of characterization in his work. Inner character is less to him than situation. In *Chocolate War,* for example, the wellsprings of Archie's evil are never adequately explained, and Jerry's motivation for his lonely rebellion, while plausible enough, is not dwelt upon at any great length. Certainly it is not the centerpiece of the narrative, as it would be in most teen novels. Adam, of *I Am the Cheese,* is more a victim than a protagonist. If we care about what happens to him, it is not because of any crucial internal decision he must make, but precisely because he is the helpless victim of processes he cannot affect, let alone control, and because we recognize the circumstances of his tragedy as part of the world we actually live in. In *After the First Death,* characterization is again—as several critics have complained—clearly secondary to the situation set out in the novel, and to Cormier's view of the commitments and choices that have brought about that situation.[2]

The book that has drawn the most critical attention is *The Choco-*

late War, possibly because it was the first, perhaps because its statement of defeat is explicit and made by the protagonist, or maybe simply because it is hard to recognize until the end just how shatteringly this novel differs from others of its genre. It looks, after all, like a school story, about schoolboys, and can be read just that way— in which case the unhappy comment by several reviewers about its negativism is understandable.[3] But of course *Chocolate War* has another life outside its familiar form: it is a metaphor, a parable of political evil and a small manual on the sources and uses of political power.

The evil in *Chocolate War* is initiated by individuals, but not contained in them. Archie and Brother Leon are manipulators: Archie manipulates the Vigils, Brother Leon manipulates his students; together, during the chocolate sale, they manipulate the whole school. Yet neither could work his will without the cooperation of others. The acquiescence of the community is essential to their power, as the classroom scene makes clear. In an episode that is a virtual cliché in school stories, Brother Leon singles out a student for torment, accusing him of cheating, mocking, and humiliating him, while the rest of the class laughs uncomfortably. If this were all, the scene would simply establish (without much originality) that Brother Leon is the kind of teacher who abuses the power of his position for some private satisfaction. But Cormier's interest here is not really Brother Leon, still less the reasons for his abuse of position. What he wants to demonstrate is the source of the power, which is, of course, the students themselves. The harassment goes on exactly as long as the class lets it; when at last one student speaks up in mild protest, the spell breaks. And it is Brother Leon himself who points the moral, asking contemptuously why no one had objected sooner, suggesting the parallel with Nazi Germany.

Still, the message of the novel as a whole is neither so simple nor so hopeful as the episode might imply. If it were, then Jerry's lone dissent would succeed, would break the combined power of Archie and Brother Leon—and would place the novel squarely in the long American tradition of the triumphant lonely hero tale. Instead, there is that final scene, which laid the cornerstone of Cormier's reputation for bleakness: Jerry carried away on a stretcher, his face too battered to allow him to speak the message he wants to convey to Goober: "to play ball, to play football, to have fun, to make the team, to sell chocolates . . . to do whatever they [want] you to do."[4] The lone dissent has not only failed, it is repudiated. The American Adam is brought low; Huck Finn turns Jim over to the slave-catchers, Gary Cooper lies in his own blood in the street at high noon—no wonder the reviewers gasped. In one brief, bitter paragraph, Cormier has abandoned an enduring American myth to confront his teenaged readers with life as it more often is—with the dangers of dissent, the ferocity of systems as they protect themselves, the power of the pressure to conform.

In his second novel, *I Am the Cheese,* Cormier dispenses with metaphor. This stark tale comments directly on the real world of government, organized crime, large-scale bureaucracy, the apparatus of control, secrecy, betrayal, and all the other commonplaces of contemporary life. Its message is, if possible, even less ambiguous than *Chocolate War*'s. The most optimistic reader will find it hard to locate an exit as the story moves to a conclusion. Adam is doomed, as his parents were; he will be "obliterated" one way or another because he is a threat to one or possibly to both the systems with which his life is entangled. There is certainly some ambiguity about the role played in this tragedy by Mr. Grey, supposedly the family's government protector. Might he have been instead their betrayer? Which side did he really work for? As the narrative rolls coldly on, it occurs to the reader that it hardly matters. And this is clearly Cormier's point. The two systems are equally impersonal, and equally dangerous to the human being caught between them. What matters to the organization—*either* organization—is its own survival, not Adam's.

I Am the Cheese is the most Kafkaesque of Cormier's three novels. The narrative technique, combined with a nearly overwhelming sense of loneliness, helplessness, and hopelessness give the novel a surreal quality. When his parents are murdered, Adam is left in a world empty of human figures; he has only memories of those few he has loved and lost. It is as though he were alone in a computer room where every machine is programmed to cancel him out; he is like a mouse in a maze, searching for an opening, unaware that every exit has been blocked. The language of the "psychiatrist's" reports, bleached of emotional accuracy, underlines the impersonal, bureaucratic character of Adam's cold enemies. And when Adam's trip to Vermont is revealed for what it is, a bicycle ride within the fenced grounds of the institution where he is confined, the sense of nightmare recalls Kafka's terrifying world.

After the First Death both reiterates and extends concepts found in the earlier books. The plot is built around an episode of political terrorism—the ultimate weapon of an outnumbered dissident group—directed against the technically superior, equally purposeful security apparatus of the established government. In the course of the story, Cormier explores the outer limits of patriotism and the inner perception of fanaticism. Here, as in the first two novels, Cormier shows privileged position and privileged information used to manipulate the weak and the unwary. Here, as in *I Am the Cheese*, the discussion of political evil is cast in fiercely contemporary terms, and the shadow of statism stretches long over the narrative.

One episode brings into sharp focus concepts central to this novel and also, I think, to Cormier's general outlook. The scene takes place between Miro, the young terrorist, and Kate, the girl who is to become Miro's "first death." The tentative human relationship created between them when Kate encourages Miro to talk about his past dissolves abruptly when Kate recognizes the depth and the terrible simplicity of Miro's dedication to his political purpose. For the sake of a country he has never seen, and never really expects to see, Miro has made himself into an instrument of guerrilla warfare. Save for his mentor, Artkin, Miro has no connection with the actual world of human life, nor does he expect any. He envisions no future for himself, takes no interest in his own qualities except as they make him an efficient weapon in a struggle whose political terms he cannot possibly know. He has no feeling for the innocent victims, past or potential, of the undeclared "war" he wages; indeed, he cannot even understand what it is Kate expects him to feel for them. In short, as Kate realizes with shock, he is "a monster." Not only monstrous, Miro is innocent as well: "The greatest horror of all was that he did not know he was a monster. He had looked at her with innocent eyes as he had told her of killing people. She'd always thought of innocence as something good, something to cherish. People mourned the death of innocence. . . . But innocence, she saw now, could also be evil. Monstrous."[5] The attitude toward innocence explicitly expressed in this passage seems to me to underlie all three of Cormier's books and goes far to explain his break with prevailing standards for adolescent novels. Like Kate, most literature for the young has assumed that innocence, particularly in the young, is desirable, and that its loss is a regrettable, if inevitable, part of the transition from childhood to adult life. The celebration of innocence is a romantic attitude, of course, and one that has been losing ground, even in children's literature, for many decades. But Cormier is forcing the pace considerably in his work and it is political, rather than personal, innocence that he is talking about. He is saying that political innocence is a dangerous quality, that it can be a kind of collaboration with evil, that innocence is often acquiescence through moral neutrality in the abuse of power by the powerful, and in the sacrifice of the individual to the political organization.

In this novel, Miro's awful innocence has a parallel in the other "monster" of the story, Ben's father, General Marchand. Like the terrorists, the General has dedicated his life to the service of his country; like Artkin, he has extended his own commitment to his son's life, which becomes forfeit to the State's needs. General Marchand has had his son observed, recorded, and cataloged throughout his developing years, so that he is able to predict Ben's behavior under any circumstances. As the dangerous game begun by the terrorists comes to a climax, the General uses that accumulated knowledge of Ben's strengths and weaknesses—uses Ben, in fact, as a pawn to win the game, and so destroys him.

One may reject the basic assumption behind this phase of the story—that it is possible to reduce a human being to an entirely predictable quantity—but I think that this is not really Cormier's main point. The point here, with the General, as with Miro, is the consequence of a surrender of moral will to the abstract concept of patriotism, which General Marchand describes as "sweet and pure and unquestioning."[6] The point is the General's willingness first to subject a human being to secret scrutiny and then to use him as though he were but one more instrument in the governmental arsenal. The fact that the human being so used is the General's son underscores the monstrousness of the action; that the General suffers doubt and remorse afterward emphasizes the political, as opposed to the purely personal, aspects of the father's choices. He does what he does, not because he hates his son, or is indifferent to him, nor because of some destructive psychological flaw in his own personality, but because he, as much as Artkin or Miro, has given himself wholly— "innocently"—to the service of the State.

The parallels are clear throughout. The detached professionalism of the terrorist is not different from the General's; Marchand himself acknowledges that "they are professionals just as I am a professional." The coldness with which Artkin murders a child or tortures a boy is neither more nor less monstrous than Marchand's choice of Ben for the mission on the bridge, or his calculated anticipation and use of Ben's break under torture: "Expediency is the rule." The violence initiated by the terrorists is matched by the equally violent response of the government, and the children are the victims of both. "Perhaps," says Artkin, "they [Americans] cherish their children more than their agencies." But they do not. No wonder Artkin and the General "recognized each other."[7]

Here again, the questions raised are not primarily concerned with personal morality. When is it that such men as Artkin and Miro and Marchand become monsters? It is not when they murder or lie or torture, but earlier, at the point where they make the initial choice to surrender their moral will to the State. They disavow their humanity in the same moment that they seal their innocence by choosing never to question nor even to contemplate questioning. Cormier makes it abundantly clear that, in the political context they have accepted, the General's decisions and Artkin's are not only logical, they are correct. It is humanly that the choices are monstrous. Ben's suicide, Raymond's murder, and Kate's death are Cormier's comment on the human cost of political abstraction. In the end, he tells us, the price is often paid by those who have been given no choice in the matter.

Cormier's teen novels are not "great books"; I doubt that they will outlast their topical relevance. But they are important books just the same. Cormier writes of things few books for the young acknowledge at all. He has evoked a political world in which evil is neither an individual phenomenon nor a personality fault explainable by individual psychology, but a collaborative act between individuals and political systems that begins when the individual gives over to the system the moral responsibility that is part of being human. He suggests that innocence can be a moral defect, that evil is (as Hannah Arendt has said) banal, and, above all, that political bureaucracies are often— perhaps always—a potential danger to individual freedom because they are fundamentally committed to their own perpetuation, which is always threatened by individual dissent.

These are aspects of contemporary reality not often set out in literature for the young, as the reactions of many reviewers attest. Yet the young are not immune to political reality. Far from it, they are its chief inheritors. Though it may be true—it undoubtedly *is* true— that adolescents are primarily interested in themselves, it does not follow that adults who write for the adolescent readers must share this narrow preoccupation. All of us, including the young, live in a political as well as a personal world. We are not safer for ignoring it.

Surely, if message there is in Cormier's work, this is the most insistent. I cannot discover that he wants to tell his readers that by recognizing their dangers they can escape them, and I do not think his books can be reduced to a positive statement about the protective virtue of political understanding. "Know your world and you will be safe" is far too bald and optimistic. Put negatively, the proposition may come a little closer; "what you fail to understand about your world can destroy you, either literally or as a human being." Certainly these novels suggest that no one will escape who does not know where the threat lies, how the annihilating process works.

Neither the issues Cormier poses nor the answers he implies belong to the same moral world as the themes of adjustment, acceptance, and understanding that undergird most adolescent fiction. Instead, his work opens again the complex questions of the function of literature and of whether that function varies with the age of the intended reader. Cormier's three adolescent novels answer for him, echoing the words of Franz Kafka: "If the book we are reading does not wake us, as with a fist hammering on our skull, why then do we read it? Good God, we would also be happy if we had not books, and such books as make us happy we could, if need be, write ourselves. But what we must have are those books which come upon us like ill-fortune, and distress us deeply, like the death of one we love better than ourselves, like suicide. A book must be an ice-axe to break the sea frozen inside us."[8]

The Transformation of Childhood in Twentieth-Century Children's Literature

>f< ><

For about two-thirds of the twentieth century, the "family story" in children's literature built upon a coherent and remarkably consistent view of the place of children in family and community and the role of adults vis-à-vis children. The basic assumptions involved hadn't changed very much since the beginning of the century. At the heart of these assumptions was the idea that children and adults were different, that there was a necessary space between childhood and adulthood that children had to grow across, so to speak. It was not a matter of separation, exactly; children were thoroughly integrated into family and community in these books—indeed, family life was the real subject of books written by such preeminent children's authors of the twentieth century as Elizabeth Enright, Eleanor Estes, and Rachel Field. Integrated into, but not occupying quite the same space: children in these stories were set apart from adult life in important ways. They were concerned with childish matters and with growing up. There was never any doubt that adults would handle the problems of the family (think of the Laura Ingalls Wilder books, for example), and there was almost always the assurance that somewhere in a child's life there was safety, security, and stability available from adults. And direction: the foundation of the relationship between children and adults was the conviction that adults had something to teach children. In sixty-some years there were of course differences in emphasis and nuance in family stories, and a steady trend toward writing for older children—twelve to fourteen, say, as opposed to eight to twelve—but on the whole, a reader of twentieth-century children's books written before the mid-1960s is more likely to be struck by the consistency than by the variety of the attitudes they express.

This continuity began to dissolve about the middle of the 1960s. As I look back, it seems to me that the breakup might be dated from the publication of *Harriet the Spy* in 1964. Without breathing hard about it, Louise Fitzhugh discarded several cherished children's literature taboos, producing a book that I think of as a major breach in the protective walls around children's books. When, in *Harriet,* an adult told a child, "You must lie" she was doing at least two things unprecedented in mainstream children's literature: First, she was repudiating a long-observed adult responsibility to be a role model and a keeper of the moral universe for children.[1] And second, she was letting a child, an unambiguous, preadolescent, eleven-year-old child, in on one of the untidy realities of the adult world, with no moral judgment attached.

It's hard to remember now the furor that *Harriet the Spy* caused in the world of children's literature—so much has happened since—but those who furored had sound instincts. *Harriet* was the breach and after Fitzhugh came the Deluge. (I should say that Fitzhugh was symptomatic, not causative.) The old relationship between child and adult had begun to shift.

Perhaps the most fundamental and certainly the least subtle change is in the relationships within families. The traditional hierarchy of parents and children has been dismantled, along with, emphatically, the system of mutual respect and affection that once bound fictional parent and child to each other in peace and contentment. The literature of the 1970s reveals an astonishing hostility toward parents, making parental inadequacies a central theme, especially (though not exclusively) in books written for the teen market. In story after story, such writers as Paul Zindel, John Donovan, Isabelle Holland, Kin Platt, and others paint devastating portraits of parents. Alcoholic mothers are legion, as are fathers who abandon their families literally or figuratively: "My father pulled that old trick of saying he was going out to buy the evening paper but went to Mexico."[2] If not Mexico, then California or New York or elsewhere; the divorce rate in children's books of the 1970s may have surpassed the national statistics.

Even when they stay, parents are rarely satisfactory. Fathers are preoccupied with success and moneymaking; mothers are selfish, neurotic, unloving, alcoholic, or addicted to pills. If this fiction is to be believed, the contemporary American family is a shambles. As one narrator says, characteristically if ungrammatically, "We were the all-American family because at the core, like every other typical family, there was rot."[3]

Family relations, particularly between the generations, have taken on a bitter flavor. "My father . . . split the scene with some broad when I was five. He has never bothered to get in touch with me." This young man's mother is alcoholic, and "in an Italian haven for remorseful drinkers," he explains laconically.[4] Zindel's unhappy fifteen-year-old narrator in *Confessions of a Teenage Baboon* introduces himself and his mother in the first few pages of the book: "My story has my mother in it, and she's what is known as a small-time shoplifter." She is also, he remarks, "loud and domineering."[5] This boy was abandoned by his father at five and has since been supported by his mother, who works as a practical nurse. His affection for her is restrained, to say the least. The optimistic proposition that children felt gratitude toward their parents, so prominent in Victorian fiction, was muted but still detectable in twentieth-century children's books through the 1950s. By the 1970s, such a concept was well-nigh unthinkable.

The misfit protagonist of Barbara Wersba's *Tune for a Small Harmonica* has "successful" parents, whose lives as their daughter describes them are sterile and whose interests do not include parenting. "[My mother's] hair had been done at George Michel's . . . her nails at

Elizabeth Arden, and her figure toned up by a French masseuse. . . . Every part of her came from a different place. . . . Every day my mother and Tippy Bernhardt did the same thing. In the morning, they shopped for two hours . . . then they would have lunch in a little bistro off Fifth Avenue, where they would discuss their friend's divorces. After that each of them would depart for a session with a masseuse, hairdresser or manicurist. . . . As for my father, who worked for Standard Oil, we never saw him. He was always in conference. Until I was eight years old, I thought Conference was a place."[6]

Lisa, Bright and Dark is the story of a teenage girl whose parents ignore the symptoms of the schizophrenia that finally claims their daughter. Lisa also has successful, upwardly mobile parents— "phonies," her friend and the narrator of the story calls them— the father "caught by hard cold cash," the mother a materialistic social climber. Separately or together, they pay "almost no attention to Lisa or Lisa's sister, Tracy."[7] The last thing these parents want to hear is their daughter's cries for help as her mental confusion overtakes her.

The books rarely suggest that the hostility children feel toward their parents is an "adolescent phase" or in any sense unjust or undeserved. On the contrary, authors are usually at some pains to make it clear that parents are not only indifferent to their children, but often openly hostile and destructive. One fourteen-year-old boy (who says his mother's "hobby" is marrying) remarks, "Mother doesn't like me. She never has." Another story records a bluntly brutal conversation between mother and son. Speaking of her divorce from his father, Roger's mother tells him, "I was the one that was stuck with you. . . . I had you on my hands all the time. . . . And you were quite a hateful child, Roger."[8]

The young protagonists' self-doubts—which are endless—are squarely laid at parental doors: "I'm not exactly the most beautiful girl in the world. . . . Just ask my mother. 'You're not a pretty girl, Lorraine,' she has been nice enough to inform me." Another fifteen-year-old introduces herself as "Suzy, the Slade daughter the father chose *not* to take to New York to live with him. My mother actually gave him his choice of girls."[9] Though the parents in such stories are clearly unhappy people whose own lives are in hopeless disarray, authors show little sympathy for them. What counts is the effect these adults have on their children and that is disastrous.

The shortcomings of parents are seldom counterbalanced by the strengths of other adults. Grandparents sometimes take over the care of abandoned children, as in Betsy Byars's *House of Wings* and Cynthia Voight's *Homecoming*, but in both these cases the task is thrust upon the grandparent rather than voluntarily undertaken. Sometimes unrelated adults offer the support or acceptance parents fail to give, as in Barbara Wersba's *The Dream Watcher* and Isabelle Holland's *Man Without a Face*. Of the latter two, however, one is an elderly woman who has fantasized the dramatic life she describes to the lonely boy who listens to her, and the other is a homosexual ex-teacher ostracized by the community. Both die before the novels end, leaving the boys they have befriended on their own again; what solace they provide is brief and ambiguous. The protagonist of *Confessions of a Teenage Baboon* claims to have found a substitute for his long-gone father in Lloyd DePardi, whom he knows for a few weeks at most. But Lloyd is thirty years old, a hard-drinking, self-confessed loser who apparently has a homosexual alliance with a sixteen-year-old neighbor boy and whose attraction for other teenagers consists in his willingness to supply them with liquor and all-night parties. Complaints from neighbors bring the police, who beat Lloyd, then offer him a choice between prosecution on morals charges or bribery payments to keep them quiet. Left alone to decide, Lloyd shoots himself, a suicide the protagonist witnesses from a hiding place. If it is hard to find reassurance here, it is harder yet to miss in this or in most of these books the insistent message that the young cannot rely on adults to solve the difficulties of life, since adults are themselves bewildered and overwhelmed by circumstance.

Kit Reed's *The Ballad of T. Rantula* is a sad, psychologically complex novel about a fourteen-year-old boy whose parents have recently separated and whose best friend commits suicide by anorexia. The story is told with unusual compassion for both parents and child as they struggle with a situation in which their separate needs, all legitimate, are in hopeless conflict. But the collapse of the traditional hierarchy of parent and child, and the cost to the child of its demise, have never been better articulated in a juvenile novel. Fred, speaking of his Harvard-professor father and his colleagues, says it all: "They have read zillions of books. . . . They have been to more lectures than the city of Boston put together, they have written enough books to stuff five dozen bookmobiles and . . . they still can't figure out the simplest little things; what's happening, how to behave. . . . I'm only the kid, Pop. How am I supposed to know?"[10]

What is lost between children and parents in these books is lost again between child and society. Though most novels of contemporary realism focus narrowly on personal events and feelings, what glimpses they give of the larger society scarcely encourage trust or confidence. The corruption that Zindel glancingly describes in *Confessions* is a major theme in Robert Cormier's *The Chocolate War,* in which a lone student is victimized by a school gang with the tacit consent of a faculty member who is using the gang to further his own ambitions. Political terrorism, bureaucratic amorality, and the helplessness of the individual in contemporary society are the central themes of Cormier's other two novels. While Cormier goes a good deal further than most writers to elaborate a vision of cold despair to young readers, he is not alone in suggesting that the adult world is a dangerous, threatening place with few shelters for the innocent. Most teen novels of recent years, and many stories for younger children as well, chronicle disintegrating families and an uncaring if not a positively threatening society.

Indeed, if security was the emotional center of the literature of earlier decades, uncertainty is at the very heart of most recent children's books. Human relationships are without permanence, and often without substance. At best, society at large is drifting, unsure of its values, unanchored by any firm belief in morality or predictability. Even a proselytizing author like Madeleine L'Engle, whose novels are a vehicle for her spiritual and moral convictions about the power of love, conveys little faith in human decency outside a cultured elite, and less confidence that the chaos of modern life can be held at bay for long. So Meg Murry, in *A Wind in the Door,* reflects on recent problems in her hometown: "Suddenly the whole world was unsafe and uncertain. . . . Even their safe little village was revealing itself to be unpredictable and irrational and precarious."[11] At worst, books like most of Zindel's and all of Cormier's describe a nightmare world of violence, betrayal, and irrationality that offers no place, not even home, where a child may grow up in safety.

Within this uneasy setting, the central characters of recent fiction exist in virtual isolation. Remembering the cheerful clumps of children in family literature of earlier decades, one realizes how often current protagonists lodge in the mind one by one: Adam, the doomed child of Cormier's bleak *I Am the Cheese;* Slake, living like a rat in the New York subway in Holman's *Slake's Limbo;* Flanders, in M. E. Kerr's *Is That You, Miss Blue?;* and John, the quintessence of loneliness and the central character of Donovan's *Wild in the World,* who sees his family die one by one and then dies himself, alone. Or one remembers pairs of kids clinging to each other for the comfort and reassurance they cannot find in adults, as in June Jordan's *His Own Where,* Rosemary Well's *None of the Above,* and most of Zindel's novels for teens.

A corollary to the isolation of the protagonists in these novels is their self-absorption. Forty or fifty years ago, authors implicitly identified one central task of growing up as the transcendence of egocentricity. The pattern of fiction encouraged children to become acquainted with their communities and their fellow human beings, to find their place in the society beyond home. Personal growth was measured and maturity defined by a child's growing understanding of and concern for other people.

Today's authors, by contrast, presuppose an adult society so chaotic and untrustworthy that no child could move toward it with confidence. Its rules are unclear, its authorities corrupt or ineffectual, its values bankrupt. Most of all, it is a society inhabited by people who are manifestly unhappy. By the same token, closeness with another human being is as likely to end in disillusionment as understanding; love is more often a source of pain than of joy in these books. Any encouragement to go outside of one's self is cautious at best, and most protagonists are, in fact, mainly preoccupied with self. Their problems, their emotions, their reactions and needs occupy the center of the literature, and neither challenge nor perspective is added by the authors. Judy Blume's enormously popular books, which mirror the egocentricity of childhood and adolescence without comment and certainly without criticism, are the best known but hardly the only examples of a general abandonment by contemporary authors of the traditional adult determination to modify the self-centeredness of children. It would be hard to overstate what a breathtaking change this represents over *all* past American literature for children.

It is impossible to read much of this fiction without raising some questions about the cumulative sense of bitterness and disillusionment that pervades it. What accounts for such a drastic revision of the traditional tenets of literature for children? What is the impulse that has toppled the age-old relation of child to adult, which assumed the superiority of adults and the need of children to learn from their elders? Authors of the 1970s have opened the secrets of the adult world to children as juvenile literature has never before done. They have demolished protective walls built more than 200 years ago to separate the child's world from that of the adult, and in doing so, have not only exposed children to aspects of adult life long considered unsuitable for them to know, but also and by the same stroke have exposed adults to the scrutiny of children who now see them portrayed in every shade and degree of failure, inadequacy, and confusion. What kind of cultural change has brought about such a development?

It is far easier to ask the questions than to answer them. Any search for the sources of cultural attitudes may encompass every influence on a society and cross the entire political and social spectrum. The enormous upheavals in American society in the 1960s and 1970s coincided with the advent of a "new realism" in literature for children, and there is undoubtedly some causal relationship, however complex. The social and political struggles of those years set in motion powerful forces for change in American society, changes that must have inevitably affected the tone and tenor of literature written for the young as they affected so many other traditionally accepted conventions.

The relationship between societal unrest and the mood of children's books, however, is not a simple one. The image of trust and tranquillity in children's books of the 1930s, for example, contrasts sharply with the anxieties of current fiction, yet the 1930s can scarcely be called a tranquil period. In a decade darkened first by economic depression, then by world war, millions of families knew that life was hard, uncertain, sometimes terrifying. Nevertheless, the 1930s produced a literature for children that promised them the shelter of adult protection, a future with hope, and the assurance that happiness was attainable—all propositions that the fiction of our own era has effectively reversed. At the very least, we must conclude that the turmoil of the past fifteen to twenty years has done more damage to traditional familial arrangements than did either depression or war in the 1930s and 1940s.

Cause and effect in cultural change are notoriously difficult to demonstrate. Confident assertions about the precise ways in which the political and social disturbances of recent years have revolutionized the concept of childhood in children's books would go well beyond my purposes in this essay and the slender evidence available. But to read the books is surely to ponder the nature, if not the exact sources, of the changes I have described in attitudes toward children, and some observations, admittedly highly speculative, about the emotional meaning behind these attitudes are irresistible.

The chief casualty of the new realism has been the clear separation between adult and child observed in more than 200 years of writing for children. And the blurring of the distinction has taken place in both directions. The child, as recipient of knowledge hitherto withheld, is increasingly treated like an adult. At the same time, adults, with their open uncertainties, their unwillingness to carry the burden of responsibility, their preoccupation with their own satisfactions, function more like children, or at least like adolescents, than ever before in juvenile literature.

Certainly the tone of the literature is authentically adolescent. Egocentric, emotional, angrily judgmental toward adults, the stories purportedly reflect the outlook of their young protagonists. But I cannot escape the feeling that the emotion these authors put into their stories of family life is their own as much as it is that of their fictional characters. Surely it is significant that the first-person narrative, which fuses the voices of author and protagonist, is all but universal in recent teen fiction. First person was rare in earlier children's books; then adults stayed firmly in their adult place, protecting, instructing, assuming the superiority of adult knowledge and judgment, and translating that sense of superiority into an unargued acceptance of responsibility for children. Even if it is no more than a literary device, the use of the first-person voice has effectively diluted the separate adult presence one could always detect in children's books of the past.

Implicit throughout the new realism is a cumulative assertion of the failure of human relations in general and of adult-child relations in particular; the persistent mood is one of resentment and despair. As conclusions, both seem to be largely unconscious on the author's part. Even in strongly realistic stories, today's authors generally accept, at least overtly, the convention that books for the young must conclude on a positive note. The endings of choice in recent fiction are hardly stridently optimistic, but most authors (Cormier always excepted) extend to their characters and readers assurances that their feelings are normal, that they will adjust and survive whatever crisis they are facing.

Yet the unspoken communication is the more powerful; it is hard to balance by such tardy and bland reassurance the bleakness that dominates the books. The aggrieved tone of the fiction overwhelms its stated sentiments, as the passionately one-sided portraits of parents project the dismay of an adolescent who has discovered that parents are human and flawed, and that the society at large is neither safe nor happy. One ends by believing that the authors are as angry with adults, as outraged by the failures of adult society, as any of their fictional characters. And one cannot but speculate that these authors, children as they are of the 1930s and 1940s, are recording the dislocation of a generation brought up to expect a contentment it cannot find in the contemporary world.

In general, realistic fiction of recent years conveys an image of adults withdrawing from parenthood, retreating, in a real sense, from adulthood. The settled hierarchy of adult-child relationships is destroyed, and with it the system of responsibility and dependency that firmly separated child and adult roles. It is no longer taken for granted that adults are moral mentors to the young. Adults in fiction, and the adults who write the fiction as well, seem to have little impulse to define the moral world for children. At most, they heap their readers with information and step back from decision, and from the responsibility that decision implies. In any case, much of the fiction tends to concentrate on a kind of therapeutic "working through" of feelings rather than on moral decision; not resolution but coping is the aim. As implicitly defined, coping means minimizing pain, tolerating disappointment, accepting one's own feelings, and, above all, limiting one's emotional investments. Insofar as the books endorse any goal, it is survival, not mastery; endurance rather than triumph. Such tepid conclusions are of course offered as realistic; I would only note the abyss that lies between such a view and that which informed children's literature of the past. Into the abyss has fallen hope, conviction, moral certainty, optimism, and, possibly, courage.

Like so much else about these novels, their moral neutrality is symptomatic of a deeper shift in the adult stance toward the young. Nothing in the literature is more striking than the sense that adults have lost confidence in their ability to tell children how to live in the world. Their unwillingness to describe and prescribe "right" behavior for children, their evident dissatisfaction with their own lives, the guilt that takes the form of inviting the condemnation of adults by children—all betray how little these authors, and the adults they speak for, believe that they are in a position to tell children how things ought to be. No matter what else they know, as the protagonist of *T. Rantula* pointed out so cogently, they seem helpless before the fundamentals of living: "what to do, how to behave." They decline to decide for children what is right because they no longer believe that they themselves know. Even experience, that time honored trump card of adults, avails them little. Adults as the fiction portrays them are lost in a world in which the rules are other than those they learned, or in which there are no rules at all.

It would be neither surprising nor unprecedented if a faltering adult confidence in contemporary society resulted in literary romanticization of the young as more sensitive and natural than adults. There is some: *Lisa, Bright and Dark* and Paul Zindel's novels reflect some neoromantic notions about children as better human beings than adults. But today's romanticizing, when it occurs, is a far cry from the late nineteenth-century vision of children pure in heart and charming in manner leading adults to a more moral life. The children of contemporary fiction work no miracles on the people or the world around them—no one believes in miracles any more—and they have few of the charms of their romantic predecessors. Indeed, given their universal self-doubts, their waspish criticism of almost everyone, and their entire preoccupation with their own, usually negative, feelings, today's protagonists are often pitiable but rarely loveable and almost never admirable. Though the style of contemporary adolescent fiction still sounds faint echoes of J. D. Salinger, few of its heroes are as warmly compassionate toward a world they never made as was the neoromantic protagonist of *Catcher in the Rye*. Even after Victorian sentimentality had passed out of fashion, a modest idealization of children persisted a long time in literature for the young, but no romantic bloom seems to have survived the chill winds of recent history.

Finally, when the awful weight of negativism is measured and the failures, disappointments, and betrayals in contemporary children's books are tallied together, another observation is hard to avoid: the literature is fundamentally antichild. Something in the eagerness of the authors to acquaint children with all the terrors of the contemporary world, in their unwillingness to offer any perspective or corrective to puerile emotions, something in the joylessness of the fiction as a whole, goes beyond the requirements of an unflinching realism designed, as its apologists claim, to prepare children for the real world. From an obscure level, and surely without conscious intention by the authors, much of current fiction communicates an adult hostility toward children and, ultimately, toward the very concept of childhood. For while childhood is in one sense a biological reality, in another it is a cultural creation. As a distinctive period of life lived under adult protection and sheltered in some degree from adult concerns, childhood exists if, and only if, adults are willing to accept the burden of responsibility such a system imposes upon them. It is too soon to know whether the adult resistance to childhood's claims that runs like a subterranean stream through recent juvenile fiction is a passing or a permanent phenomenon. What is certain, I think, is that contemporary American culture is profoundly ambivalent about children, unsure whether they are dependents, companions, or adversaries. Children's literature reveals that ambivalence, perhaps better than almost anything else.

Epilogue

The social revolutions of the 1970s transformed children's literature. Old taboos fell, subjects excluded from children's books for years appeared everywhere. Death, divorce, alcohol and drugs, racism and sexism as identified social evils, and, eventually, sexuality became commonplace in literature for the young.

So much seems a predictable response to the changes taking place in the society at large, where conventional rules were being rewritten at a breathtaking rate. But the literature also broke with some of its oldest traditions in less foreseeable ways. Until the mid-1960s, family was virtually sacrosanct in children's books. Traditional children's fiction nearly always assumed family as the secure foundation of children's lives.

The decade of the 1970s was extraordinarily hard on this conception. In the name of a "new realism," fiction dwelt relentlessly on adult failure, weakness, irresponsibility, and limitation, portraying children as victims of their parents' inadequacies. Collectively, literature of the 1970s seemed to say—certainly to teenagers—that adults and children had lost touch with one another; that the confusion natural to growing children was matched by the confusion of their parents, who were bewildered by a changing society and uncertain of their ability to help themselves, let alone their children. Always allowing for some exceptions, it is fair to say that 1970s fiction, especially that written for adolescents, was overwhelmingly negative.

The 1980s opened a very different era, socially and politically, and one would expect children's fiction to respond to those differences. The question is not whether the literature changed in the last dozen years, but how and in what direction. Has fiction since the 1970s rehabilitated the American family, and if so, how does that family look in today's literature for the young? Are we back in the 1950s with intact, hierarchical families, strict gender roles, and narrowly middle-class values? Has a more conservative social climate restored the implicit value once put on conformity? How does individuality fare now? What has children's literature in the 1980s and 1990s made of the "new realism" of the 1970s?

The answers are not simple, as one might guess, but some are clear. Family has most surely been reinstated; the value of family is a recurrent theme in contemporary literature. But, just as emphatically, there has been little reactionary return to the idealized families of the past. The concept of family has expanded to include single parent families, families of grandparents and children, blended families of second marriages, even unrelated people who care about one another. The configuration of the family now is far less important than the fact of its existence. Robert Frost's poem said that "home is where, when you go there, they have to take you in." Many an author of contemporary children's books uses a definition something like that. Whatever and whoever the people around a child, if they function as a family—that is, if they provide the emotional support and continuity the child needs to grow—then they are a family. Literature of the 1970s told children they were on their own; post-1970s books say that they cannot be.

Cynthia Voigt's *Homecoming* was a kind of forecast. In this very popular 1981 novel, four children, left without parents, walk from Connecticut to the Eastern Shore of Maryland to reach a grandmother they have never known. They find a reclusive woman who has no wish to take on the responsibility for four young lives, but the children understand that she is their only chance to survive as a family, and they persist until she accepts them. In her sequels to *Homecoming* Voigt continues her exploration of this and other families, good and bad, past and present, always showing her readers that it is commitment, not form or convention, that makes a family.

The sheer necessity of family is also the theme of Ouida Sebestyen's *Far from Home* (1983) and, for that matter, of Virginia Hamilton's *Sweet Whispers, Brother Rush* (1983), though it is always difficult to push Hamilton's work into categories. Sebestyen's story is of a young boy who, with his aging grandmother, goes to live in a boarding-house, where the motley collection of people living there becomes his family. Though he finds his father there, too, the relationship between them does not develop in a conventional way, and a coincidence that sounds sentimental is really not. Mostly, the story is just matter-of-fact about the human need for others.

Sweet Whispers is a powerful blend of realism and fantasy that confronts the fact of child abuse with remarkable humanity. Tree, a young teenager, takes the major responsibility for her mildly re-tarded older brother while her mother, who works as a private duty nurse, is away from home for days at a time. When the ghost of a long-dead cousin shows Tree glimpses of the past, she learns that her mother abused the boy when he was younger. In a 1970s book, such a revelation would have put the guilty parent beyond redemption, but Hamilton is never so predictable. Angry as Tree is, she loves her mother and needs her; the family will never be conventional, but the ties of love and need and learned tolerance suffice to hold it together.

Attitudes toward difference, individuality, and nonconformity have also shifted. Fiction in the 1970s was full of protagonists who de-scribed themselves as "different," loners who claimed (in remarkably stunted first-person narrative) to be brighter than their peers. They were an unhappy lot, since in a 1970s novel, "difference" all but in-sured a painful alienation from family, peers, and community. The underlying assumption was that nonconformity, even of a mild sort, invited retaliation.

These attitudes have been modified in recent fiction. Numerous young characters in today's fiction manage to be intelligent and indi-vidual without putting themselves at odds with the world; most of them coexist in reasonable peace with family and friends. Alienation has become a less obligatory state of mind for the young; the Salinger effect may have run down at last.

The influence of the women's movement on children's fiction is a question that deserves more attention than I can give it here. Traditionally, children's literature has often allowed girls central roles, but it has also held them firmly to conventional gender expectations. That has not changed as much as one might suppose. While it is true that there is more declared support for "strong female characters" among publishers and authors, it is also true that departure from the old models is often more apparent than real. Dicey Tillerman (of *Homecoming* and its sequels) is strong and resourceful when she assumes responsibility for the children her mother has abandoned, but the maternal role is one that has been conceded to many young girls in children's fiction; Voigt is not breaking new ground here.

Robin McKinley's two novels of adolescence-cum-high-fantasy have been hailed as feminist because her girl protagonists train as warriors and in other ways tread some paths well worn by traditional male heroes. A closer look, however, finds some very familiar conventions. The novels are basically romances, whose heroines, in spite of their achievements in the masculine arena of fighting skills and battle courage, are really validated by a man's romantic interest in them. Moreover, these are not aggressive or even confident girls by any standards. On the contrary, McKinley's nearly interchangeable heroines are diffident and unsure of themselves, misfits in their own societies, however extraordinary by another set of rules. And though they learn to value their own qualities, their choices are only selectively untraditional. The protagonist of *The Hero and the Crown* (1984) leaves home in classic hero tale form, travels far and has many adventures, and, through prodigious feats of bravery and skill, recovers the lost crown that will save her kingdom from its enemies. Talisman in hand, she rides through the great final battle—and gives it to the young man she subsequently marries. McKinley assures us that her heroine does not *want* to govern, but feminism is rocked all the same. It is harder than it looks, apparently, to set aside the old patterns and harder yet to devise new ones.

Nevertheless, at their best, recent portraits of girls have a variety, individuality, and ease that contrasts with the narrowness of pre-1970s literature and, equally, with the self-consciousness of many early efforts to strengthen girls' literary images. Girls can be nonconformist now without being condemned, subtly or otherwise. Girls can know their own minds and act with courage and initiative without either apology or defiance and can even accept help or comfort without thereby backing into secondary roles. Rarest, but perhaps most significant, is the fictional adolescent girl who can move toward self-knowledge without taking male attention as the measure of her worth. It does not happen often, but it does happen in post-1970s literature.

Books for the young, like American politics, tend toward middle ground. The literature absorbs change, and presents it again with its sharper edges blunted. Today's authors, with both the pre-1970s inhibitions of children's book publishing and the anxious literary pessimism of the 1970s behind them, are free to write about contemporary life with new frankness, to look for meaning past the surface of a society in transition. Some have taken the opportunity, some have not; but overall the literature seems to have arrived at a complexity of outlook missing in the first decade of the "new realism."

Middle ground is not necessarily exciting terrain. While it seems to me that the literature has matured in a freer atmosphere, I would not claim that the number of authors stretching the outer limits of the literature is a large one. Virginia Hamilton does, but she always has, taking chances and experimenting since the beginning of her career. Robert Cormier, on the other hand, whose first three adolescent novels made bold use of the literary license of the 1970s, retreated in the 1980s. Perhaps he listened too well to his critics, or perhaps he has nothing left to say. Whatever the reason, although the tough language and the jaundiced view of human nature persists in Cormier's recent books, the political subtext is gone and with it the challenge of idea. It is a net loss for adolescent literature.

A literature as large as that produced for young readers is never monolithic. If most authors have chosen to take a positive approach to the social changes of the past twenty years, there are also dissenters. Richard Peck, author of many novels for and about high-school-aged readers, makes it clear in *Princess Ashley* (1986) that he finds contemporary relations between parents and children dangerously permissive. And indeed, his story of overprivileged, underdisciplined teenagers and their uncaring parents is a harsh morality tale. The one responsible parent in the novel is obviously speaking for the author when she blames adolescent freedom for the disasters that end the story.

In something of the same mode, Bruce Brooks takes the view that American family life will soon make no provision at all for childhood. His futuristic tale with its double-entendre title, *No Kidding* (1988), supposes a time when a huge proportion of America's parents succumb to alcoholism and irresponsibility, leaving their children to fend for themselves, take care of one another, and get along as well as they can without adult supervision. Brooks's story is subtler and a good deal more original than Peck's, but his misgivings about the decline of adult responsibility toward children are much the same.

There's no way to summarize the trends and changes of an enormous literature in a few words. What is most apparent is that the turbulent 1970s conferred a new freedom on children's literature, and while the authors of that decade did not, on the whole, use that freedom very imaginatively, today's authors sometimes do. Picture books are full of experimentation; nonfiction, at its best, melds the visual and the textual into illuminating new ways of presenting information. Current fiction inevitably includes vast reaches of familiar territory—school stories, romances, mysteries, and teen fiction carefully designed to avoid all strain or surprise. But at the frontiers, there is experimentation here, too. Unconventional narrative forms, from Cormier's *I Am the Cheese* to Macauley's *Black and White* and Spinelli's *Maniac Magee,* capitalize on the modern reader's familiarity with the storytelling techniques of film and television. Content as well as form continues to evolve. The airtight categories of traditional children's literature have become permeable; a more flexible, more complex view of human relationships has become possible. Certainly, given the demise of virtually all taboos, the literature is open to many more aspects of human experience than it once was. As the most daring authors test the definitions of what is marketed as children's literature, the boundaries between children's and adult literature, always movable, blur, shift, and sometimes seem to disappear altogether.

Notes

$\searrow \mathbf{f} \mathbf{\mathcal{K}}$

American Girlhood in the Nineteenth Century:
Caddie Woodlawn's Sisters

1. Carol R. Brink, *Caddie Woodlawn* (New York: Macmillan, 1935), 240.

2. See Barbara Welter, "The Cult of True Womanhood, 1820–1860," *American Quarterly* 18 (1966), 151–74, for a survey of the concept of womanhood in the period.

3. Caroline Briggs, *Reminiscences and Letters,* ed. G. S. Merriam (Boston: Houghton Mifflin, 1897), 6.

4. Caroline A. Creevey, *A Daughter of the Puritans* (New York: G. P. Putnam, 1916), 15; Elizabeth R. Allan, *A March Past,* ed. Janet Allan Bryan (Richmond: Dietz, 1938), 60; Briggs, *Reminiscences and Letters,* 54.

5. Creevey, *A Daughter of the Puritans,* 15, 16.

6. Sarah Bonebright, *Reminiscences of Newcastle, Iowa* (Des Moines: Historical Department of Iowa, 1921), 180; Anna L. Clary, *Reminiscences* (Los Angeles: Bruce McCallister, 1937), 47.

7. Una Hunt, *Una May* (New York: Charles Scribner's Sons, 1914), 24.

8. Hunt, *Una May,* 23; Allan, *A March Past,* 70.

9. Ellen Mordecai, *Gleanings from Long Ago* (Savannah: Braid and Hutton, 1933), 4, 5, 10.

10. Frances E. Willard, *Glimpses of Fifty Years* (Chicago: Woman's Temperance Publishing Association, 1889), 25.

11. Lucy Larcom, *A New England Girlhood* (Boston: Houghton Mifflin, 1889), 30, 104.

12. Bonebright, *Reminiscences of Newcastle, Iowa*, 183, 162. Note her distinction by age rather than by sex.

13. Alice Kingsbury, *In Old Waterbury* (Waterbury, Conn.: Mattatuck Historical Society, 1942); Mordecai, *Gleanings from Long Ago*, 39; Hunt, *Una May*, 52.

14. Rachel Butz, *A Hoosier Girlhood* (Boston: Gorham Press, 1924), 52, 83; Laura E. Richards, *When I Was Your Age* (Boston: Lauriat, 1894), 202.

15. Butz, *A Hoosier Girlhood*, 16; Larcom, *A New England Girlhood* (Chevy Chase: Corinth Books, 1961), 166, 167; Mordecai, *Gleanings from Long Ago*, 140.

16. Willard, *Glimpses of Fifty Years*, 69.

17. For the direct parallel with Louisa's feelings about her sister Anna's marriage, see *Louisa May Alcott: Her Life, Letters, and Journals*, ed. E. D. Cheney (Boston: Little, Brown, 1928), 80.

18. Louisa May Alcott, *Little Women* (1868–69; reprint in one vol., Boston: Little, Brown, 1915), 164, 217, 226.

19. Louisa May Alcott, *Jack and Jill* (1880; reprint, Boston: Little, Brown, 1928), 5.

20. Ibid., 41, 201.

21. Ibid., 85.

22. Ibid., 228, 321, 322.

23. Ibid., 220.

24. Ibid., 323.

25. Ibid., 310, 198.

26. Susan Coolidge [Sarah Woolsey], *What Katy Did* (1872; reprint, New York: Garland, 1976), 11, 12, 32.

27. Ibid., 185, 181.

28. Ibid., 272, 273.

29. William Blake, "Visions of the Daughters of Albion," in *The Prose and Poetry of William Blake*, ed. E. Erdman and H. Bloom (Garden City: Doubleday, 1965), 48.

30. Kate Douglas Wiggin, *Rebecca of Sunnybrook Farm* (Boston: Houghton Mifflin, 1904), 320.

31. Wiggin, *New Chronicles of Rebecca* (Boston: Houghton Mifflin, 1907), 278.

32. Lucy Breckinridge, *Lucy Breckinridge of Grove Hill: The Journal of a Virginia Girl, 1862–1864*, ed. M. D. Robertson (Kent, Ohio: Kent State University Press, 1979), 25, 31.

33. Quoted in P. M. Spacks, *The Adolescent Idea* (New York: Basic Books, 1981), 120.

34. Wiggin, *New Chronicles of Rebecca*, 84.

Nancy Drew and Her Rivals: No Contest

1. I've made no attempt in this essay to review the controversies over authorship of pseudonymous series books; my interest was in the contents. Some recent research now supports Mildred Wirt Benson's claim to have written the first twenty-five or thirty Nancy Drew stories, though Harriet Stratemeyer Adams always took full credit for the series. Certainly there is continuity in the characterization through the first ten to fifteen years of the series, the period I covered, but whether that is attributable to Benson as author or to Adams as editor is less clear. Both the Kay Tracey and the Penny Nichols series are also claimed by Benson. As noted in the essay, Kay Tracey has the Stratemeyer style, but Penny Nichols sounds quite different. If Benson wrote all three, the differences may reflect editorial control. The facts of authorship, however, are irrelevant for present purposes, since I am concerned with what the books said to readers.

The secondary literature on series books is widely scattered. Much of it is published in specialized journals such as *The Yellowback Book* and *The Dime Novel Round-up*. Only the *Round-up* is indexed in standard sources and that only recently. For those interested in the Stratemeyer authors, Deidre Johnson's *Stratemeyer Pseudonyms and Series Books* (Westport, Conn.: Greenwood Press, 1982) is indispensable. There are also two useful book-length studies: Bobbie Ann Mason's *The Girl Sleuth* (Old Westbury, N.Y.: Feminist Press, 1975) and Carol Billman's *The Secret of the Stratemeyer Syndicate* (New York: Ungar, 1986). For a discussion of authorship claims, see Anita Susan Grossman, "The Ghost of Nancy Drew," *Ohio Magazine* 10 (December 1987), 41–43, 82–84; and Deidre Ann Johnson, "Continued Success: The Early Boys' Fiction of Edward Stratemeyer and the Stratemeyer Syndicate" (Ph.D. diss., University of Minnesota, 1991), 80, 82.

2. Frances K. Judd, *The Secret of the Red Scarf* (New York: Cupples and Leon, 1934), 4, 30.

3. Ibid., 12.

4. Frances K. Judd, *The Mystery of the Swaying Curtains* (New York: Cupples and Leon, 1935), 197, 70.

5. Carolyn Keene, *Password to Larkspur Lane* (New York: Grosset and Dunlap, 1933), 203.

6. Judd, *Scarf*, 46.

7. Frances K. Judd, *The Green Cameo Mystery* (New York: Cupples and Leon, 1936), 60; Judd, *Swaying Curtains*, 174.

8. Joan Clark, *Penny Nichols Finds a Clue* (Chicago: Goldsmith, 1936), 86, 144, 182.

9. Joan Clark, *Penny Nichols and the Black Imp* (Chicago: Goldsmith, 1936), 34, 98, 99.

10. Ibid., 192.

11. Ibid., 193, 194.

12. Lillian Garis, *Terror of Moaning Cliff* (New York: Grosset and Dunlap, 1935), 35; Garis, *The Secret of the Kashmir Shawl* (New York: Grosset and Dunlap, 1939), 27.

13. See, for example, Garis, *Kashmir Shawl*, 85, 116; *Terror*, 56, 90, 98, 115, 222.

14. Sainsbury also wrote a series with Bill Bolton (Dorothy Dixon's boy-friend) as protagonist and a number of sports and adventure stories, sometimes under the pseudonym Charles Lawton.

15. Dorothy Wayne, *Dorothy Dixon Solves the Conway Case* (Chicago: Goldsmith, 1933), 47, 54.

16. Ibid., 132.

17. Dorothy Wayne, *Dorothy Dixon Wins Her Wings* (Chicago: Goldsmith, 1933), 184–186.

18. Wayne, *Conway Case,* 214.

19. Ibid., 57.

20. Margaret Sutton, *The Unfinished House* (New York: Grosset and Dunlap, 1938), 112.

21. Ibid., 114.

22. Dorothy Wayne, *Dorothy Dixon and the Mystery Plane* (Chicago: Goldsmith, 1933), 191.

23. Carolyn Keene, *The Sign of the Twisted Candle* (New York: Grosset and Dunlap, 1933), 44.

24. Carolyn Keene, *The Clue of the Broken Locket* (New York: Grosset and Dunlap, 1934), 196.

25. Carolyn Keene, *The Hidden Staircase* (New York: Grosset and Dunlap, 1930), 11; Keene, *The Secret at Shadow Ranch* (New York: Grosset and Dunlap, 1931), 4; Keene, *The Secret of the Old Clock* (New York: Grosset and Dunlap, 1930), 6.

26. Carolyn Keene, *The Mystery of the Ivory Charm* (New York: Grosset and Dunlap, 1936), 13; Keene, *Password to Larkspur Lane* (New York: Grosset and Dunlap, 1933), 89; Keene, *The Message in the Hollow Oak* (New York: Grosset and Dunlap, 1935), 13.

27. Keene, *Old Clock*, 133.

28. Keene, *Larkspur Lane*, 204.

29. Carolyn Keene, *The Clue in the Old Diary* (New York: Grosset and Dunlap, 1932), 136; Keene, *Ivory Charm*, 2.

30. Keene, *Hidden Staircase*, 59; *Nancy's Mysterious Letter* (New York: Grosset and Dunlap, 1932), 70–71.

31. Keene, *Shadow Ranch*, 64, 65, 136, 179.

32. Keene, *Larkspur Lane*, 163, 164.

33. Ibid., 169, 192.

34. Ibid., 164, 138.

35. Carolyn Keene, *The Haunted Bridge* (New York: Grosset and Dunlap, 1937), 161, 169, 171, 171.

36. See Carolyn Keene, *The Ghost of Blackwood Hall* (New York: Grosset and Dunlap, 1948), 52.

37. Annie L. Mearkle, "The Woman Who Wants to Be a Man," *Midland Monthly* 9 (1898), 176.

Girls' Novels in Post–World War II America

1. The distinction between teen and children's fiction was signaled in 1946 by *Booklist*'s decision to review books for children and young adults separately.

2. A useful overview of the statistics of postwar adolescent life can be found in chapter 1 of James Gilbert, *A Cycle of Outrage* (New York: Oxford University Press, 1986).

3. Mary Stolz, one popular author of girls' books, is an exception to some, though not all, of the generalizations in this essay. Stolz's protagonists are usually older (out of high school), a difference that seems to have allowed her greater frankness about some subjects. Stolz and Florence Crannell Means, who broached racial problems in their books, deserve essays of their own.

4. Beverly Cleary, *Fifteen* (New York: Scholastic Book Services, 1956), 3.

5. Lenore Mattingly Weber, *Meet the Malones* (New York: Thomas Y. Crowell, 1943), 41.

6. Cleary, *Fifteen*, 37.

7. Madeleine L'Engle, *Meet the Austins* (New York: Vanguard, 1960), 158; Rosamund DuJardin, *Class Ring* (Philadelphia: Lippincott, 1951), 20.

8. Betty Cavanna, *Accent on April* (New York: William Morrow, 1960), 122.

9. Beverly Cleary, *Jean and Johnny* (New York: William Morrow, 1959).

10. Weber, *Meet the Malones*, 187, 185.

11. Charles Strickland and Andrew M. Ambrose, "The Baby Boom, Prosperity, and the Changing Worlds of Children, 1945–1963," in *American Childhood*, ed. Joseph Hawes and R. Hiner (Westport, Conn.: Greenwood Press, 1985), 536.

12. See Cleary, *Fifteen*, and Weber's *Malone* books for settings; the cotton dress is mentioned in Betty Cavanna, *Going on Sixteen* (Philadelphia: Westminster Press, 1956), 219.

13. Madeleine L'Engle, *The Moon by Night* (New York: Farrar, Straus and Giroux, 1963), 37, 38.

14. Erik Erikson, *Childhood and Society* (New York: W. W. Norton, 1950), 263; Gilbert, *A Cycle of Outrage*, 199, quoted in Margaret Mead, *Culture and Commitment* (Garden City, N.Y.: Natural History Press), 51.

15. Lenore Mattingly Weber, *Beany Malone* (New York: T. Y. Crowell, 1948), 42.

16. See Beverly Cleary, *Sister of the Bride* (New York: William Morrow, 1963); and Mary Stolz, *Who Wants Music on Monday?* (New York: Harper and Row, 1963), for examples.

17. Mary Stolz, *Ready or Not* (New York: Harper and Row, 1953), 81.

18. Cleary, *Jean and Johnny*, 50, 51.

19. Cleary, *Fifteen*, 150; Stolz, *Ready or Not*, 208, 223.

20. Almost any book by DeLeeuw or Cavanna will demonstrate this point.

21. The complexities of adult feelings about adolescence in the 1950s are well explored in Gilbert, *A Cycle of Outrage*.

22. Barbara White, *Growing Up Female: Adolescent Girlhood in American Fiction* (Westport, Conn.: Greenwood Press, 1985), 137, 141, 143, 145.

23. Cleary, *Sister of the Bride*, 124.

24. See Elaine Tyler May, *Homeward Bound* (New York: Basic Books, 1988), 9.

25. Elizabeth Donvan, "The Age of Narcissism," in *American Childhood*, ed. Joseph Hawes and R. Hiner, 594.

26. See Carl Degler, *At Odds* (New York: Oxford University Press, 1980), 429.

Bad Boys: Tom Bailey and Tom Sawyer

1. Thomas Bailey Aldrich, *The Story of a Bad Boy* (New York: Garland, 1976), 7, 8.

2. Leslie Fiedler, *Love and Death in the American Novel*, rev. ed. (New York: Stein and Day, 1966). See chapter 9.

3. Mark Twain [Samuel L. Clemens], *The Adventures of Tom Sawyer* (New York: Harper and Brothers, 1985), preface.

4. Aldrich, *Bad Boy*, vi.

5. Edward Eggleston, *The Hoosier Schoolmaster* (New York: Grosset and Dunlap, 1871), 50.

6. Aldrich, *Bad Boy*, 77.

7. Ibid., 85.

8. Ibid., 151.

9. Twain, *Tom Sawyer*, 199.

10. C. J. Sommerville argues this thesis persuasively in *The Discovery of Childhood in Puritan England* (Athens: University of Georgia Press, 1992).

Children's Literature for a New Nation, 1820–1860

1. Washington Irving, *The Legend of Sleepy Hollow,* quoted by Leo Marx in *The Machine in the Garden* (New York: Oxford University Press, 1964), 3.

2. William Cardell, *The Happy Family,* 2d ed. (Philadelphia: T. T. Ash, 1828), 4.

3. Ibid.

4. William Cardell, *Story of Jack Halyard,* 3d ed. (Philadelphia: Uriah Hunt, 1825), ix.

5. Samuel Goodrich, *Parley's Book of Fables* (Hartford· White, Dwier, 1836), 6.

6. *Self-Willed Susie and Her Sister Lena* (New York: Carleton and Porter, American Sunday School Union, 1860), 150.

7. Lydia Maria Child, ed., *The Juvenile Miscellany,* 3d ser., no. 2 (Boston: John Putnam, 1832), 225.

8. Joseph Alden, *The State Prisoner* (New York: Love and Tippett, 1848).

9. William Cardell, *Story of Jack Halyard,* 26.

10. See Aunt Friendly, *Bound Out* (New York: Anson D. F. Randolph, 1859).

11. Horace Bushnell, *Christian Nurture* (New Haven: Yale University Press, 1947).

12. *Filial Duty Recommended and Enforced* (New York: O. Scott, 1847), 4.

13. Clara Arnold, ed., *A Juvenile Keepsake* (Boston: Phillips, Sampson, 1851), 57.

14. Catherine Maria Sedgwick, *Conquest and Self-Conquest* (New York: Harper and Brothers, 1843), 55.

15. See, for example, *Little Mary: A Story for Children from Four to Five Years Old* (By 'A Mother') (Boston: Cottons and Barnard, 1831).

16. *Alfred Raymond* (Philadelphia: American Sunday School Union, 1854), 5.

Child and Conscience

1. Elizabeth Randolph Allan, *A March Past* (Richmond: Dietz, 1938), 2.

2. Carroll Smith-Rosenberg, "The Female World of Love and Ritual," *Signs*, vol. 1, no. 1 (Autumn 1975), 1–29; Nancy Cott, *The Bonds of Womanhood* (New Haven: Yale University Press, 1977).

3. John S. C. Abbott, *The Mother at Home; or, The Principles of Maternal Duty* (London: J. Mason, 1834), 15.

4. *Original Moral Tales Intended for Children and Young Persons* (Boston: Bowles and Dearborn, 1828), 205, 213.

5. Mrs. Child [Lydia Maria], *The Mother's Book* (Boston: Carter and Handee, 1831), 46.

6. *A Juvenile Keepsake*, ed. Clara Arnold (Boston: Phillips, Sampson, 1851), 110.

7. Catherine Maria Sedgwick, *Home* (Boston: James Monroe, 1827), 18, 20.

8. [Lydia Maria Child], *Emily Parker* (Boston: Bowles and Dearborn, 1827), 5.

9. Jacob Abbott, *Franconia Tale No. 3* (New York: Harper and Brothers, 1850), 22.

10. [By a New Pen], *Belle and Lilly* (Boston: Crosby, Nichols, 1857), 87.

11. Maria J. McIntosh, *Ellen Leslie* (New York: Dayton and Newman, 1842), 84.

12. Sedgwick, *Home*, 26, 27.

13. Child, *Mother's Book*, 61.

14. Bernard Wishey, *The Child and the Republic* (Philadelphia: University of Pennsylvania Press, 1968), 43.

15. Abbott, *Mother at Home*, 58, 59.

16. T. S. Arthur, *Maggy's Baby and Other Stories* (Philadelphia: Lippincott, Grambo, 1852), 18.

17. Laura E. Richards, *When I Was Your Age* (Boston: Estes and Lauriat, 1894).

18. Richards, *When I Was Your Age*, 55.

19. Jeanette L. Gilder, *The Autobiography of a Tomboy* (New York: Doubleday, Page, 1900), 209.

20. Alice Eliza Kingsbury, *In Old Waterbury: The Memoirs of Alice E. Kingsbury* (Waterbury, Conn.: Mattatuck Historical Society, 1942).

21. William Dean Howells, *A Boy's Town* (New York: Harper and Brothers, 1890), 247.

22. Laura E. Richards, *When I Was Your Age* (Boston: Estes and Lauriat, 1894), 41.

23. Adela Orpen, *Memories of Old Emigrant Days in Kansas, 1862–1865* (London: William Blackwood and Sons, 1926), 9.

24. Cornelia Raymond, *Memories of a Child of Vassar* (Poughkeepsie, N.Y.: Vassar College, 1940), 13, 14; Richards, *When I Was Your Age*, 90, 102.

25. Caroline A. Stickney Creevey, *A Daughter of the Puritans* (New York: G. P. Putnam's Sons, 1916), 17.

26. Eleanor H. Abbott, *Being Little in Cambridge* (Boston: Phillips, Sampson; New York: D. Appleton-Century, 1936), 76, 80, 126, 133.

27. James Weldon Johnson, *Along This Way* (New York: Viking Press, 1933), 14, 15.

28. Ulysses S. Grant, *Personal Memoirs,* quoted in *American Childhoods,* ed. D. McCullough (Boston: Little, Brown, 1987), 74, 76.

29. Howells, *A Boy's Town,* 13.

30. Johnson, *Along This Way,* 15.

31. Isabella M. Alden, *Memories of Yesterdays* (Philadelphia: J. B. Lippincott, 1931), 40.

32. Henrietta Skinner, *An Echo from Parnassus* (New York: J. H. Sears, 1928), 88.

33. Raymond, *Memories,* 13.

34. Virginia Terhune Van de Water, *The Heart of a Child* (Boston: W. A. Wilde, 1927), 121–23.

35. Una Hunt, *Una May* (New York: Scribner's Sons, 1914), 39.

36. Lucy Larcom, *A New England Girlhood* (Boston: Houghton Mifflin, 1889), 75–77.

37. Rachel Butz, *A Hoosier Girlhood* (Boston: Gorham Press, 1924), 43.

38. Johnson, *Along This Way,* 15.

39. Howells, *A Boy's Town,* 16.

40. Skinner, *Echo,* 92, 93.

Children, Adults, and Reading at the Turn of the Century

1. Harvey Fergusson, *Home in the West* (New York: Duell, Sloan and Pearce, 1944), 93.

2. Mary Ellen Chase, *A Goodly Heritage* (New York: Henry Holt, 1932), 72.

3. Ibid., 225, 226.

4. Ibid., 228, 229, 230.

5. Helen Rosen Woodward, *Three Flights Up* (New York: Dodd, Mead, 1935), 253; H. L. Mencken, *Happy Days* (New York: Knopf, 1940), 175; Una Hunt Drage, *Young in the Nineties* (New York: Charles Scribner's Sons, 1927), 123.

6. Edna Ferber, *A Peculiar Treasure* (New York: Doubleday, Doran, 1939), 52; Woodward, *Three Flights Up*, 255.

7. Chase, *A Goodly Heritage*, 46, 37.

8. Una Hunt, *Una May* (New York: Charles Scribner's Sons, 1914), 119, 76; Ferber, *A Peculiar Treasure*, 52; Woodward, *Three Flights Up*, 25.

9. Edward Martin, *The Luxury of Children and Some Other Luxuries* (New York: Harper and Brothers, 1904), 2.

10. See Jackson Lears, *No Place of Grace: Anti-Modernism and the Transformation of American Culture, 1880–1920* (New York: Pantheon, 1981); Stanley Coben, "The Assault on Victorianism in the Twentieth Century," in *Victorian America*, ed. D. W. Howe (Philadelphia: University of Pennsylvania Press, 1976), 160–81.

11. Edith Wharton, "A Little Girl's New York," *Harper's Magazine*, March 1938, reprinted in D. McCullough, ed., *American Childhoods* (Boston: Little, Brown, 1987), 169.

12. Marie L. Sandrock, "Another Word on Children's Reading," *Catholic World*, vol. 50, no. 30 (August 1890), 678.

13. Sidney Lanier, *The Boys' King Arthur* (New York: Charles Scribner's Sons, 1880), 35.

14. Quoted in T. J. Jackson Lears, *No Place of Grace* (New York: Pantheon, 1981), 105.

15. Quoted in Janet Dunbar, *J. M. Barrie: The Man Behind the Image* (Boston: Houghton Mifflin, 1970), 170.

16. Kate Douglas Wiggin et al., "The Best Books for Children," *Outlook*, vol. 69, no. 7 (December 1901), 873.

17. Russel Nye, *New Voices in American Studies* (Bloomfield, Ind.: Purdue University Press, 1953), 68, 60.

18. Wiggin, "Best Books," 872; H. W. Boynton, "Books New and Old,"

Atlantic Monthly, vol. 91, no. 643 (January 1903), 699; Marie L. Sandrock, "Another Word," 676.

19. Sandrock, "Another Word," 676.

20. Boynton, "Books New and Old," 699.

21. And so they remain: witness today's battles over literary canons.

22. Claude G. Leland et al., *The Library and the School* (New York: Harper and Brothers, 1909), 14.

23. Sandrock, "Another Word," 680; *Book Review Digest* (1911), 493; Henry James, "Robert Louis Stevenson," *Century Magazine*, vol. 35, no. 6 (April 1888), 877; "Reviews of New Books: Fifty of the Season's Best Books for Children," *Literary Digest*, vol. 43, no. 23 (December 2, 1911), 1046.

24. Leland et al., *Library and School*, 8.

25. Harriet H. Stanley, comp., *Five Hundred and Fifty Children's Books* (Chicago: ALA Publishing Board, 1910).

Images: American Children in the Early Nineteenth Century

1. For a detailed study of early nineteenth-century children's fiction, see Anne Scott MacLeod, *A Moral Tale: Children's Fiction and American Culture, 1820–1860* (1975; reprint, Hamden, Conn.: Archon, 1990). Chapter 3 discusses the ideal child of this fiction.

2. A number of historians have mined these interesting sources. I have drawn on the bibliography in Richard L. Rapson's article "The American Child as Seen by British Travelers, 1845–1935," *American Quarterly*, vol. 17, no. 3 (Fall 1965), 520–34, adding a number of other, non-British sources. Gillian Avery's recent essay "The Puritans and Their Heirs," in *Children and Their Literature*, ed. G. Avery and J. Briggs (New York: Oxford University Press, 1989), 95–118, explores some of these accounts.

3. Quoted in Rapson, "The American Child," 527. Similar comments abound in travel literature. See, for example, Fredrika Bremer, *The Homes of the New World*, vol. 2 (New York: Harper and Brothers, 1856), 455, 469, Frances Trollope, *Domestic Manners of the Americans* (New York: Knopf, 1949), 212ff., 213; Francis J. Grund, *The Americans* (Boston: Marsh, Capen, and Lyon, 1837), 133, 134.

4. Quoted in Rapson, "The American Child," 521.

5. Frederick Marryat, *A Diary in America*, ed. Sydney Jackman (1838; reprint, New York: Knopf, 1962), 351.

6. Lady Emmeline Stuart-Wortley, *Travels in the United States*, Bandry's

European Library (Paris: A. and W. Galignani, 1851), 67; Edward Strutt Abdy, *Journal of a Residence and Tour in the United States of North America from April 1833 to October 1834*, 3 vols. (London: J. Murray, 1835), vol. 1, 73.

7. *The Working Man's Advocate*, 1 (March 1830), reprinted in *Annals of America*, vol. 1 (Chicago: Encyclopaedia Britannica, 1968), 388.

8. John Muir, *My Boyhood and Youth* (Boston: Houghton Mifflin, 1913), 176–77.

9. Hamlin Garland, *A Son of the Middle Border* (New York: Macmillan, 1917), 86, 87; U.S. Bureau of the Census, *Historical Census of the United States, Colonial Times to 1970*, Bicentennial ed., part 1 (Washington, D.C., 1975) (see chapter D: Labor). Similar accounts are too numerous to list, but for a vivid description, see Ward Bradford, *Biographical Sketches* (Fresno, Calif., 1891), 9–11 (privately printed).

10. Henry Conklin, *Through Poverty's Vale* (Syracuse, N.Y.: Syracuse University Press, 1974).

11. Adela Orpen, *Memories of Old Emigrant Days in Kansas, 1862–1865* (London: W. Blackwood, 1926), 92, 93. See also Caroline H. Dall, *Alongside* (Boston: Thomas Todd, 1900), 31 and 49, especially for early responsibilities. General descriptions of girls' work are also numerous. See especially Sarah Brewer Bonebright, *Reminiscences . . .* (Des Moines, Iowa: Historical Department of Iowa, 1921), 184ff., and William Reed, *Life on the Border* (Fall River, Mass.: R. Adams, 1882), 16–19.

12. See Robert Bremner et al., *Children and Youth in America*, vol. 1, *1600–1865* (Cambridge, Mass.: Harvard University Press, 1970), 483–595. An especially vivid description of a boy's sea apprenticeship may be found in Frederick P. Harlow, *The Making of a Sailor* (Salem, Mass.: Marine Research Society, 1928).

13. William Matthews, *Adventures in Giving* (New York: Dodd, Mead, 1939), 12. Stephen Knight, *Reminiscences . . .*, 231, 232, reprinted in Bremner, *Children and Youth*, 606.

14. Harriet Robinson, *Loom and Spindle* (Boston: T. Y. Crowell, 1889), 37, 39.

15. U.S. Bureau of Labor, *Report on the Condition of Women and Child Wage-Earners in the United States* (Washington, D.C., 1910), 77.

16. Lucy Larcom, *A New England Girlhood* (Boston: Houghton Mifflin, 1889), 154; Robinson, *Loom and Spindle*, 40. For additional background on Larcom's experience in the mills, see Daniel Dulaney Addison, *Lucy Larcom: Life, Letters, and Diary* (Boston: Houghton Mifflin, 1894).

17. Muir, *My Boyhood*, 177; Robinson, *Loom and Spindle*, 39.

18. Domingo Faustino Sarmiento, *Travels in the United States in 1847*, trans. M. A. Rockland (Princeton, N.J.: Princeton University Press, 1970), 159; Grund, *The Americans*, 136, 137.

19. Henry Bradshaw Fearon, *A Narrative of a Journey Through America*, 2d ed. (London: Longman, Hurst, Rees, Orme and Brown, 1818), 375.

20. Alexis de Tocqueville, *Democracy in America*, trans. Henry Reeves (New York: D. Appleton, 1899), 205, 210, 211.

21. Ibid., 210, 211.

22. Larcom, *New England Girlhood*, 193.

The Children of Children's Literature
in the Nineteenth Century

1. Maria Edgeworth, *Rosamund: A Sequel to Early Lessons* (Philadelphia: J. Maxwell, 1821), preface.

2. ———, *The Birthday Present and the Basket Woman* (London: G. Routledge, n.d.), 21.

3. *The Child's Portfolio* (New York: Mahlon Day, 1823).

4. Jacob Abbott, *Rollo at Play* (Boston: T. H. Carter, 1833), 9, 10.

5. Edward K. Spann, *The New Metropolis: New York City, 1840–1857* (New York: Columbia University Press, 1981), 24.

6. Oscar Handlin, *Boston's Immigrants, 1790–1880* (New York: Atheneum, 1977), 59.

7. Louis Auchincloss, ed., *The Home and Strong Diaries of Old Manhattan* (New York: Abbeville Press, 1989), 138, 139.

8. Spann, *The New Metropolis*, 262.

9. Charles Loring Brace, *The Dangerous Classes of New York and Twenty Years among Them* (New York: Wynkoop and Mallenbeck, 1872), 330.

10. Quoted in Spann, *The New Metropolis*, 262.

11. *The Youth's Companion*, a weekly journal, was founded in 1827 by Nathanial Willis, to entertain and "insensibly instruct" children and also advise parents on the moral and religious nurture of their children. It had a large circulation among middle-class American families for nearly a century. The *New York Ledger* was a popular weekly, founded by Robert Bonner in 1851, featuring romance, simple essays, and columns by popular journalists. Its audience was adult, but younger and less church-oriented than that of the *Youth's Companion*.

12. *Youth's Companion*, vol. 27, no. 52 (April 19, 1855), 207; [Sara Parton], *Little Ferns for Fanny's Little Friends* (Auburn, N.Y.: Derby and Miller, 1854), 94.

13. [Parton], *Little Ferns*, 48, 49.

14. Brace, *Dangerous Classes*, 65.

15. Louisa May Alcott, *Little Women* (New York: Little, Brown, 1915), 125.

16. Horatio Alger, *Ragged Dick and Mark, the Match Boy* (New York: Collier Books, 1962), 42, 44.

17. Ibid., 12 (introduction by Rychard Fink).

18. Martha Finley, *Elsie Dinsmore* (New York: Dodd, Mead, 1893), 35, 36.

19. Ibid., 246.

20. Laura E. Richards, *Captain January* (Boston: Estes and Lauriats, 1989), 7.

21. Ibid., 5.

22. Ibid., 26.

23. Ibid., 56, 63, 64.

Family Stories, 1920–1940

1. Christine Jope-Slade, *St. David Walks Again* (New York: Harper and Brothers, 1928), 25.

2. Ibid., 26.

3. Ibid., 59, 62.

4. Edith Ballinger Price, *John and Susanne* (New York: Century, 1926), 60.

5. Ibid., 133.

6. Mabel L. Robinson, *All by Ourselves* (New York: Dutton, 1925), 253.

7. Margaret Ashmum, *Mother's Away* (New York: Macmillan, 1927), 166.

8. Bertha Cobb and Ernest Cobb, *Dan's Boy* (Newton Upper Falls, Mass.: Arlo, 1926), 156, 168.

9. Arthur Pier, *David Ives* (Boston: Houghton Mifflin, 1911), 28.

10. Grace Carroll, "Yes, I Know," *Horn Book*, vol. 6, no. 3 (August 1930), 229, 239.

11. This was as true of the many 1930s stories set in other countries or other periods as it was of contemporary stories with American settings.

12. Elizabeth Coatsworth, *Alice-All-by-Herself* (New York: Macmillan, 1937), 74.

13. Elizabeth Enright, *Thimble Summer* (New York: Holt, Rinehart and Winston, 1938), 7.

14. See Grace A. Johnson. "The World as It Is for Young People," *Horn Book*, vol. 11, no. 6 (November–December 1935), 303.

15. Margaret T. Raymond, "Bread for Adolescence," *Horn Book*, vol. 11, no. 5 (September 1935), 302.

16. Elizabeth Enright, *The Saturdays* (New York: Holt, Rinehart and Winston, 1944), 21.

17. Eleanor Estes, *The Moffats* (New York: Harcourt, Brace and World, 1944), 51.

18. Russell Baker, *Growing Up* (New York: Congden and Weed, 1982), 42.

19. Baker, *Growing Up*, 117.

Censorship and Children's Literature

1. This is an ideal more often achieved, of course, by the middle and upper middle classes than by those below. Nevertheless, if lower-class families rarely had the means or the space to make the ideal practicable, they often embraced the concept and deplored their inability to protect their children from too much knowledge too soon; see Oscar Lewis, *The Children of Sanchez* (New York: Penguin Books, 1964), 499.

2. Philippe Aries, *Centuries of Childhood* (New York: Random House, 1965).

3. Dee Garrison, *Apostles of Culture* (New York: Macmillan Information, 1979); see chapter 4.

4. Norma Klein, *Mom, the Wolfman, and Me* (New York: Pantheon Books, 1972).

5. See, for example, Judy Blume, *Are You There, God? It's Me, Margaret* (Englewood Cliffs, N.J.: Bradbury Press, 1970), and Judy Blume, *Then Again, Maybe I Won't* (Scarsdale, N.Y.: Bradbury Press, 1971).

6. Council on Interracial Books for Children, *Human (and Anti-Human) Values in Children's Books* (New York: Racism and Sexism Center for Educators, 1976), 11.

7. Edward B. Jenkinson, *Censors in the Classroom* (Carbondale: Southern Illinois University Press, 1979), 9.

8. American Library Association, *Newsletter on Intellectual Freedom* 30 (January 1981), 1, 5, 23–216.

Ice Axes: Robert Cormier and the Adolescent Novel

1. George Orwell, "The Prevention of Literature," in *In Front of Your Nose*, ed. Sonia Orwell and Ian Angus (New York: Harcourt Brace Jovanovich, 1968), 65. Notable exceptions to this general rule are James Forman's numerous novels set against strongly political backgrounds. Most of the moral questions posed, however, are personal. This essay, which was originally published in 1981, refers to the three adolescent novels Cormier had published at that time.

2. See, for example, Lorraine Hirsch, Book Reviews, *Christian Science Monitor*, June 1, 1979, p. 22.

3. See, for example, *Junior Bookshelf* 39 (June 1975), 194–95, and Norma Bagnall, *Top of the News* 36 (Winter 1980), 214–17.

4. Robert Cormier, *The Chocolate War* (New York: Pantheon, 1974), 248.

5. Robert Cormier, *After the First Death* (New York: Pantheon, 1977), 130.

6. Ibid., 134.

7. Ibid., 194, 204, 193.

8. Franz Kafka to Oskar Pollak, January 24, 1904, printed in Franz Kafka, *Letters to Friends, Family, and Editors* (New York: Schocken, 1977), 16.

The Transformation of Childhood in Twentieth-Century Children's Literature

1. Louise Fitzhugh, *Harriet the Spy* (New York: Harper and Row, 1964), 275.

2. Paul Zindel, *Confessions of a Teenage Baboon* (New York: Harper and Row, 1977), 7.

3. Sandra Scoppettone, *The Late Great Me* (New York: Putnam's, 1976), 10.

4. Angier Bradford and Barbara Corcoran, *Ask for Love and They Give You Rice Pudding* (New York: Bantam, 1979), 2, 23.

5. Zindel, *Baboon*, 2, 30.

6. Barbara Wersba, *Tune for a Small Harmonica* (New York: Harper and Row, 1976), 15, 16.

7. John Neufeld, *Lisa, Bright and Dark* (New York: Phillips, 1969), 29.

8. Isabelle Holland, *The Man Without a Face* (New York: Lippincott, 1972), 4; Kin Platt, *The Boy Who Could Make Himself Disappear* (New York: Chilton, 1968), 48.

9. Paul Zindel, *The Pigman* (New York: Harper and Row, 1968), 9; M. E. Kerr, *Love Is a Missing Person* (New York: Harper and Row, 1975), 8.

10. Kit Reed, *The Ballad of T. Rantula* (Boston: Little, Brown, 1979), 19.

11. Madeleine L'Engle, *A Wind in the Door* (New York: Farrar, Straus and Giroux, 1972), 33.

Index

Abbott, Eleanor, 108
Abbott, Jacob, 104, 105, 108, 155
Abbott, John S. C., 101, 106
Abbott, Madcline, 108
Abdy, Edward, 129
Accent on April, 54
Adams, Harriet Stratemeyer, 30, 35, 41, 44, 45, 47
Adolescence, 14, 25, 27, 29, 49, 58; post–World War II, 50, 51, 52, 62; rebellion in, 58, 59, 62; identity in, 58, 59; in adult literature, 63
Adolescent literature, 14, 183, 189, 190, 211, 214; for girls, 14, 49, 54–61; post–World War II, 50, 55, 56; voice in, 54, 61
Adventures of Tom Sawyer, The, 69, 70, 76, 90
Aesop's Fables, 120
After the First Death, 190, 193
Alcott, Louisa May, 14, 15, 16, 18, 20, 21, 23, 25, 116, 117, 123, 125, 149, 150, 151

Alden, Isabella, 109
Aldrich, Thomas Bailey, 69, 70, 72, 73, 116
Alger, Horatio, 77, 78, 79, 81, 82, 83, 122, 149–52, 160, 161
Alice-All-By-Herself, 167
Allan, Elizabeth, 7, 8
Ambition, 16, 19, 25, 55, 60, 95, 96, 97
American Library Association, 186
American Revolution, 92, 95
Andersen, Hans Christian, 120, 126
Andersen's Fairy Tales, 116
Anne of Green Gables, 22, 24, 158
Anti-modernism, 118
Arabian Nights, The, 120, 121
Arendt, Hannah, 196
Areopagitica, 173
Are You in the House Alone? 184
Aries, Philippe, 174, 175
Atlantic Monthly, The, 120
Autobiographical novels, 15, 69, 90, 151

235

Autobiography, ix, 5–7, 19, 100, 126, 131; of women, 5, 6, 9, 100, 101; of children, 6, 100, 106, 107, 110; of men, 109, 113
Autonomy: in Nancy Drew mysteries, 39, 40, 41; adolescent, post–World War II, 62; children's sense of, 136, 139; children's moral, 137, 138
Awakening, The, 125

Baker, Russell, 171
Ballad of T. Rantula, The, 202, 208
Barred Road, The, 57
Baum, Frank, 122
Beattie, Ann, 70
Beim, Jerrold, 180
Bell Jar, The, 63
Ben Hur, 126
Benson, Mildred Wirt, 33, 40, 219 (n. 1)
Billman, Carol, 219 (n. 1)
Black and White, 215
Blackboard Jungle, 62
Blackmore, Richard Doddridge, 118
Blake, William, 23
Bleak House, 116
Blue Denim, 62
Blue Willow, 168
Blume, Judy, 182, 183, 184, 204
Bonebright, Sarah, 7, 11
Bonham, Frank, 180, 184
Boston, Mass., 147
Boys' King Arthur, The, 118
Brace, Charles Loring, 147, 148
Breckinridge, Lucy, 28
Briggs, Caroline A., 6, 7
Brink, Carol, 3, 16
Brontës, the, 116, 124
Brooks, Bruce, 215

Burnett, Frances Hodgson, 77, 78, 80–83, 119, 154, 155, 160
Burton, Sir Richard, 120
Bushnell, Horace, 94
Butz, Rachel, 11, 12, 111
Byars, Betsy, 202

Caddie Woodlawn, 3, 6, 12, 16, 19
Campfire Girls series, 126
Captain January, 119, 154, 158
Captain Marryat. See Marryat, Frederick
Captains Courageous, 163
Cardell, William, 90
Carroll, Grace, 166, 168
Catcher in the Rye, 209
Cavanna, Betty, 54, 184
Censorship, 173; in children's books, 174, 177, 181, 185; in schools, 183
Centuries of Childhood, 175
Century Magazine, 119
Chase, Mary Ellen, 114, 115
Child, Lydia Maria, 103, 104
Childhood: romantic views of, 78, 102, 117, 119, 120, 154, 156; adult views of, 175, 176; twentieth-century views of, 181
Childhood and Society, 58
Child nurture: during nineteenth century, 5–12; theories of, 91, 94, 103–6, 113, 150; in children's fiction, 95, 96, 167
Chocolate War, The, 190, 191, 192, 203
Chopin, Kate, 125
Civil War, 72, 75, 92, 148
Clarke, Rebecca Sophia. See May, Sophie
Clary, Anna L., 8

Class, 50, 53, 62, 80, 81, 83, 120, 155, 156, 158, 161, 169
Cleary, Beverly, 52, 57, 64
Clemens, Samuel. *See* Twain, Mark
Coatsworth, Elizabeth, 166, 167
Cobb, Lyman, 106
Comic books, 178
Confessions of a Teenage Baboon, 200, 202, 203
Conklin, Henry, 132
Continued Success: The Early Boys' Fiction of Edward Stratemeyer and the Stratemeyer Syndicate, 219 (n. 1)
Coolidge, Susan. *See* Woolsey, Sarah C.
Cooper, James Fenimore, 116, 124
Cormier, Robert, 189–96, 203, 204, 207, 214, 215
Cott, Nancy, 100
Council on Interracial Books for Children, 183
Crane, Stephen, 125
Creevey, Caroline, 7, 108

Daily Telegraph, 120
Daly, Maureen, 180
Dana Girls series, 35
Dan's Boy, 163
Defoe, Daniel, 124
DeLeeuw, Adele, 57, 59
Depression, economic, 157, 158, 166, 170, 171, 205, 206
Dickens, Charles, 116, 117, 124
Dickinson, Emily, 126
Dime novel, 121, 149, 177
Dime Novel Round-up, The, 219 (n. 1)
Divorce, 56, 64, 200, 201, 210
Donovan, John, 182, 200, 204

Don Quixote, 124
Dorothy Dixon series, 37, 38
Dr. Dolittle, 184
Drage, Una Hunt. *See* Hunt, Una
Dream Watcher, The, 202
Dreiser, Theodore, 125
DuJardin, Rosamund, 54
Duncan, Lois, 184
Durango Street, 184

Edgeworth, Maria, 101, 113, 143, 144
Edgeworth, Richard Lovell, 144
Eggleston, Edward, 71
Eight Cousins, 150
Eliot, George, 116, 124
Elsie Dinsmore, 117, 122, 152, 153
Emile, 145
England, 79, 80, 129
Enright, Elizabeth, 166, 168, 198
Erikson, Erik, 58, 59
Estes, Eleanor, 166, 168, 198
Evans, Mary Ann. *See* Eliot, George
Evil Tendencies of Corporal Punishment, The, 106

Families, in children's fiction: nineteenth century, 5; twentieth century, 199, 200, 203, 211, 215; relations in, 199, 200, 202, 203, 207
Family stories, children's, viii, 158, 166, 169, 198
Fantasy, 212, 213
Far From Home, 212
Farquharson, Martha. *See* Finley, Martha
Fearon, Henry Bradshaw, 137
Feminine Mystique, The, 65
Feminism, 15, 41, 43, 47, 213

Ferber, Edna, 116, 117
Fergusson, Harvey, 114, 116
Fern, Fanny. *See* Parton, Sara
Fiedler, Leslie, 69
Field, Rachel, 166, 198
Fifteen, 52
Finley, Martha, 122, 153
Fitzgerald, F. Scott, 125
Fitzhugh, Louise, 199
Five Little Pepper series, 116, 160
Forever, 184
Franconia tales, 105
Freud, Sigmund, 29, 47, 153
Friedan, Betty, 64
Frost, Robert, 211

Gallic Wars, The, 115
Garis, Lillian, 36
Garland, Hamlin, 132
Gates, Doris, 166, 168
Gender roles, 18, 21, 25, 27, 29, 45,
    47, 48, 55, 63, 104, 165, 213; role
    reversal, 43–46
"Ghost of Nancy Drew, The," 219
    (n. 1)
Gilder, Jeanette, 107
Girl of the Plains Country, A, 165
Girl Sleuth, The, 219 (n. 1)
Goldsmith Publishing Company, 37
Goodrich, Samuel G., 90, 177
Grant, Ulysses S., 109
Great Depression. *See* Depression,
    economic
Grimm's Fairy Tales, 120
Grosset and Dunlap, 36, 39
Grossman, Anita Susan, 219 (n. 1)
Grund, Frances, 136

Hall, G. Stanley, 118
Hamilton, Virginia, 212, 214

Handlin, Oscar, 147
Hans Brinker and the Silver Skates,
    116
Harper's Bazaar, 116
Harriet the Spy, 184, 199
Haunted Bridge, The, 46
Hawthorne, Nathaniel, 116, 120
Headman, 184
Hemingway, Ernest, 30, 125
Hero and the Crown, The, 213
His Own Where, 204
Holland, Isabelle, 182, 200, 202
Holman, Felice, 204
Home, 104
Homecoming, 202, 211, 213
Hoosier Schoolmaster, The, 71, 91
Horn Book, 125
House of Wings, 202
Howe, Julia Ward, 12, 106, 107, 108
Howe, Samuel Gridley, 12, 106, 107
Howells, William Dean, 107, 109,
    112, 125
Hunt, Una, 8, 110, 116

I Am the Cheese, 190, 192, 193, 204,
    215
Intellectual freedom, 174, 179, 183,
    185
Irving, Washington, 87, 124
Is That You, Miss Blue?, 204

Jack and Jill, 16, 19, 20, 22
Jacksonian period, 88, 89; anxiety
    in, 88, 89, 93, 96, 97; optimism
    in, 88, 95; juvenile literature of,
    89–93, 95, 96, 97
James, Henry, 123, 125
Jean and Johnny, 55
John and Susanne, 162
Johnson, Deidre Ann, 219 (n. 1)

Johnson, James Weldon, 109, 111
Johnston, Anne Fellows, 83
Jordan, June, 204
Judd, Frances K., 32
Judy Bolton series, 38, 39
Juvenile delinquency, 57, 63

Kafka, Franz, 192, 196
Kay Tracey series, 32
Keene, Carolyn, 35
Kerr, M. E., 204
King Arthur, 126
Kingsbury, Alice, 11, 107
Kingsley, Charles, 120
Kipling, Rudyard, 119, 126
Klein, Norma, 182, 184
Krug, Judith, 186

L'Engle, Madeleine, 54, 57, 63, 203
Lamb, Charles and Mary, 115
Lang, Andrew, 120
Lanier, Sydney, 118
Larcom, Lucy, 10, 12, 15, 110, 135, 139
Larkspur Lane. See Password to Larkspur Lane, The
Last of the Mohicans, The, 117
Lerner, Max, 58
Lewis, Sinclair, 125
Lisa, Bright and Dark, 201, 208
Little Black Sambo, 184
Little Colonel series, 83
Little Lord Fauntleroy, 78, 82, 83, 114, 119, 154, 159
Little Princess, A, 82
Little Women, 15, 23, 26, 27, 75, 90, 116, 149, 150, 151, 180
Locke, John, 102, 113
London, Jack, 126
Lorna Doone, 118

Lothrop, Margaret. *See* Sidney, Margaret
Lowell, James Russell, 109, 120
Lowell mills, 134, 135, 139

Macauley, David, 215
McKinley, Robin, 213
Maine, 115
Malory, Thomas, 118
Maniac Magee, 215
Man Without a Face, 202
Marriage, age of, 51, 56, 64, 165
Marryat, Frederick, 129
Mary Poppins, 184
Mason, Bobby Ann, 219 (n. 1)
Matthews, William, 133, 134
May, Sophie, 116
Meaker, Marijane Agnes. *See* Kerr, M. E.
Means, Florence Cranall, 180, 221 (n. 3)
Meet the Malones, 52
Melody Lane series, 36
Mencken, H. L., 116
Michelet, Jules, 28
Milton, John, 173
Missouri Compromise, 92
Moffat family stories, 168
Montgomery, L. M., 22, 24, 25, 26, 27
Moral didacticism, 75, 90, 93, 95, 96
Mordecai, Ellen, 9, 11, 13, 16
More, Hannah, 29, 113
Mother's Book, The, 103, 105
Muir, John, 131, 132, 135

Nancy Drew series, 30, 48
New Chronicles of Rebecca, 26
New England, 77, 110, 111, 133

New England Girlhood, A, 10
Newsletter on Intellectual Freedom, 186
New York, N.Y., 77, 147, 152, 162
New York Ledger, 147, 229 (n. 11)
New York Mirror, 112
No Kidding, 215
None of the Above, 204

Old Fashioned Girl, An, 150
Old Mortality, 63
Oliver Twist, 126
Orgetorix, 115
Orpen, Adela, 108, 132
Orwell, George, 190
Outlook, 120
Oz series, 122

Parley, Peter. *See* Goodrich, Samuel G.
Parton, Sara, 147, 148, 152
Password to Larkspur Lane, The, 45, 46
Patty stories, 123
Peck, Richard, 214
Penny Nichols series, 33, 40
Peter Pan, 119, 120
Phil, the Fiddler, 152
Pier, Arthur, 164
Pilgrim's Progress, The, 116, 124
Plath, Sylvia, 63
Platt, Kin, 200
Porter, Katherine Anne, 63
Princess Ashley, 214
Pyle, Howard, 118

Ragged Dick, 78, 152
Rags-to-riches stories, 149, 151, 160, 161
Randall, Rebecca, 29

Raymond, Cornelia Morse, 108, 109
Realism, 48, 75, 125, 126, 168, 181, 189, 209, 212; "new," 205, 206, 207, 208, 211, 214
Rebecca of Sunnybrook Farm, 22, 119, 123, 158, 164
Rebel Without a Cause, 62
Reed, Kit, 202
Richards, Laura E. Howe, 12, 107, 108, 154, 155
Ripley, Sarah Alden, 115
Rip Van Winkle, 124
Robin Hood, 118, 120
Robinson, Harriet H., 134, 135
Robinson Crusoe, 117, 120, 124
Romanticism, 75, 125, 151, 166, 194; in children's fiction, 146, 150, 151, 154, 155, 158; neo-romanticism, 208, 209
Rose and the Ring, The, 124
Rousseau, Jean-Jacques, 102, 113, 144

Sainsbury, Noel E., Jr., 37, 38
St. David Walks Again, 159, 160
St. Nicholas; A Magazine for Boys and Girls, 116, 119, 168
Salinger, J. D., 209, 212
Sarmiento, Domingo Faustino, 136
Saturdays, The, 169
Scoppettone, Sandra, 182
Scott, Sir Walter, 117, 118, 120, 124
Sebestyen, Ouida, 212
Secret Garden, The, 119
Secret of the Stratemeyer Syndicate, The, 219 (n. 1)
Sedgwick, Catherine Maria, 104, 105
Self-Willed Susie, 90
Sentimentality, 146, 148, 152, 166

Seventeenth Summer, 180
Sex roles. See Gender roles
Sexuality, 58, 59, 61, 180, 182
Shakespeare, William, 115, 116, 154, 159
Sidney, Margaret, 160
Sister Carrie, 125
Sister of the Bride, 64
Skinner, Henrietta, 109, 113
Slake's Limbo, 204
Slavery, 92
Slow and Sure; or, From the Street to the Shop, 151
Smith-Rosenberg, Carroll, 100
Spinelli, Jerry, 215
Star Bright, 158
Steffie Can't Come Out to Play, 184, 185
Stevenson, Robert Louis, 116, 123
Stolz, Mary, 60, 221 (n. 3)
Story of a Bad Boy, The, 69, 70, 76, 91
Story of Doctor Dolittle. See Dr. Dolittle
Stratemeyer, Edward, 30, 38, 42, 122
Stratemeyer, Harriet. See Adams, Harriet Stratemeyer
Stratemeyer Pseudonyms and Series Books, 219 (n. 1)
Stratemeyer series, 32
Stratemeyer Syndicate, 30, 36, 47
Stuart-Wortley, Lady Emmeline, 129
Sutton, Margaret, 38, 39
Sweet Whispers, Brother Rush, 212
Swiss Family Robinson, The, 115, 117

Taboos, 179, 180, 210

Tales from Shakespeare, 115
Tanglewood Tales, 120
Teen culture. See Adolescence, post–World War II
Teen novels. See Adolescent literature
Thackeray, William Makepeace, 116, 117, 124
Thimble Summer, 168
Tocqueville, Alexis de, 83, 137, 138
Tomboys, 164
Tom Sawyer. See Adventures of Tom Sawyer, The
Tom Swift series, 126
Travel accounts: of foreigners, 128; American children in, 128, 129, 130, 136
Tune for a Small Harmonica, 200
Twain, Mark, 69, 70, 72, 74, 76, 119, 125

Van de Water, Virginia Terhune, 110
Vassar College, 108
Victorianism, 117, 118; anti-Victorianism, 118. See also Anti-modernism
Voigt, Cynthia, 202, 211

Walker, Jimmy, 173
Warner, Susan Bogart, 152
Washington, George, 92, 111
Water Babies, 116, 120
Wayne, Dorothy. See Sainsbury, Noel E., Jr.
Weber, Lenore Mattingly, 59
Webster, Jean, 123
Wells, Rosemary, 204
Wersba, Barbara, 200, 202

Wetherell, Elizabeth. *See* Warner, Susan Bogart
Wharton, Edith, 118
What Katy Did, 20, 22, 75
White, Barbara A., 63
Whittier, John Greenleaf, 115, 120
Wide, Wide World, The, 153
Wiggin, Kate Douglas, 22–27, 120, 121
Wilder, Laura Ingalls, 199
Wild in the World, 204
Willard, Frances E., 10, 13, 15
Wind in the Door, A, 203
Wirt, Mildred. *See* Benson, Mildred Wirt
Woman, 28
Woman's sphere, 4, 12, 16, 29, 64, 101. *See also* Gender roles
Women's Christian Temperance Union, 10
Wonder Book for Boys and Girls, A, 117, 120

Woodward, Helen Rosen, 117
Woolsey, Sarah C., 20, 21, 25
Work: women's, 4, 5, 6, 64, 132; nineteenth-century children's, 9, 131–39; twentieth-century teenager's, 51, 52; men's, 57; in fiction, 59, 60, 163, 164; rewards of, 81, 135
World War I, 118, 157, 160
World War II, 157
Wyse, Francis, 128

Xenophobia, 36

Yellowback Book, The, 219 (n. 1)
Youth's Companion, The, 147, 229 (n. 11)

Zindel, Paul, 182, 184, 200, 202, 203, 204, 208